Here Comes the Sun

The Spiritual and Musical Journey of George Harrison

Joshua M. Greene

WILEY

John Wiley & Sons, Inc.

Published by John Wiley & Sons, Inc., Hoboken, New Jersey
Published simultaneously in Canada

Credits appear on page 297 and constitute an extension of this copyright page.

For general information about our other products and services, please contact our Cus-tomer Care Department within the United States at (800) 762-2974, outside the United States at (317) 572-3993 or fax (317) 572-4002.

Wiley also publishes its books in a variety of electronic formats. Some content that ap-pears in print may not be available in electronic books. For more information about Wiley products, visit our web site at www.wiley.com.

Library of Congress Cataloging-in-Publication Data:

Greene, Joshua M., date.
    Here comes the sun : the spiritual and musical journey of George Harrison /
Joshua Greene.
        p.   cm.
Includes bibliographical references and index.
ISBN-13 978-0-471-69021-4 (cloth)
ISBN-10 0-471-69021-X (cloth)
1. Harrison, George, 1943- 2. Rock musicians—England—Biography. I. Title.
ML420.H167G74 2006
782.42166092—dc22

                                                                    2005028947

Printed in the United States of America
10 9 8 7 6 5 4 3 2 1

To George
for undertaking the journey
with determination, integrity, and love.

The great souls are always singing My glories.

—Bhagavad Gita, 9:13–14

Contents

Photographs follow page 120

Preface

The seeds for this book were planted in 1970 during a recording session with George Harrison at EMI Studios in London. This was during my Christmas break from college, just at the time George was producing an album of Sanskrit hymns with devotees from the Radha Krishna Temple. On a visit to the temple, I happened to mention that I played organ in a university band, and the devotees invited me to sit in.

We arrived at EMI in the early afternoon. George looked up from behind a mixing console and smiled. He appeared very relaxed. His long brown hair hung loose around his shoulders. He wore blue jeans and an open vest with a purple Om button pinned to it. The devotee men wore saffron-colored robes wrapped Gandhi-style around the waist and tucked in front and back. The women wore silk saris draped over their hair. George came over and exchanged hugs with some of the devotees. He and I shook hands. Then George and his devotee friends started chatting about chanting sessions they'd had and laughing about people's reactions to a singing group with shaved heads.

"You know," he said after a while, "this studio is costing us forty pounds an hour. We better get started." That impressed me. He may have been one of the most successful pop stars in the world, but he was quite practical. George took up his guitar, and the devotees positioned themselves behind traditional Indian instruments, including a two-headed mridanga drum, a stringed tambura, and brass hand cymbals. I sat down at a hand-pumped keyboard harmonium in the middle of the floor while technicians positioned microphones around us. George signaled the sound room, gave us a nod, and the devotees began singing a medley of Indian prayers. Respecting the album's devotional purpose, he kept voices prominent and instrumentation simple. During a crescendo, from force of habit I fell into an embellished riff. George looked up and calmly raised an eyebrow.

"Really?" he seemed to say, an impish grin challenging me to disagree.

It was just a moment, but in retrospect it summarizes my impressions of a man who understood that simplicity lies at the heart of spiritual life. As the medieval Indian philosopher Chanakya put it, "Eloquence is truth stated concisely." That's a skill I have had to learn from scratch. For George, it was bred in the bone.

Nonetheless, the spiritual message that pervaded his life after the Beatles was not always understood. What was he trying to say about souls and karma and getting "liberated from the material world"? Why had he committed himself so deeply to a spiritual journey? And where did it take him? In putting together this story, I've tried not to embellish on what George thought or felt. Some interpretation was required, as happens in all biographies, and when that became necessary I based my judgment on recorded conversations, verbatim quotes, first-person accounts, or, on occasion, my own experience from thirty-five years of bhakti-yoga practice.

No assumption has been made regarding readers' familiarity with George's early life or his career as a Beatle, and the first few chapters cover this well-documented period. Childhood influences, no less than teachers and traditions, helped determine the path he took as an adult; his extraordinary success with history's most successful pop group underscores how remarkable it was that he took to a spiritual path at all.

It was clear to me after conducting a number of interviews that George's simple virtues were more important to people than his inner complexities. What people remembered about him was his *external* life. Everyone interviewed talked about his selfless and generous nature, and hardly anyone talked about his theology. He was a spiritual doer; people liked that about him. In the past, developing an inner life meant retreating into mountains or caves to escape the world's distractions. In his later years, George did want that kind of retreat for himself, yet he remained active and used his fame and resources to serve others. That was innovative behavior for someone on a spiritual path in those days, and it helped redefine "holy people" as individuals deeply engaged in the world they long to transcend.

Sadly, his efforts "to get a message through," as he sang in *Living in the Material World*, were not always well received. Critics panned him, claiming he was exploiting his Beatles fame to preach about God. The record-buying public deserted him. Fans invaded his home. Some even physically attacked him and his family. George desperately wanted to help the world. Eventually, he wanted just as much to leave it behind forever.

Of the many books George studied on his spiritual journey, one he found most helpful was Hinduism's principal text, the Bhagavad Gita (Song of the Supreme). The Gita is a call to action in which the speaker, Krishna—the Sanskrit name for God—instructs His warrior-disciple Arjuna on the eve of a great battle in about 3000 B.C. Arjuna's efforts to reclaim his family's kingdom from the hands of usurpers have failed, and war is inevitable. Krishna encourages Arjuna to follow his duty and fight the aggressors, but the compassionate warrior prefers to retreat and meditate. To inspire him to action, Krishna describes five basic truths of traditional Indian belief: the immortality of the soul, the impermanence of the material world, the influence of time, the relationship of the soul to God, and active devotion as the highest path. Arjuna accepts Krishna's challenge to "stand and fight," and the battle is waged and won. In her preface to a tribute published shortly after George's death, Olivia Harrison compared her late husband to Arjuna, saying that George faced his own battles with similar spiritual courage and unwavering conviction.

All practicing Hindus honor the Bhagavad Gita, even though Krishna never describes Himself as Hindu. Nor did George, who from an early age looked askance at organized religion. His spiritual passion grew from what the Gita calls "the most secret of all secrets": knowledge that the soul lives on after leaving its physical body. If prepared by a life of devotion, a soul can come face-to-face with the Divine.

Here is the story of a man who gave up one of the most spectacular careers in entertainment history for that goal of seeing God face-to-face and who succeeded beyond his greatest expectations. The sound track of his spiritual journey begins with the explosions of battle and ends fifty-eight years later with the harmonies of eternal peace. And like all good stories, this one starts when the hero was just a child.

1

Beginnings

Before there was anything there was the One.
When the universe came into being,
The One became many.

—Rig-Veda

Years later, looking back, George Harrison found it strange that his soul entered his mother's womb in Liverpool in 1943 amid the sounds of battle—air raid sirens, German bomb attacks, English Spitfires shrieking by overhead racing to meet enemy planes—and wondered how he came to be in that family, in that house, at that time.

The final months of World War II were days of scarcity and rationing, and people of every class were scraping by. Harold Harrison's bus-driver salary barely covered basics, so when his wife, Louise, was pregnant with their first child, Harold and his brother-in-law Johnny built her a radio. They twisted wires and connected tubes and screwed the whole concoction into a wooden enclosure. After giving up her job at a local green-grocer's, Louise spent much of her time listening. She twisted the wooden dial to broadcasts of Irish folk songs, English dance-hall tunes, and music of foreign lands, wearing down the batteries until Harold had to leave them at a nearby electrical shop to be recharged. Louise gave birth to a daughter, whom they named after her. Three years later came Harold Jr., and then their second son, Peter. During her fourth and last pregnancy—with

1

George—Louise's favorite program was a weekly broadcast called Radio India. Every Sunday she tuned in to mystical sounds evoked by sitars and tablas, hoping that the exotic music would bring peace and calm to the baby in her womb.

George Harrison was born on February 25, 1943, at 12:10 A.M. in his family's house in a working-class section of Liverpool called Wavertree. By age three he had already developed the large ears, thick eyebrows, and lopsided smile that would be signature features throughout his life. "A tiny, squalling, miniature replica of myself," Harold proclaimed proudly, not foreseeing all the ways his youngest would break the mold. Harold was a man of his generation, a father for whom there was a right way and a wrong way to all things and who was determined to see his daughter and sons grow to adulthood as respected and productive members of their community. Louise, a careful housekeeper, was unstintingly considerate of everyone's feelings and dedicated to providing as sane a home for her children as their modest circumstances would allow. Behind their house she planted an apple tree and tall purple delphinium and fragrant lavender bushes. She kept a henhouse and cooked and cleaned and dedicated herself to the enterprise of raising healthy, happy offspring.

"Even though there wasn't much money," George's sister, Louise, recalled, "Mum made sure we knew we weren't peasants, that we came from educated stock and had great potential in life. She taught us to think, to question things, to always be kind, never kowtow to big shots or lord over the lowly. We were never to cringe in fear but neither were we to become bullies toward anyone. And we took care of one another. If there was only one apple, we'd each get a quarter."

Not many homes had central heating in postwar Britain, so George's mother bathed him in a battered zinc tub filled with water heated on the stove. Scrubbed and dressed, he would entertain a constant traffic of family and friends with songs and skits. Like many Liverpudlians, Louise came from a large Irish family; when the Harrisons gathered for parties they crowded around Harold's wind-up gramophone and let loose with full-throated renditions of old favorites. One of George's earliest memories was standing on a leather stool and singing folksinger Josh White's "One Meatball" to his family's great delight.

"He had these animal puppets," his sister, Louise, said, "and he'd do skits with them for us. He was funny and outgoing and the family doted on him. He had fun growing up and was always the center of attention." Inside their little house, childhood was a pleasant time.

Outside, life was not as happy. German bombs had left Liverpool in ruins, and the city struggled under the weight of its own debris. George and his friends played in the remains of buildings and shops, rummaged through wreckage, dared one another to jump from demolished roofs, and manufactured bows and arrows from bits of broken wood and flattened bottle caps. Dodging cars and trucks was a popular game, although it often left slower kids with broken legs or worse. "It was rough then," remembered Bill Harry, who grew up near George and later founded *Mersey Beat* magazine. "There were gangs—the Chain Gang, the Peanut Gang. On your way to school, they'd stop you and search your pockets for money. I remember one guy throwing me to the ground while three others kicked the hell out of me. They'd smash bottles and stick them in people's faces. The violence was extreme because kids imagined themselves stuck there for the rest of their lives and felt hopeless."

George kept his defenses up. In Dovedale Junior School he practiced running fast and kicking a soccer ball hard. In those days, solving problems lacked subtlety, and a quick punch was the most expedient way of dealing with bullies.

In 1949, after being on a waiting list for several years, the Harrisons moved to a larger house in Speke, a state-subsidized development forty-five minutes by bus from central Liverpool. When six-year-old George walked out of his new house and looked up, he saw planes arriving at Liverpool Airport to the south, descending with a drone through skies tinted dark gray by smoke from a nearby industrial zone.

To the north, cars kept up a constant hum on the A561 highway. To get away, George would hop on his brother Peter's bike and pedal off. There were places a young boy could bike to, such as Carr Mill Dam, big as a lake with grassy slopes, where the sky overhead regained some of its natural blue. He watched long-tailed ducks land with unceremonious belly flops on the placid water and tracked white-fronted geese as they glided by in search of food. At other times he would walk to Halewood, near the spot where his school bus stopped, to skim rocks across a pond that sprouted sticklebacks like wayward tufts of hair. Occasionally Harold bundled his wife and children off to a little rented cottage in the countryside, where George ran after bugs and forest animals, picked wildflowers, and luxuriated in open spaces while Harold and Louise supervised.

"He had a lot to thank his parents for," George's sister-in-law Irene said years later, considering how carefully they protected him. "They worried constantly." In their eyes, their youngest was a trusting, soft-natured child who needed looking after.

As a boy, George had dreams that frightened him. The dreams started with a sensation of being very small. The sensation grew more and more intense, and things around him went faster and faster until he awoke, scared. It was an experience that followed him into adulthood. During recording sessions at Abbey Road Studios, when no one was around, he would use the sound booth as a place to meditate, and the sensation would return. In boyhood he shook away such uncomfortable thoughts by hopping on his bike and riding off through the farmlands of the Cheshire plain to the east or along the mud cliffs that stretched out along the Mersey River. Back in nature, he felt good again. He loved plants. With his keen powers of observation, he might have become a botanist if school hadn't been so boring.

More interesting to him were fast cars, which also promised escape from the debris of Liverpool. On weekends, as a kid he would take a box camera to racetracks and snap photos, and if he found a manufacturer's plate welded to any of the cars, he would send off a letter asking for brochures and pictures.

But more than cars, more than biking away from the mud and rubble, more than anything else, George wanted to make music. Arriving back home from junior school, he'd crank up the gramophone and sing along to country songs by Jimmie Rodgers, urban blues tunes by Big Bill Broonzy, ballads by country-and-western singer Slim Whitman, and a wide assortment of English music-hall numbers. "It's hard to realize that there are kids like I was," he said, "where the only thing in their lives is to get home and play their favorite records." He warbled lyrics to songs about broken hearts and lonely nights and waiting for trains that never came. He sang silly tunes with names such as "I'm a Pink Toothbrush, You're a Blue Toothbrush" and yodeled along with Hank Williams on "Blue Yodel 94" until the musical stew grew so mouthwatering that he couldn't be without it for long.

When George was ten, a classmate offered to sell him a beginner's guitar for three pounds, ten shillings. It was a lot of money in those days, but George's mother bought it for him. His father had a friend who ran a pub and played guitar, and he showed George how to finger chords to tunes from the twenties and thirties such as "Dinah" and "Whispering." George tried the new chords out for his mother, twisting the guitar pegs until each string came as close to true as he could manage, positioning his fingers to best effect. The instrument's cheap wooden neck bent, and his fingers bled from pushing down on the strings.

"I'll never learn this," he said.

"You will, son," Louise encouraged. "Just keep at it." She sat up with him until he quit, teary-eyed, at two o'clock in the morning. He looked at the toy instrument and chafed.

"You don't understand about guitars, do you, Mum," he said.

"No," she admitted, "but if you stick to it I'm sure you'll make it." Louise remembered all the things she had wanted as a girl, but with so many children needing attention, her parents hadn't encouraged her. "I'll help you buy a new guitar," she told her youngest.

As a young man, before joining the Liverpool bus company, Harold Harrison had trained to be a bursar for the Cunard Steamship Lines. Then he saw how much more money stewards earned working in first class and managed to get himself transferred. He knew the value of a solid job and, despite having offered some initial encouragement, balked at his son's growing interest in music.

The other Harrison children were practical about their careers. Their daughter attended teachers' training college. Harry and Peter completed full apprenticeships, and by 1955 Harry was a mechanic, while Peter did panel beating and welding. If all else failed, Harold reasoned, maybe George could become an electrician and open a repair shop with his brothers. His Christmas gifts to twelve-year-old George included a set of electrical tools. The war had taken its toll, and screwdrivers were what a sane man gave his youngest son, something dependable.

George had no taste for manual labor, but he did benefit from his father's ability to reason problems out to their solution. Popular myth has painted George as a bus driver's son, but Harold was more than just a driver—he was in charge of scheduling all the buses in Liverpool: nearly six thousand buses and eighty different routes through town. "He scheduled them all so that connections were made in the most efficient manner," daughter Louise said. "Not many people understand how brilliant he was."

As for religion, George had as little interest in it as he did in manual labor. His dad was a lapsed Anglican, while his mother maintained her Roman Catholic traditions and did what she could to instill a sense of faith in her children. Still, religion made no sense to George. "I was raised Catholic," he told photographer Murray Silver, "but even as a kid I couldn't understand the claim that Jesus was the only Son of God when, in fact, we all are."

Young George appreciated that Christ died for the sins of others but snickered at the irony of seeing pubs located across from every church in the city. How convenient, he thought. People can drink themselves under the table and then cross the street to make amends with a fiver on the collection plate. By the time of his first Holy Communion at age eleven, he had grown sufficiently disenchanted to skip Confirmation, deciding that he'd "confirm it later" for himself.

Despite his lack of interest in formal education, George was a bright child and the only one in his family to gain admission to Liverpool Institute, a local secondary school that catered to the city's academic elite, those who passed the Eleven Plus examination. Acceptance to the institute meant possibly gaining entrance to a university. Those who failed the entrance exam usually left school to look for an apprenticeship or earn money as laborers electrifying the railways between Liverpool and London. For George, starting at Liverpool Institute at age twelve was "when the darkness began." Even physically, the place was dark. Once it may have boasted an imposing Greek facade, carved balustrades, elegant wooden railings, and bright natural light, but years of neglect had robbed it of its grace. Chips of paint drooped from window ledges and clouds of dust blanketed corners and corridors. He felt that his new teachers, most of them aging war veterans or inexperienced college graduates, had nothing to teach him. They only wanted to turn students into "rows of little toffees" with their meaningless lessons in algebra and history. He would arrive at school in one of his brother Harry's hand-me-down sports jackets, pointy blue suede shoes, hair stacked and combed to perfection, take a seat in the rear, and begin doodling cello guitars with big "f" holes. Warnings from his teachers followed: start working or you'll be expelled. George replied with silence.

Arthur Evans, one of George's teachers, remembered, "Harrison was the greatest surprise to me of all during the Beatles' meteoric rise to fame. My memory of him was of a very quiet, if not even introverted little boy who would sit in the farthest corner and never say a word, or even look up."

Friends, though, saw him in a different light. "He had a wicked sense of humor," remembered schoolmate Rod Othen, "always in mischief—and he didn't suffer fools gladly." The headmaster's threats, Othen recalled, merely drove George farther away from any interest in studies and provoked his nascent sense of righteous anger. "George was antibullying. There was a kid in school who smelled so bad that the master's punishment for anyone who disobeyed was to make the offender sit next to him. George would voluntarily take the chair next to the smelly kid. He befriended him."

The institute's reputation as one of Liverpool's finer schools did nothing to diminish George's disgust at being there, and he failed one class after another. Often he would sneak off to spend his days at the movies—another place of escape that would later become important in his life. "I cannot tell you what his work is like," wrote the headmaster, "because he has not done any." Eventually, having received one too many miserable report cards, he dropped out of school completely.

"Hadn't you better get a job or something?" his father hinted again and again, until George finally interviewed with the Youth Employment Centre and took a position as apprentice electrician at a shop called Blackler's for one pound, fifty pence per week. At Blackler's he barely did his work, preferring darts in the basement while waiting for the day to end so he could race home to play his guitar.

Young George was frequently ill, and his poor health provided him with plenty of sick days and consequent practice time. He suffered from tonsillitis and at thirteen developed nephritis, an inflammation of the kidneys that sent him to the hospital for six weeks.

He hated the hospital. Cockroaches crawled across the floor and up onto his sheets while he slept, and the doctors were not the best: good ones left Liverpool in search of better pay.

He couldn't have blamed them. Detesting confinement, he believed in getting out, too, and in moving on to places ripe with opportunity. Childhood in Liverpool was an impatient time, made bearable by imagining the possibilities of something more. Like many young people in Britain after the war, George dreamed of discovering bigger worlds. And though the day would come when he could imagine nothing worse, at age thirteen, he could imagine nothing better than a career in rock and roll.

Over British radio in 1956 came a new kind of music. Rock and roll was earthy, sexual, angry, loud, self-absorbed, defiant—a perfect outlet for adolescents seeking freedom from postwar constraints. Grownups looking for calm after World War II were outraged. Psychologist Francis J. Braceland, then president of the American Psychiatric Association, called the new music "a communicable disease . . . cannibalistic." Proper children should be studying science and math, the argument went, not gyrating their hips and screaming at the top of their lungs.

George was thirteen and out of the hospital when rock and roll entered his life by way of Fats Domino's "I'm in Love Again," Elvis Presley's "Heartbreak Hotel," and Little Richard's "Tutti Frutti." The music sent shivers down his spine and fueled a desire to join a band. In those days anybody could put a band together. One kid drummed on a washboard, another plunked a broom-handle bass, a third faked chords on guitar, another blew into a gob iron (which was what they called a harmonica), and they dubbed themselves a band. By the end of the 1950s, more than three hundred bands across Liverpool were scratching out hit tunes in "jive hives," ballrooms and town halls booked by enterprising local promoters, as well as in youth clubs, ice rinks, church halls, coffee bars, and pubs. Records from America arrived in the seaport city before anywhere else in Britain. George listened carefully to these new tunes at parties and record shops, puzzling through unfamiliar chords and guitar licks. While parents swooned over Bing Crosby and dreamed of earning more money, boys such as George swooned over Elvis Presley's "Hound Dog" and dreamed of becoming musicians.

The bus that had taken George back and forth to his dreary school was a double-decker like the one his dad drove. George met Paul McCartney in 1956 on the upper deck, where Paul sat so he could smoke a pipe and feel like the poet Dylan Thomas. Paul was nine months older and a grade ahead at Liverpool Institute. He read plays by Samuel Beckett and Tennessee Williams, loved musicals and Fred Astaire, and imitated his dad's renditions of "Lullaby of the Leaves" and "Stairway to Paradise" on their piano. "If you want to learn," Paul's dad said, "you've got to learn properly—and if you do, you'll get invited to parties." When George demonstrated for Paul how many guitar chords he knew, they began practicing together. Paul was playing with a group called the Quarry Men.

"I got this friend," he told the group's leader, John Lennon. "He's a bit young, but he can play 'Raunchy' really well."

John was three years older than George and attended the nearby College of Art. Not sure whether he was an artist or a rebel, John wore a beret by day and a leather jacket by night. George strummed "Raunchy" for John on a bus ride home in February 1958, and it sounded just like the rock instrumental by Alabama guitarist Bill Justis.

"You're in," John said.

Joining a band in 1950s Liverpool meant becoming part of a team. Joey Molland, who went on to fame as guitarist in the band Badfinger, remembered what it was like. "There was a sense of staying together and not deserting the ship. Your band was like your family. You worked with them. We were raised like that," he said, "with the history of England and the commitment to the English way of life and character. An Englishman is known for sticking it out through good and bad and believing that things will work out in the end. We had to have that attitude in Liverpool because you'd be taking your dad's suit to the pawnshop on Monday and getting it out on Friday when he got paid, and during those four days in between the family had to survive. I guess the sense of loyalty is an extension of that."

That loyalty came in handy, especially when dances ended in a brawl, as they often did. Boyfriends had a hard time tolerating the attention their girls gave to band members.

George, Paul, and John tried rehearsing at John's house, where he lived with his aunt Mimi. John's father had deserted the family when John was four. John's mother, Julia, funny and gorgeous with long red hair, pursued a social life that made raising a child impractical. Julia's sister Mimi was well off, but she never had children of her own and insisted on chastising her nephew and his musician friends. "The guitar is all right for a hobby, John," she said, "but it won't earn you any money." Her judgment of George Harrison was just as severe. "You always seem to like the lower-class types, don't you, John," she said.

"Shut up, Mimi," John said, and then he screamed. Screaming was real. It made people's hair stand on end. He loved Little Richard's scream *"Ooooooo tutti frutti,"* but didn't like living at his aunt's. He preferred being with his mother, who was witty and played banjo and let the boys practice in her bathroom, where the acoustics were good. Mimi put brakes on him, he felt, and never let his band in the front door. "You watched your p's and q's around her," said Quarry Man bass player Len Garry.

George wanted to find the group some place other than Mimi's to rehearse and convinced his parents to let them practice at their house, where the group could play records on brother Harry's portable player. During rehearsals, Louise cheered them on and fed them cookies and sometimes a little taste of whiskey.

At first John made fun of younger George, who had big ears and was always fawning over him and his girlfriend, Cynthia. John "was a bit embarrassed about that," George recalled, "because I was so tiny. I only looked about ten years old." One way to even the odds, George surmised, was to wear the right clothes. Harold went into shock one day on discovering his son wedged into an old pair of John's hand-me-down jeans. They were the tightest pants Harold had ever seen. Seeing a look of disapproval on his father's face, George leaped into the air and landed at his feet. "How can I do my ballet without tight jeans?" he asked, prancing around some more until his parents had to laugh.

"George never gave us any cheek," said his mother, Louise, "but he always got round us."

The youngest band member admired John's worldliness, his apparent sexual prowess and aggressive self-assurance, but he never let John's sarcasm get the better of him. George would simply talk back and "give him a taste of his own," as George said.

A few months after George and John met, John's mother, Julia, died in a car crash. A drunken policeman was behind the wheel. After that, "John always had a thing about authority," his half-sister Julia said.

George offered his condolences. It was George's first encounter with death, and it shook him. "George was terrified that I was going to die next," his mother recalled. "He'd watch me carefully all the time. I told him not to be so silly. I wasn't going to die." George had come on the scene after John and Paul had already built a friendship, one that grew stronger with Julia's death. Paul's mother had died of breast cancer when he was fourteen. When John's mother died, it created "an almost inseparable bond between him and Paul," said John's half-sister Julia. They practically "grew into each other's pockets. It cemented their friendship in a deep way."

George was the only Beatle to grow up without divorce or early death—Ringo's mother divorced when Ringo was three—and George's happy childhood helped compensate for being the youngest in the group. As a band, they grew better. As friends, they grew closer, and despite the unique bond between John and Paul, there was no mistaking their cohesiveness, never any uncertainty over their commitment to one another. George thrived in the industry of their musicmaking and the intimacy of their shared lives. If they fought, they made up, usually with a laugh. "That was one thing to be said about us," he said. "We were really tight, as friends. We could argue a lot, but . . . in the company of other people or other situations we'd always stick together."

Friendship between George and his new bandmates was reinforced by hard work. They rehearsed constantly. If one of them heard a good new song, he'd tell the others and they'd take a bus to NEMS, Liverpool's largest record shop, where customers could play records before deciding to buy. The biggest song of 1956 was Bill Haley's "Rock Around the Clock," the theme song to the film *Blackboard Jungle.* Liverpool theaters admitted no one under sixteen. In later years Paul remembered helping baby-faced George get in by grabbing a fingerful of soil from Louise's garden and painting a mustache on George's upper lip. The ruse worked, and off they went to the movies to learn another tune for their repertoire.

As for gigs, they accepted any offer that allowed them to play for an audience. If a sponsor complained about their not having a drummer, they would argue that the rhythm was "in the guitars." Their ambition knew no limits—any venue would do, including men's clubs, pubs, and amateur competitions. They were nearly the last to audition at one talent show when, by 11:00 P.M., the judges were too drunk to tell one group from another and awarded top prize to an old lady who played spoons.

"We shouldn't have lost to her," the boys grumbled on the bus home. "She wasn't that good."

George had recently turned seventeen when the Silver Beatles, as they called themselves then, were offered a two-week gig in Scotland. It was a big opportunity, a chance to see how they could do on the road. But if George were going to spend that much time away, he would have to quit his job. "Would you pack in work and have a go at this if you were me?" he asked his brother Peter.

"You might as well," Peter said, thinking of his younger brother's passion for music and his misery at work. "There's nothing to lose."

George turned in his overalls at Blackler's electrical store. G. J. Peat, one of the managers, wagged a finger. "Mark my words, George Harrison. One day you'll crawl back on your knees pleading for your job." It was a chance George was quite willing to take.

George, John, and Paul enlisted a friend, Stuart Sutcliffe, who played bass, and a drummer who worked a forklift at a nearby bottling company, and the group set out for Scotland with visions of their name in lights. The tour turned out to be a depressing string of one-night stands, scarce food, and an abundance of misfortunes. A near-fatal car accident, coldwater flats, and meager publicity brought the tour to a less than glamorous end, and they returned to Liverpool disappointed and hungry but not defeated.

Allan Williams, who ran a coffee bar and managed a few local bands, offered them a slot at his club, the Jacaranda. "The night they first played here," he said, "George came up to me earlier in the day—he was only seventeen at the time—and said, 'Hey, Al, have you got a broom?' I told him the floor was clean enough, but he said, 'and a mop as well?' I found out why that evening. You see, they were so poor in those days that they didn't have microphone stands. Their girlfriends used to tie the mikes on the broomsticks and they'd be sitting in the front row holding up these brushes and things all night long."

Girlfriends came with the territory. If girls flocked to the front of the stage when a band played, if they let themselves be impressed into service holding broom handles or ironing a band member's clothes, it was because rock and roll struck hard below the belt.

"I don't think teenagers get that sensation anymore," said *Mersey Beat* magazine founder Bill Harry. "There are too many choices. Back then we focused our whole attention on the Beatles or Rory Storm and the Hurricanes or Kingsize Taylor and the Dominoes because they were unbelievable. They took your breath away."

George had plenty of girlfriends. When he was younger, there was Jennifer Brewer, who had a beaming white smile and wore her hair in a pageboy. Then there was Rory Storm's sister, Iris Caldwell, who filled out her bra by stuffing it with cotton padding. A few years later, there was a girl who studied with John at the Art College. George thought she looked like his favorite actress, Brigitte Bardot, with blond pigtails, and managed to "shag" her at a party one night. John found out, and after that he paid George a little more respect.

"Don't get yourself trapped alone with a female you don't know," Harold warned his youngest son, always cautious about that sort of thing, "or with a female you can't trust. You'll find yourself in a paternity suit."

"We weren't promiscuous," Bill Harry explained. "First of all, it was hard to get condoms. Plus, there was no place to go. Where would a boy go with his girlfriend if they wanted to make love? There were alleys—we used to call them jiggers— but if a fellow took a girl there and tried to do it with her, she'd usually say, 'I'd get off at Edge Hill.' Edge Hill was the station just before the last train station, which was Lime Street. So when a girl said that, she was saying, 'you'd better be satisfied with coitus interruptus, because that's as far as I go.' To be pregnant and unmarried was such a stigma that families would have the daughter move away for a time and make some excuse about going on vacation."

Satisfied by their trial run at the Jacaranda, a few weeks later Allan Williams gave the Silver Beatles the oddest engagement of their young career: playing backup for Janice, a stripper who would only disrobe to live music and who referred to George as "that nice boy with the bony face."

Williams had booked a few Liverpool groups at clubs in Hamburg and was looking for new acts to send across the English Channel. He offered the Silver Beatles a chance to travel, provided they could find a permanent drummer. George contacted Pete Best, a friend who played with a group called the Blackjacks, and the band was ready for Germany.

Harold Harrison bristled at the thought of his son in such a place. Germany was dangerous and a wartime enemy only a few years back. Besides, there were no guarantees in the music business.

Still, a salaried job, however modest, at least offered some security. George's mother convinced Harold to let him go, and George loved her for it, for defending his right to choose his own way in life even if there were risks, for helping his father understand that this was something he had to do, that it was useless trying to keep him tied to Liverpool. His mom and dad were no strangers to entertainment—they enjoyed a reputation as two of Liverpool's best ballroom dancers—and Harold could even take pride in seeing his son transform a passion into a career.

George's parents swallowed their fear, handed him a can of scones, made him promise to write, and waved their son good-bye. Seventeen-year-old George Harrison's world of familiar, predictable routines was about to give way to an unfamiliar, unpredictable world—of sex, drugs, and rock and roll.

2

George among the Savages

And now for something completely different.

—*Monty Python*

After hastily arranging passports and visas, George and his bandmates set out for Hamburg on August 16, 1960, in Allan Williams's rickety Austin van. They ferried across the English Channel, motored their way south through Holland, and two days later arrived in the Reeperbahn, Hamburg's red-light district. The streets were crowded with transvestites, gangsters, gunrunners, gaudy clubs, seedy restaurants, and garish porn shops. Though it was utterly lawless and devoid of scruples, a rough place to start a career, it was the most exciting place George had ever seen.

Club owner Bruno Koschmider had named his venue the Indra, after India's rain god. Apart from its name, the club had nothing in common with spiritual realms: the place was a dump. The five boys shared a filthy little space in the back of a nearby movie theater and began their first set the day after their arrival. They played to a dark, empty room and took turns at the door inviting people in, joking in broken German, encouraging their few customers to come back soon. At first the Beatles, as they now called themselves, moved onstage in a restrained and mannerly fashion, like the neatly choreographed groups they knew back in England.

"Make a show, boys!" Koschmider would scream. *"Mach Schau!"*

George may have been more reserved than the others, but he responded with equal gusto. The boys jumped on and off their tiny stage, danced with the sparse audience, and ran around the room stamping their feet like madmen. Customers took up the chant—*"Mach Schau! Mach Schau!"*—slamming fists and beer steins on wooden tables. The band responded by yelling back, pretending to beat each other up, grabbing bites of sandwiches between songs, and joking with customers in the front row. John was cheeky and rude and occasionally screamed "Heil Hitler!" from the stage.

"John was mean and fresh," said Icke Braun, a German friend from the band's Hamburg days, "but when you knew him he had a good heart. Paul was always funny, always with an open, smiling face. And George was quiet, mostly the subject of John's meanness—although he could laugh out loud, too, when others got theirs."

George later described these early stabs at music in Hamburg as little more than "thump-thump-thump," but the audiences loved it. The first week there were thirty people a night, the second week forty, and a month into their contract a hundred people were packing the club every night, jammed together like sardines. Two months into their stay, complaints from neighbors about noise forced the Indra to eliminate live music and resume its former function as a strip club, and the Beatles moved to Koschmider's other venue, the Kaiser Keller. No respectable Hamburger ever frequented these dens of iniquity, but Koschmider's regulars—a demimonde of prostitutes and knife-wielding thugs—loved the Beatles.

George had his own fans among these ruffians, who called him *das liebschen Kind* (the darling child), and shouted for him to sing. At those times, John invited George to take the lead, and he would give his best rendition of a song by Elvis Presley or Carl Perkins.

George couldn't believe his luck. He had a live audience in front of him, a little money in his back pocket, and girls on both sides. He was seventeen, abroad for the first time in his life; and best of all, he was improving as a guitarist.

"The thing was, by playing all night you did get good," remembered Tony Sheridan, the singer/guitarist credited with making "English Mersey" music popular and a frequent performer in Hamburg back then. "The Kaiser Keller was a black hole in hell. You'd go down there for a week and not come up. And if you weren't good, people left within a minute because next door there were strip clubs and all kinds of entertainment, so you had to be really good, energetic, and original—so you did get good, and getting good gave you a good feeling."

Playing all night meant having to be awake all night. The drug of preference was Preludin, a habit-forming stimulant readily available from a little old lady who sold a handful of pills for a few German marks out of bathrooms up and down the street. "We had no respect for our constitutions," Sheridan said. "We were going on very little food, often very little sleep . . . and on those days when you really didn't want to play, you'd pop a pill and it was, 'Hey, let's get the fuck up on that stage, man.'" It was thirsty work as well. Swilling beer and other alcohol sent up to the stage by satisfied patrons became the easiest way of staying quenched.

After a long night of playing, George and his mates would often walk to other clubs to listen as visiting bands finished their all-night sets. At other times they headed straight back to their shabby quarters. They slept on bunks, John on top and George on the bottom in one bunk, Paul on top and Stu on the bottom in another, and rarely without female company. Girls working the clubs would assign numbers to each boy and then toss dice to see which one they would try to sleep with, and on the pretext of offering to do their laundry the girls would traipse back to their room. Some mornings, the clothesline from the boys' window hung heavy with wash. The room looked like a youth hostel.

The group's six-week contract was extended by popular demand. At fifteen pounds per week, George was earning more than his dad, but that did little to compensate for his being so far from home.

Local photographer Astrid Kirchherr sensed that George missed his family. After visiting the club several times and coming to know him better, she would invite him and his bandmates to her studio for a hot meal and a bath. On these occasions Little Georgie, as she called him, made jokes at his own expense.

Astrid's Christmas present to John was an edition of the collected writings of the Marquis de Sade.

"What's mine, then?" George asked with typical self-mocking humor. "Comics?"

In later years, George remembered Hamburg with contradictory emotions. On occasion he would describe it as the worst of times, "living in squalor with things growing out of the sink" and fuming about "Where's my share? Why can't I have some?" At other times he would describe Hamburg as the best of times, a tough and effective training period that prepared him for the success to follow.

"Oh, you just wait till we're as big as the Shadows," he enthused over breakfast at their favorite eatery after a night of hard labor at the Kaiser Keller.

"Oh, no, no, no, no," John replied between bites of pancakes with lemon and sugar. "Not the Shadows," who were only famous in England. "We want to be as big as Elvis."

Defying their agreement with Koschmider, the Beatles began jamming in another club with Tony Sheridan and his group the Jets. "They came to see me . . . and I recognized them as being blood brothers by their outward appearance," Sheridan recalled, "cowboy boots, black jeans stuck inside their boots—which is what we thought all cowboys did—leather jackets, their hair done up in a James Dean or Elvis thing, and I thought, 'Great! Guys after my own heart.'"

But Koschmider was outraged. He terminated the Beatles' contract and saw to it that the police learned George's true age: seventeen. The authorities charged George with being underage and working without a permit and gave him twenty-four hours to leave Germany.

The next day, George sat silently in Astrid's car as she and Stuart Sutcliffe drove him to the station. It was unbelievable. Not only had he been living like a refugee in hovels filthy beyond description, not only had he given up his chances back home to come here and work till all hours of the morning for pennies, but now he had to suffer the embarrassment of getting himself and his mates fired. Not because he couldn't play well or refused to do so, and not because he wouldn't do his share of cutting up like an idiot to keep patrons amused, but because he was underage, too young to play with grownups. Maybe his dad was right. If he stayed home, he could be in business with his brothers. There would be problems, no doubt, but the money would be steady: there were always cars needing repair. And the family would be there. At home they'd love him and respect him and care for him. No more getting put down for being a kid. No more customers stabbing each other, no more filthy beds, no more dirty sex and fearing that some horrible disease would make him sick. He'd find some nice girl and settle down, have kids, and tell them about Hamburg and the foolishness of youth, the futility of pursuing a dream. A solid job with a house and family.

But could he really abandon his dream and ever sleep soundly again? Maybe the others would hold it against him for having lost them their gig, but they were a team. Didn't they share everything equally, including dreams?

The car pulled up to the train station. Astrid and Stuart accompanied George to the gate. He threw his arms around Astrid in a gesture of emotion she had never seen from him before. "My darling Little Georgie," she remembered, "looking all lost."

It was a long trip back to Liverpool. Clutching a bag of apples and biscuits that Astrid had given him, George struggled under the weight of his amplifier, suitcase, and guitar. He arrived home on November 22, 1960, exhausted, discouraged, and penniless, having spent whatever money remained on train fares, porters' tips, and taxis. The others straggled back a few weeks later, just as broke and just as dispirited. John withdrew, doubting that nightclubs and seedy bars were really what he wanted in life. Paul, finding no alternative, took a job in an electrical factory, winding wire into coils. The Beatles made no contact with one another for several weeks.

By mid-December 1960, George and John had put their disappointment over Hamburg behind them. John told him not to think himself the only one responsible for their having to leave: Paul had also provoked authorities by setting fire to a condom that blackened the wall in their quarters. One problem with getting the band going again was that Stuart Sutcliffe had fallen in love with Astrid and remained in Germany, so they were shy one member. Undaunted, they went looking for work. Through Allan Williams, who had landed them the Hamburg job, they met disc jockey Bob Wooler, and Wooler offered to let them play for a dance north of Liverpool. George and John took a bus to the factory where Paul wound cables.

"We got a gig," George told him.

Paul shook his head and looked around the electrical company yard. "I've got a steady job here," he said, "seven pounds a week. . . ." Then, realizing the harsh sentence he had just imposed on himself, he changed direction. "Sod it, I can't stick to this lot," he said, and joined them as they headed out the door.

On the evening of December 27, 1960, Litherland Town Hall was packed. "As soon as I announce you," Wooler told the group, "go straight into the first number." The curtains parted, and Wooler got only as far as *Direct from Hamburg* when Paul launched into "Long Tall Sally" by Little Richard. The boys played it like they had for fans in the Reeperbahn, brash and unrestrained. *"Oooh-oooh baby, havin' some fun toniiiite."* George let loose with a solo that bent his guitar strings to the snapping point.

From offstage, Wooler stared down into a sea of silent, bewildered faces, and that worried him. When audiences went quiet, it usually meant they were about to boo an act offstage. This crowd was simply stunned. Everyone knew the Little Richard song—it was a popular dance number—but the sound coming out of the Beatles was an absolute explosion.

All hell broke loose. Spurred by the pounding music and the band's infectious energy, kids rushed to the front of the stage. They stomped, they screamed, they waved their arms and bounced off walls. George, John, Paul, drummer Pete Best, and Chas Newby standing in for Stu on bass swapped looks. They were used to applause and cheers, not screams and riots. The pandemonium energized the band, and as the screaming escalated, so did their playing. This was what George had wanted from music all along, a chance to connect with fans and have fun playing guitar and singing.

Afterward the kids swarmed around, asking questions and marveling at how well the band "direct from Hamburg" spoke English. In his column for the local music newspaper *Mersey Beat,* Wooler wrote with surprising prescience that the Beatles had created "the excitement, both physical and aural, that symbolized the rebellion of youth. . . . I don't think anything like them will happen again." The Litherland performance marked a turning point for the Beatles. In the next three months they would perform more than forty gigs and establish themselves as Liverpool's premier rock combo.

Shortly after the dance, Wooler proposed that the group make his place, the Cavern, their permanent home so that fans would always know where to find them, and the group began lunchtime performances in February 1961. The Cavern was a former vegetable warehouse on a narrow street in Liverpool's produce district. No one needed directions to find the place: the stuffy basement was so thick with youngsters that their body heat generated a cloud of steam by the front door. Patrons entered by sidling down a stone staircase barely wide enough for one and walking into a dingy brick basement with a low ceiling and a shallow wooden stage. There were no curtains or carpets, no tables, and only a few chairs. There was no ventilation, and condensation dripping from bricks occasionally short-circuited equipment. When that happened, the Beatles led everyone in a chorus of "Comin' 'Round the Mountain" or a round of Sunblest bread commercials, or else they found some other jokey way to keep crowds laughing until the electricity was restored. Paul might walk out with shredded newspaper sticking out of his trouser legs. John might traipse onstage wearing cellophane bags around his shoes. George might come out wearing a collar and tie and nothing else above the waist. Half their job, it seemed, was ad-libbing.

Some Beatles chroniclers have commented that it was here, within hand's reach of clamoring fans, that the band members shaped their unique personalities. John would stand with legs spread wide, the collar of his black leather jacket raised, his guitar riding high on his chest, exuding arrogance and virility. Paul worked a different magic on the girls down front, charming them with his good looks, sweet voice, and polite patter; being half of the band's songwriting team added to his allure. George contented himself with being on the sidelines.

Paul was spending so much time by then writing songs with John that it detracted from time Paul used to spend with George. When John received one hundred pounds from family for his twenty-first birthday, it was Paul he invited to come on a trip to Spain. They never went farther than Paris, but the gesture made clear their allegiance to each other.

The Beatles' originality rested, for the moment, with Lennon and McCartney.

Between February 1961 and August 1963, Wooler introduced the Beatles to Cavern regulars nearly three hundred times, welcoming them with a hearty "Hi there, all you cave dwellers.

Welcome to the best of cellars." The crowds grew bigger until two hundred or more packed in at every lunch.

Some fans couldn't afford the entrance fee and, not wanting to see anyone disappointed, George would see to it that at least a few found places anyway. "Don't tell her I gave it to you," he would whisper to the Cavern doorman, pointing to a hopeful fan and slipping him a few shillings. George championed other bands as well, defying usual rivalries by recommending this guitarist or that pianist to club management.

George's mother, Louise, became a regular, and when her son stepped forward to sing "Sheik of Araby" or another of the few songs in his repertoire, she cheered with the enthusiasm of a young fan. Louise was sitting in the audience one afternoon when John's aunt Mimi showed up to check on what John had been doing with his days.

Louise recognized her and called out, "Aren't they great?"

"I'm glad someone thinks so," Mimi huffed. "We'd all have had lovely, peaceful lives but for you encouraging them."

George remained generally stoic onstage, his one recognizable gesture being a rhythmic twitching of one leg in time to the music. When asked why her son rarely smiled or said anything, Louise gave George's reply: he was the lead guitar. If the others made mistakes while joking around, no one would notice. He, on the other hand, couldn't afford mistakes. All that determined practice as a young boy was beginning to pay off.

Chemistry among the band members was exciting, fun, infectious, and their bookings at other local venues increased. Still, despite the Beatles' growing popularity, no agents came calling, no press attended their performances, and nothing suggested they would ever rise above the confines of their little cellar.

In April 1961, George, John, Paul, and Pete returned to Hamburg to play the Top Ten Club, an upscale version of Koschmider's dive. Before finishing this tour, the Beatles provided backup on a studio recording by Tony Sheridan.

On October 28, 1961, a teenager walked into NEMS Department Store in Liverpool and asked the record department manager, Brian Epstein, for a copy of the record. Epstein scoured his memory and came up blank. "Terribly sorry," he said. "Never heard of it. Or the group." That a customer should ask for a record he did not recognize galled the Beatles' future manager. As son of the store's owner, he took pride in maintaining a complete inventory of all available pop records.

After a round of calls to suppliers, Epstein learned that "My Bonnie" had been recorded in Germany. He called his German supplier and ordered twenty-five copies. When the records sold out in less than an hour, his instincts were aroused. He inquired further and discovered that the band came not from Germany but Liverpool and were in fact playing just around the corner.

"It was dark, damp, and smelly, and I regretted my decision immediately," Epstein recalled of his lunch-hour visit to the Cavern with his assistant Alistair Taylor on November 9, 1961. The Beatles came onstage. Epstein and Taylor stood at the back and watched. Not neat or tidy, Epstein thought. They smoke in public, pretend to hit one another, turn their backs on the audience—still, what enormous energy. After the show he went backstage.

"Hello there," George said. "What brings Mr. Epstein here?" Although they had never been introduced, George knew Epstein from the band's many visits to his store. George scanned the well-dressed visitor. Rich, he thought, and very posh. Epstein explained his instincts about "My Bonnie" and ended their first conversation with handshakes and a promise to return. He and Taylor retired to Peacock's, a nearby restaurant, for lunch.

"What did you think?" Epstein asked his young assistant.

"They were bloody awful," Taylor said. "But *fantastic.*"

"I tend to agree," Epstein said. "Alistair, do you think I could manage them?" Neither of them even knew what a management contract looked like.

A few weeks later, after phoning music industry contacts for details about managing a rock and roll band, Epstein invited the group to his office. Paul didn't show, and Epstein asked George to call him at home.

"He's in the bath," George reported.

Epstein simmered. Why would anyone take on such an irresponsible group of teenagers? "This is disgraceful. He's going to be late for a very important meeting."

"Late," George agreed, "but very clean."

Eventually Paul arrived, and the party relocated to a nearby milk bar, where Epstein made his proposal. "You need a manager," he said, and offered to take up the task. They agreed to terms: 25 percent agent's fee. Because George was still a minor, Epstein had to secure permission from his father. Epstein's gentlemanly demeanor impressed Harold and Louise when he came to visit. They granted him permission to sign George on, and Epstein took charge of their son's career.

Epstein began by typing up instructions spelling out where and when the boys were expected to be for each engagement. Please do not smoke or eat onstage, he asked, and play your best numbers, not just the ones you like. He explained that joking with girls in the front row made other people feel ignored, and when they finished a set they should bow from the waist, the way he had learned to do at the Royal Academy of Dramatic Arts. Under Epstein's leadership their fees at the Cavern doubled from seven to fifteen pounds per date. Bookings expanded farther and farther away from Liverpool. Epstein's makeover worked magic, and soon four greasy Beatles reincarnated as an ensemble of groomed artists.

Besides a neater appearance and better pay, George's new manager provided him with greater self-confidence. When they met, George was just a boy who played music because it was fun and because nothing in his constricted world of docks and vegetable markets offered a more exciting future. But he needed someone more mature to guide him, and Epstein's faith in his prospects helped George see how to make the most of his talent. In turn, George inspired the others to keep the fires burning. We're bound to make it, he told them, if we just keep going.

Epstein became George's role model: a full-fledged adult at age twenty-seven who possessed everything George never had, including a well-to-do family, a successful business, and a gentleman's bearing. For his part, Epstein found in George and in the other Beatles things he desperately wanted in his own life: excitement, irreverence, and creative energy.

Most of all, they provided him with friendship, which for a gay man struggling for acceptance in a homophobic culture was not always available. Epstein eventually explained his sexual orientation, which never altered George's affection for him. In later years George spoke only of Epstein's kindness and concern for the group's success and how he had shaped their image and taken care of them personally and professionally.

Brian Epstein would never be content merely to earn his boys more money. He wanted them to be superstars, and that required a careful plan of attack. His strategy was first to land them a recording contract, then upgrade the band from playing clubs to bigger and bigger venues.

After a seemingly endless round of rejections, Epstein at last landed the group an audition at Decca Records in London. On New Year's Day 1962, the Beatles arrived at the Decca studios and set up for their audition. A red light went on, a technician signaled, and they began. Paul's voice cracked from nervousness, and George picked up the beat with "The Sheik of Araby," rocking on his guitar and charging across a lyrical desert in search of his one true love. The session ended without event, and the group returned to Liverpool and to their daily grind at the Cavern. In March, Epstein received an invitation to meet with Decca executive Dick Rowe.

"Not to mince words," Rowe said, "we don't like your boys' sound. Groups are out. Four-piece groups with guitars particularly are finished. You have a good record business in Liverpool," Rowe said. "Stick to that."

Epstein hid his disappointment behind a brazen reply. "You must be out of your mind," he said. "These boys are going to explode. I'm completely confident that one day they will be bigger than Elvis Presley." Epstein's faith in the Beatles was admirable, but Rowe's eyes rolled. Elvis was king. No one in the history of music had ever sold as many records, earned as much money, or gained as wide, large, or faithful a following. If ever a phrase could destroy a speaker's credibility, Epstein had just uttered it.

That evening, the manager for what would become the most successful group in entertainment history called his boys to a meeting. Then he boarded a train at Euston Station, nursing his wounds, and disembarked two hundred miles later at Lime Street Station, Liverpool. George, John, Paul, and Pete sat with him in a coffee shop and listened to what had happened. Over the next few months, the Lime Street Station coffee shop became a confessional where Epstein admitted one failure after another at Phillips, EMI, Columbia, or whatever label he had just visited. He was applying every negotiating skill at his disposal, but there were hundreds of bands in early 1960s England vying for the attention of a handful of London record labels.

George understood how hard it was for Brian to admit defeat. Epstein's father had criticized his son for wasting time with a rock group instead of doing real work, a refrain George had begun to hear regularly from his own father. Neither George nor Brian had ever been a good student, which added to their list of shared disappointments. Still, Epstein persevered, booking the Beatles wherever he could, including another stint in Hamburg, to begin on April 11.

On April 10, Stuart Sutcliffe died, the victim of a brain hemorrhage resulting from an attack weeks earlier after a dance. Astrid wandered out of the hospital, dazed and alone. She cabled Stuart's mother, who flew with George to Hamburg later that day. John, Paul, and Pete Best had arrived earlier to prepare for their club job, expecting to have Stu back in the group. At the airport, Astrid told them the news through tears. Paul and Pete wept, and John cried hysterically.

George gathered them together for their show that night. They played somehow, but said little and did not have the strength for gags. Out of respect for their friend, the band declined to return to England for the funeral. They were becoming more popular by then, and had they turned up, Tony Sheridan said, "it could have turned things into a three-ring circus."

George hadn't encountered death this close before. Stuart was twenty-one, two years older than himself. They were friends, played music together, shared a room and a career. George had stood next to him onstage just a few weeks before. Stuart wasn't that skilled a musician, but he looked good, which was why some jealous thug had attacked him back in Liverpool and given him a brain hemorrhage. What was it that twisted life into such cruel shapes? Everybody loved Stuart. Could there have been gentler fellow? It made no sense. What good did it do working so hard for something if fortune played so whimsically with the outcome?

In June, during an engagement at Hamburg's Star Club, their fortune turned. A telegram arrived from Epstein. CONGRATULA-TIONS, BOYS. EMI REQUESTS RECORDING SESSION. PLEASE RE-HEARSE NEW MATERIAL. George was stunned. A recording session was not yet a contract, but for a homegrown Liverpool rock and roll band it was as miraculous as turning lead into gold.

On June 6, 1962, the band arrived at EMI Studios in Abbey Road. Producer George Martin listened carefully as the group sailed through one of John and Paul's early compositions, "Love Me Do," and four other numbers. He was particularly impressed by Paul's voice and George's solid lead guitar work. Martin deemed the Beatles a balanced band that might provide good backup for some name artist. Very nice, he said; he would let them know. The boys returned to Liverpool, not knowing what to make of Martin's cryptic review and fearing this would be a repeat of their Decca disappointment.

Three months later, word came that George Martin wanted to produce the Beatles' first record. This was it, their chance to go big time. If diligent efforts such as Brian's could reap such results, then maybe George needed to assume a more active role in helping determine the group's future. After some serious closed-door discussion, he and Paul agreed that, to make the most of the opportunity, they needed to replace Pete Best with Ringo Starr, a drummer whom they had befriended in Hamburg.

Born Richard Starkey, Ringo had grown up in the Dingle, a densely packed square mile of out-of-work Liverpudlians, crowded pubs, and violent gangs. At ten he developed pleurisy and spent a year in the hospital, where doctors kept their young patients active by teaching them music. It was there that Ringo discovered drums.

Ringo assimilated rhythms effortlessly and was a better drummer than Pete Best. He was also witty and brash, more like George and the others in personality and style. George may have liked Pete, but business was business and if he was ever going to realize his destiny in music, he was prepared to make hard choices. He convinced Epstein to go along with the plan and then called Ringo to tell him the job was his.

In August, Ringo Starr took his place behind the drum kit, causing a near riot at the Cavern, where fans viewed Pete's removal as outright sabotage.

George wanted it clear that his choice had been sound. Over drinks with Epstein and Allan Williams at the Blue Angel, a club nearby the Cavern, George turned to the *Mersey Beat* magazine founder and asked, "Allan, tell me, who do you think is the best drummer, Peter Best or Ringo?"

"Ringo," Williams said immediately, "every time."

"There, you see," George said to Epstein with a smile. "What did I tell you?"

That afternoon at the Cavern, a disgruntled patron gave George a black eye—not the last time he would feel backlash from acting on what he believed. Ringo fit in seamlessly, and the newly configured Beatles arrived at Abbey Road Studios on a blustery September morning to make their first record.

Tall and professional, George Martin fulfilled his role as head of EMI's Parlophone label with style, wearing a tie and jacket and giving directions in impeccable queen's English. He brought the boys into the control room and told them what they should and should not do during their sessions. The four sat there quietly.

"Well, we've laid into you about what sort of standards we expect from you as recording artists," Martin said. "Is there anything that you want to say to us? Anything you don't like?" It was an opportunity too good to resist. George glanced mischievously at his mates and then grinned at Martin.

"Yeah," he said. "I don't like your tie."

It was a nice tie, black and white with horses, one of which George Martin was particularly proud. He looked at his engineer, Norman Smith, then at the group. Everyone broke up. George Martin produced recordings of such offbeat comedians as Peter Sellers, Peter Ustinov, and the Goons. "We just fell about laughing," Smith recalled, relieved to discover that the Beatles shared a brand of humor that was Parlophone's stock in trade.

"Love Me Do" was released a month later and climbed to number seventeen on the U.K. charts. On October 5, 1962, George heard his work for the first time on radio and "went shivery all over." Even though it wasn't a number-one hit, that first bit of plastic was a heady payoff for two years of slogging it out in clubs. Then it happened all at once—a rush of radio and television appearances, more dates away from Liverpool, and the most votes in that year's *Mersey Beat* popularity poll.

For nineteen-year-old George, the attention was, in his own words, "a thrill beyond compare." Yet, unlike some teenage musicians who mistook popularity for privilege, he heeded his manager's advice and remained a gentleman. He even apologized to an audience in Exeter for the group's late arrival, hoping that "our fans were not disappointed with the show we put on."

With the Beatles' jump in ratings, Epstein put an end to their Hamburg-era style of dress by convincing the group to wear custom-tailored mohair suits and ties. "Yeah, man, I'll wear a suit," John said. "I'll wear a balloon if someone's going to pay me. I'm not in love with leather *that* much." Epstein's fashion advice was practical, not frivolous. His target for the band now was television, which by that year was in more than 80 percent of all British homes, and on TV neatness counted.

In December 1962 Epstein landed them an appearance on an important TV show called *Thank Your Lucky Stars*. The broadcast took place on one of the coldest nights on record. Everything froze: motors, snowplows, even the English Channel. No one ventured outdoors, concerts and sports events were canceled, and movie houses and entertainment venues closed their doors. People went mad for the Beatles that year, at least in part because the group debuted on a night when all of England was home watching television.

The momentum of the Beatles' career continued to build. On February 6, 1963, the group showed up for a gig in the North English town of Bedford. From the moment they arrived, things felt different to them. The crowd by the stage door was larger, louder. George and his mates sat in their cars waiting for doormen to clear a path. Inside, the tension was greater than ever, and the audience restless during opening acts. At last the openers finished and a hush descended over the auditorium. The houselights dimmed, and the curtains swung open to reveal the Beatles onstage. The crowd started screaming as never before.

"It sounded like pigs were being slaughtered," said Andrew Loog Oldham, a freelance publicist who was there that evening and who would later be known as the manager of the Rolling Stones. "I was standing at the side of the stage next to Brian, and the effect was like being hit with a steamroller—a wall of noise, which drowned our voices, drowned the band, swamped everything."

George stood with his mates at the center of the adulation. The moment epitomized everything he had ever hoped to achieve: the excitement of making music, cheers washing over him from adoring fans.

Oldham looked over at Epstein, who stood smiling, his chin resting in his hand, and he sensed more than heard the words Epstein mouthed as he gently nodded his head.

"It's starting. Just like I said it would. It's starting."

3

A Price to Pay

It's just as though it's a different person.
—*George, 1964*

B y April 1963, the Beatles were eliciting shrieks and screams wherever they went. That month their third single, "From Me to You," reached number one. Their next, "She Loves You," reached number one a few months later. In October they starred on *Sunday Night at the London Palladium* and were seen by more than fifteen million television viewers. Crowds at their live concerts continued to swell. Thousands of fans parked all night outside box offices hoping to secure tickets. In Sweden, police with dogs on leashes were needed to protect the group from fans who broke through the barricades, climbed onstage, and threw themselves on the four men. The Beatles' arrival back in London stirred even greater chaos. Thousands of fans choked the airport. Beatlemania, as the press called the hysteria, had begun.

On November 4, 1963, the Beatles sang before the queen at the Royal Command Variety Performance, England's most prestigious charity event, where they shared the bill with such world-renowned stars as Marlene Dietrich and Maurice Chevalier. "I don't want to sound ungrateful," George told the press afterward, "but why are the Beatles on the same stage as a mass of show business greats? . . . We're just four normal folk who have had a couple of hit records." George's greater concern was for fans who could not afford the high ticket prices. "On an occasion like this," he said, "we would have liked some of our fans in the audience, to make us feel more at home. After all, it was those people who made it possible for us in the first place."

After the show, Marlene Dietrich told Epstein, "They are so sexy. They have the girls so frantic for them, they must have quite a time." Epstein remained silent, but his assistant Alistair Taylor later commented that she wasn't wrong. "After every concert, the best-looking female fans would be given instructions as to how to get back to the hotel. It was one of the perks of the job, and the boys liked their perks. . . . They had this amazing power to point and say, 'You, you, you, and you,' and lovely young women would arrive at the hotel simply begging for sex."

That month, their next single, "I Want to Hold Your Hand," went straight to number one, with advance orders for more than a million copies. In December, the Beatles were voted Top Vocal Group of the Year, and seven of their records were in the top twenty, an unprecedented feat.

Beatlemania continued to spread, and grownups searched frantically for explanations of what was happening. At an annual meeting of the Church of England, a bishop railed that the band was a "psycho-pathetic group" whose one-week's wages could build a cathedral in Africa. Another countered that he was a fan and thought it all healthy fun. A third garnered attention in the press when he asked the Beatles to tape "O Come, All Ye Faithful, Yeah, Yeah, Yeah" for Christmas. They declined. A psychologist writing in the *Daily Mirror* made a safe guess that the Beatles were "relieving a sexual urge" in youngsters. Taking that insight to a higher realm, the *Observer* printed a photo of the Greek fertility goddess Amorgos, who possesses a vaguely guitar-like shape, and declared that the resemblance proved guitars were sex symbols with precedents "dating back about 4,800 years before the Beatles Era."

The madness escalated. Before one concert in Plymouth, authorities turned hoses on screaming fans to control them.

No one thought to turn hoses on journalists whose over-heated catchphrases also threatened to spin out of control. One music critic lauded the band's "flat submediant key switches" and their work's "Aeolian cadence . . . like Mahler's 'Song of the Earth.'" A writer for London's *Sunday Times* declared John and Paul "the greatest composers since Schubert." A reporter asked John what he thought of the group's "unresolved leading tones" and "false modal frames."

"We're gonna see a doctor about that," John said.

George savored his success with the Beatles but was beginning to realize the price he had to pay. Fame made him stand out. Strangers claimed to love him. People had things to sell him and favors to ask. Young girls wrote him about their fantasies. Businessmen dangled schemes before him, and reporters clamored to broadcast his every move. That August he wrote his first Beatles song, "Don't Bother Me," voicing his distrust of all the attention and a desire to keep a space of his own. Please go away, he sang, I just want to be alone.

In 1963 it all still seemed more or less manageable. "You get used to it," George told a London reporter, "signing autographs, waving at people."

What about wealth? the reporter asked. Had that made a difference in the way George and his family lived?

George thought of his dad, who was still reluctant to spend money on anything unnecessary. "No," he said, shaking his head, "not so far, anyway. Except for holidays and things like that. You know, we can just get the money out of the bank and go wherever we want!" Not many people had bank accounts in those days, which were reserved for businesses and the truly posh.

You are one of the reputed deep thinkers in this group, the reporter said. Is this the peak of your life? What happens to you after this is over?

"Well," George calculated, not minding the deep-thinker part but wanting to avoid sounding smug, "I suppose we'll stay doing this sort of stuff for a couple of years. I mean, naturally we won't be able to stay at this level. But, umm, we should have another two years at least, I think."

What happens then? the reporter asked.

"Probably I'll have a little business or something like that. I don't know," he said. "You can't really tell."

"It's funny," George told a Manchester television reporter. "You see your pictures and read articles about George Harrison . . . but you don't actually think, 'Oh, that's me. There I am in the paper.'" He smiled and added, "It's just as though it's a different person."

He raised his eyebrows, looked off to the side as though considering what to say, and then smiled at his inability to find a way of explaining either to himself or his interviewer what it felt like to see himself through the eyes of the public. For now it was all good fun, and the money and fame were his childhood dream come true.

On January 3, 1964, talk-show host Jack Paar aired footage of the Beatles on the *Tonight* show. The clip focused on John at the microphone and George on guitar before a screaming audience of young fans. "I'm interested in the Beatles as a sociological phenomenon," Paar quipped. "They're from the toughest part of England and they're kind of witty. Someone asked them what was exciting about growing up on the docks of Liverpool. Their answer was, 'Just staying alive, that's exciting.' Ed Sullivan will have them live in February."

On February 7, 1964, the Beatles left London for their first trip to America. By 6:30 A.M. radios across the United States were tracking the approach of their Pan Am flight like that of an enemy bomber. "The Beatles left London thirty minutes ago. They're thirty minutes out over the Atlantic Ocean, heading for New York. It is thirty-two Beatles degrees." As the plane touched down at Kennedy International Airport, noise from a crowd assembled to greet them overtook the roar of the jet's turbo engines, and from his window George looked out on a scene that had him doubting his eyes. More than ten thousand screaming fans had assembled, singing "We Love You Beatles, Oh, Yes, We Do."

As the plane touched down and discharged its famous passengers, the fans went wilder. A policeman on duty shook his head. "I see it," he said, "but I don't believe it." An airport spokesperson added, "We've never seen anything like this here before, never. Not even for kings and queens." At an airport press conference the four men generated enough quips to keep everyone laughing.

"What do you think of Beethoven?" one reporter asked.

Ringo took the bait. "Great. Especially his poems."

"How do you find America?" asked another.

"Turn left at Greenland," John said.

"Was your family in show business?" asked a third.

"Well," John replied with a grin, "me dad used to say me mum was a great performer."

After a few minutes of banter, the Beatles left for Manhattan in Cadillac limousines. George shared his limo with press aide Brian Sommerville and watched as police on motorcycles flanked the entourage, sirens blaring, red lights spinning. The limos headed west on the Van Wyck Expressway. Skyscrapers loomed in the distance. Kids zoomed by, waving and screaming, dangling cardboard signs from their car windows. A white convertible sped past with the word "BEETLES" fingered onto its dusty door.

"Did you see that?" Sommerville asked, incredulous.

"They misspelled 'Beatles,'" George whispered with a grin, nursing a sore throat.

The caravan crossed into Manhattan. Hundreds of fans had gathered outside the Plaza Hotel. Guards from the Burns Detective Agency covered every entrance. Signs waving in the brisk morning air—"ELVIS IS DEAD" and "COME OUT BEATLES"—which brought smiles of satisfaction to Brian Epstein and John Lennon, who had both predicted the Beatles would eventually surpass the king. The screaming started as soon as their limos pulled up to the Fifth Avenue entrance.

The Beatles and their entourage scrambled up the steps and into a waiting elevator. George went promptly to bed. His sister,

Louise, had arrived that afternoon from her home in Illinois and ministered to him with hot tea. The Plaza Hotel physician showed Louise a vial of medication that George was advised to take every hour.

"Would you see to it?" he asked with a note of desperation. "You're probably the only female in the city who could function around him normally."

Two days later, ten thousand spectators jammed Broadway waiting to see the Beatles arrive at CBS Television Studio 50, later known as the Ed Sullivan Theater, for their first performance in America. More than 50,000 fans had written in hoping to secure seats in an auditorium that held only 728. Inside, teens waiting for the band to come onstage jumped up and down, tore their hair, howled, and let forth what one reporter described as "a sound as though of anguish, death, and destruction." Old-timers on the television crew looked at one another in disbelief. Even Elvis had not prompted such hysteria. Sullivan appeared from the wings, pushing the air with his hands, urging peace.

"Stop it," Sullivan yelled, "or I'll get a barber!" Backstage, Sullivan asked Paul, "Are you nervous?"

"Not really," Paul said with a shrug.

"You should be," Sullivan shot back. "Seventy-three million viewers will be watching you."

McCartney froze. That was more than a third of the population of the United States. George appeared his usual laconic self, unfazed by the whole affair. Then the Beatles took the stage.

Popular biographies of the band tend to describe the euphoria that greeted them that night as a reaction from Americans traumatized by recent events and desperately in need of relief. President Kennedy had been assassinated less than three months before the Beatles' Ed Sullivan debut. Days later, Kennedy's assassin was murdered on live television. Riots over any number of grievances, including jobs, education, and segregation were breaking out every week. Families struggled with the anxiety of fathers and sons shipping out to fight in Vietnam. Americans were so afraid of Soviet nuclear attack that the sonic boom from a passing jet would send people diving under the nearest table. Despite months of peaceful civil rights marches, no new desegregation law had yet been enacted, and protests nationwide turned deadly. Americans were living with violence and uncertainty every day, and for the first time in history, television broadcast images of the carnage every night. Adults could offer no explanation for why the world was tilting so far askew, leaving young people to define for themselves who they were and what they believed.

That night on *The Ed Sullivan Show*, these baby boomers, as the postwar generation would later be dubbed, saw four boys riding above the paranoia, and they fell in love. Fears faded, hormones flowed, adrenaline gushed, and pulses throbbed. The Beatles ended their first set with "She Loves You," and the song's emphatic closing words, "Be Glad." No one had told young people they could be glad again.

With all that love came a whole lot of money. For rekindling their sense of hope, consumers spent more money on Beatles paraphernalia than could be accurately counted. *Life* magazine had recently run a cover story declaring, "A New $10 Billion Power: the U.S. Teenage Consumer." Baby boomers had become the largest and most influential market force in America, and the Beatles were beneficiaries. Merchandise and paraphernalia—wigs and wallpaper, dolls and figurines, chewing gum and candy, caps and shirts, belts and boots, balloons and buttons, sheets and pillowcases, photographs and pencil sharpeners, toothbrushes, towels, and everything in between—an entire industry of Beatles stuff flooded stores and street corners. In 1964, Beatles merchandise in the United States alone generated more than $50 million in sales. In the week following their *Ed Sullivan Show* performance, the band's records accounted for a major percentage of the entire year's record industry sales, as they would for years to come.

The day after their departure from the United States, the Beatles were featured on the cover of *Newsweek,* and their return to the United Kingdom was celebrated like a national holiday. Crowds thronged the airport. Madame Tussaud's museum put wax figures of George, John, Paul, and Ringo on display, and their photos appeared on the front page of newspapers nationwide. Ringo enjoyed a unique honor. By write-in votes he was elected vice president of Leeds University over a former lord chief justice.

Ringo's mother, Elsie, awoke one Sunday morning to find a crowd knocking at her front door. A busload of fans had traveled overnight from London to visit Ringo's home.

"Well, what could I do?" said Elsie. "I fetched them all in and gave them tea and biscuits. I thought it was marvelous—all that way, just for our Ritchie. They never ate anything. They just wrapped them up, to take back as souvenirs. They wanted to see his bed as well," she said. "They'd lie on it, moaning."

George's family, too, responded to his meteoric rise with pride. Harold's hesitations were swept away in the deluge of his son's success, brothers Harry and Pete basked in the reflection of their kid brother's glow, and mother Louise looked after George's fans. Each week she traveled to Beatles Fan Club headquarters in Liverpool to pick up batches of promotional photos. Then she returned home and stayed up late answering fan mail longhand, often writing two thousand letters per month. Shelves along one wall of their new home displayed gifts sent from around the world. On another wall hung a gold plaque from the United Beatles Fans of Pomona, California, that read: "Presented to Harold and Louise Harrison for the time and effort they have shown to Beatle People everywhere."

On George's twenty-first birthday, nearly one million cards, letters, and gifts arrived at the Harrison house in Wavertree— seven truckloads of mail that filled the entry of their home for weeks. It was, according to the postal department, the most mail ever delivered to one address outside of the royal family. On George's birthday, screaming fans surrounded his parents' house. Girls kissed the doorknob.

"Have you got to put up with this all the time?" a policeman asked Louise. "I'd go mad."

It amused George that his success had transformed his parents into local celebrities. The gods had transported him to entertainers' heaven, and relocation benefits included upgrading his parents to peers of the realm. Instead of "There goes Harry," now it was, "There goes George's dad." His mother had been similarly elevated.

"People always think we must be different now, because of George," Louise said. "We went to a fan's wedding the other day, and people said, 'How can you enjoy yourselves with the likes of us?' They expect us to wear mink all the time."

George loved being able to pay them back for all they'd done for him. Harold was still working as a bus driver. George asked him how much he was earning.

"Ten pounds, two shillings," his father said.

"A day?" George asked.

"A week," Harold said. This was after thirty-one years of service. George fumed.

"Dad, please retire. I'll give you three times that to do nothing. It'll put another ten years on your life."

Harold accepted, both retirement and being proven wrong about the music business. So far, it seemed to George, success had few drawbacks, though one in particular was beginning to concern him. "What annoys us," he told the teen magazine *Rave* in June, "is that people treat us sometimes as if we are just things and not human beings."

George started living like the rock royalty he had become. He and Ringo moved to London and shared an apartment—forty-five pounds per week, a fortune back then, but one that allowed them the luxury of private bathrooms. It was an amazing time. Within walking distance were jazz clubs and nightclubs and every imaginable kind of ethnic restaurant—foods they had never tasted before, French and Middle Eastern and Jewish. It was the sixties, and colors exploded everywhere, riotous colors, on the streets and in display windows, pinks and purples, yellows and oranges and reds. George and Ringo would wear outrageous clothes and stay up all night in clubs such as the Saddle Room, where Prince Philip was a member. By 4:00 A.M. they would have drunk enough to take the club's horse and coach rather than risk driving home.

Making it as a Beatle was particularly satisfying because they had done so despite the prejudices usually encountered by bands from Liverpool. "The whole of England's music industry was in London," Bill Harry recalled. "In America, you had Detroit, Los Angeles, New York, Nashville—different centers doing different kinds of music. Here, everything was concentrated and controlled by London, and London never let anyone get in if they had a Liverpool accent. People with Liverpool accents were considered thieves and robbers. You couldn't get a decent job. You'd have to work in the factories or on the docks. The Beatles' success for us was Liverpool's success."

George bought expensive shoes and wore tailored shirts and ordered fancy cars. Ever since he was a kid, he had dreamed of going places fast, and one of his first purchases was a dark green Jaguar XK140 with a 190-horsepower engine and a top speed of 210 miles per hour. In the months that followed, he added an Aston Martin DB5, an Aston Mini, and a black Mercedes with one-way windows and contoured seats.

To the press he denied having changed much. "I'm still an eggs and chips man," he told the *Daily Mail* in April 1964. "I've had caviar and I like it. But I'd still rather have an egg sandwich. The only difference now is that when I say things like that, the Egg Marketing Board sends me a dozen for free."

More success followed when the Beatles starred in their first movie, *A Hard Day's Night*, which began shooting three weeks after their Ed Sullivan appearance. Filming had hardly started when George spied a beautiful nineteen-year-old cast member named Pattie Boyd. Pattie had blond hair, long legs, a brilliant smile, and wide blue eyes that conveyed an air of childlike vulnerability. She asked George for his autograph, and at a loss for any other way to communicate his feelings, he marked little hearts under his name. The stunning young model was out of the league of a Liverpool bus driver's son who never finished school, but she was just right for a Beatle.

George's initial infatuation was adolescent—he claimed Pattie reminded him of his favorite film star, Brigitte Bardot—but he quickly discovered that in this vivacious young woman he had found a compatible partner. At an early age, Patricia Anne Boyd had, like George, established a successful career. As a top model in a decade preoccupied with looks and fashion, she frequently appeared on the covers of leading publications such as *Vogue* and *Seventeen*. It was her appearance in popular television commercials that had landed her a part in the Beatles' film *A Hard Day's Night*, which in turn led to her partnership with George.

From the start of their relationship in March 1964, she played an active role in George's busy life. In a typical month, they would attend recording sessions, gather with friends, meet with record industry executives, have meals with fellow entertainers, and occasionally vacation to places such as Hawaii or Tahiti. They attended Allen Ginsberg's thirty-ninth birthday party and made a hasty retreat when the beat poet greeted them in the nude. They went clubbing with the Moody Blues, attended premieres of films such as *Alfie* with Michael Caine, and smiled when friends would refer to "George-and-Pattie" instead of "George," as though they were a single entity.

So syncopated were their movements that marriage occurred without a hint of fanfare, a logical addition to their crowded calendar. George's proposal came on Christmas day 1965, while driving to a party at Brian Epstein's home.

"We were just motoring along," Pattie recalled, "listening to the radio when suddenly he very calmly told me he loved me and wanted us to get married. I think I just said yes or some such nonsense. But believe me, inside I was doing cartwheels. We really were very much in love."

George jumped out of the car, went in to consult with Epstein, and returned ten minutes later. "It's all right," he said. "Brian has said we can get married in January. Off we go." They were married three weeks later and honeymooned in Barbados.

"When George got together with Pattie," his father Harold told reporters, "Mrs. Harrison and I were delighted. Of course, to the rest of the world it might have been 'Beatle Marries Model,' but to those that really knew them it was clear that this was a genuine modern-day love story."

While George's partnership with Pattie blossomed, his partnership with the Beatles was beginning to feel old. He had not completed any compositions since "Don't Bother Me," in part because he was uncomfortable promoting his own song ideas too aggressively and in part because they simply weren't welcomed. John and Paul had agreed to be songwriting partners as early as 1957, before George joined the Quarry Men, and until 1970 Lennon and McCartney would continue to share equal credit even if only one of them had composed a song.

Their monopoly on Beatles songs seemed impenetrable, and George's isolation from the creative dimension of the group preyed on him. "It was a shyness, a withdrawal," said the boy who used to doodle guitars in class. "I always used to take the easy way out."

Prior to the Beatles' first trip to America, *Mersey Beat* magazine founder Bill Harry used to badger George about doing more writing. "At least you can try," he would say. "Why should it always be Lennon-McCartney?" George replied that if he did write he'd want to take his time rather than create something corny. Some time later, Harry went to see the group perform at the ABC Blackpool auditorium. George walked up to him with a smile.

"I want to thank you," George said. "I was going down to the club one night in Liverpool and thinking, 'I don't want to bump into Bill and have him push me again about writing a bloody song.' So instead I stayed home and started writing. I called it 'Don't Bother Me.' So, thanks very much. I've already earned seven thousand pounds off that one." From then on, he carried a tape recorder with him on tour, and in the isolation of his hotel room he recorded ideas for songs, often late into the night.

✳　✳　✳

Despite constraints on his creative talents, George's career spiraled upward as the number of Beatles fans exploded past anything in entertainment history. In August 1964 more than a
hundred thousand people lined the streets of Amsterdam to
catch a glimpse of them driving from the airport to their hotel.
In Adelaide, Australia, the number tripled: three hundred thousand fans—half the population of the city—lined the route of
their caravan. When their film *A Hard Day's Night* debuted that
year, attended by Princess Margaret and the Earl of Snowden, so
many onlookers jammed into Piccadilly Circus that central
London came to a complete standstill. In five years, George had
skyrocketed from a row house in working-class Liverpool to the
top of the material mountain. Contrary to his earlier prediction
that the group might have no more than two years of success, it
seemed now like the rocket would never come down.

Reporters frequently asked the band whether all this adulation made them think of themselves as gods. "Whenever we start
thinking like that," they quipped, "we just look at Ringo and
that brings us back down to the ground." That ability to turn the
mirror on one another and laugh had been bred in Liverpool.

"We made fun of ourselves since we figured someone was
going to do it anyway, and we might as well do it first," said
George's sister, Louise. "There was no such thing as a bigheaded
Liverpudlian. As soon as you presented yourself as a big shot, all
of Liverpool would jump on you. 'Who do you think you are?'"

When on tour, George wrote to his sister about all the exciting things that were happening to the Beatles, and he would add
"Big Head" at the end of his sentences, "just to bring himself
down again and let me know that he wasn't taking it seriously,"
she said. "He said to me many times, 'We're not great musicians,
you know. We're still just learning. And none of us knows how
to read music. None of us is particularly good-looking, and
none of us has a fantastic personality. We're just ordinary kinds
of guys.' He had a practical, realistic way of looking at things."

Looking at his career in that practical, realistic way, George
was beginning to see little to be happy about. Newsreels and

movies of the day may have depicted his life as fun and games, but nothing could have been farther from the truth. "A good romp? That was fair in the films," he wrote in his autobiography, *I, Me, Mine*, "but in the real world . . . we didn't have any space . . . like monkeys in a zoo."

On their 1964 U.S. tour alone, the Beatles covered twenty-five cities in thirty-two days, played to a total of half a million people, and flew forty thousand miles. Between 1961 and 1965 they made seven tours of the United Kingdom, three of America, one of Europe, and two around the world. They played more than fourteen hundred club dates, often as many as three in a day, in addition to fifty-three radio shows, thirty-five television programs, and one of the most prolific and grueling record outputs in pop music history.

George's world became claustrophobic, shrunk to the confines of hotels and cars and stages and recording booths. On those rare occasions when he had a day off, the impositions of fame followed him home. His friend Andrew Oldham lived not far away, but to pay a visit George needed to take two cabs to outwit fans. To see a movie with friends, he had to rent a private screening room and organize arrivals and departures like a military maneuver. Celebrities and VIPs insisted on seeing him, usurping any personal time he may have had. George rebelled.

"I'm not meeting Shirley Temple," he shouted at press aide Derek Taylor on one leg of an American tour. "I don't know Shirley Temple. She doesn't mean anything to me."

Usually George just gave in to the caricature of himself depicted by reporters and offered quick retorts and quotable one-liners.

"What do you do when you're cooped up in your rooms between shows?"

"Ice skate."

It was simply the fastest way to get reporters off his back. Wit and irony came naturally to him, but occasionally the incessant preoccupation with his every move sent him over the edge. In January 1964, an argument with Beatles press agent Brian Sommerville over adding more interviews to his calendar had George so exasperated that he threw orange juice in Sommerville's face. The press agent retaliated by boxing George's ear. Six months later, at a nightclub in Los Angeles, George threw a drink at a photographer whom he had warned not to take pictures.

George could afford to go anywhere he wanted now, and yet the world felt once again too small, as it had when he was growing up in Liverpool. His life consisted of sleeping in hotels, eating tepid food, and wasting time playing cards while waiting to sing the same tunes that no one could hear above the screams. A married man, he still had to put up with young girls constantly sneaking into his hotel room, where guards had to be posted at every elevator and exit. Even on his short retreats back home to Esher, the intrusions continued. George and Pattie returned home one night to find that two girls had broken in and were hiding under their bed and giggling.

It was the hysteria that had George most terrified. During a concert in Kansas City in September 1964, hundreds of screaming fans broke through police barriers and attacked the band's mobile dressing room. The van rocked backward and forward until at last it pitched over with a groan. To restore order, police retaliated by attacking the mob with rubber billy clubs.

As the Beatles' fame continued to grow, so did George's concern over what might happen to him in public. When sponsors scheduled a ticker tape parade for the band prior to a concert in San Francisco, he refused to take part.

"I was getting very nervous," he told a reporter years later. "I didn't like the idea of being too popular. They used us as an excuse to go mad, the world did—and then they blamed it on us." George's sister, Louise, remembered watching one night in Chicago as police hustled the group out a window of their hotel room—the only way they could reach the concert hall next door without being mobbed. As he stepped out onto the fire escape, George looked back at her.

"It was like the eyes of a deer," she said, "looking into the barrel of a gun."

There was also a constant parade of disabled children. Convinced their charges would be cured if only a Beatle would bless them, caregivers arrived at concerts with handicapped youngsters—deaf, blind, paraplegic, babies missing arms or legs—in wheelchairs and oxygen tents. A tangle of unfortunate young people reached out to George as he worked his way toward the stage.

"What do they think that we can do?" he lamented. How could anyone think God had chosen him as a vehicle of mercy? He had always been modest, not given to grandiose displays, let alone capable of divine dispensations. Certainly he felt for the children. Some quirk of fate had spared him from their plight, and he was grateful. But how could he change things? For the past two years, people had assumed that because he was now a mythic figure he had acquired special powers. It was part of the price he paid for being taken as a god: exaggerated expectations from worshipers.

Crueler, John poked fun at the fans' disabilities, flapping his hands together in imitation of their awkward applause and stumbling about onstage. His antics failed to amuse George, who found little about their career amusing anymore.

By early 1965, George had stopped laughing. The Beatles had managed to survive the circumstances of their career thanks to a limitless supply of friendship and an ability to laugh at anything, even tragedy—but the humor had gone out of their lives.

"Never again," he told Epstein. "This is it." Touring had become a sideshow of artistic futility, and John, Paul, and Ringo agreed. Their concert days were over.

"Sorry, lads," Epstein said. "We've got something fixed up for Shea Stadium. If we cancel, you are going to lose a million dollars."

Shea Stadium on August 15, 1965, was a gaping, howling maw filled with fifty-six thousand people, the largest crowd ever assembled for an entertainment event. The entire world seemed to have descended on the Flushing, New York, arena. Caged in behind a high wire fence was an undulating, writhing sea of Beatlemaniacs illuminated by ten thousand spotlights. The band arrived by helicopter atop a nearby World's Fair building, then scrambled into a Wells Fargo armored truck that drove them inside the stadium. They stepped out of the truck, and from the stands spewed an apocalyptic roar. Police held their ears against the pain. Within minutes, emergency nursing stations beneath the stands were filled to overflowing with girls who had fainted from their own screaming.

Stadium concerts had never happened before. No singer or group could fill so large a space. Originally conceived for baseball, football, and other relatively nonmusical events, the acoustics inside Shea Stadium were poor. For the Beatles' concert, the Vox sound company created customized amplifiers with their usual thirty watts of power boosted to a spectacular one hundred watts. Nothing helped. The Beatles' performance was swallowed up by an all-engulfing noise that drove the arena's two thousand guards to despair. Screams overwhelmed anything coming off the stage. George, John, and Paul heard nothing of what they played and watched one another, trying to stay in sync. Ringo followed the tapping of their feet and the bobbing of their rear ends in a vain effort to keep the beat. It was absurd. John gave up and began playing the keyboard with his elbows. George and Paul fell into a fit of hysterics.

Beneath the giddiness of their predicament festered a sobering certainty that the world as they knew it was coming to an end. The audience was a raging animal, far away, straining against wire barriers. George was estranged from his fans, a condition that contradicted the very purpose that had drawn him to work with John and Paul and Ringo as a group: to entertain up close, to be with the people.

"Does it bother you that you can't hear what you sing during concerts?" a reporter asked John the next day.

"No, we don't mind," said John. "We've got the records at home."

When a reporter asked George how he felt about the near riot at Shea Stadium, he replied, "It was very impersonal. Worst of all . . . we really didn't care anymore."

The Beatles had been brought onstage at Shea Stadium by radio personality Bruce Morrow. Later inducted into the Radio Hall of Fame, Cousin Brucie, as he is known, befriended the Beatles in part by strongly promoting their records on American radio—playing "I Want to Hold You Hand" as many as ten times in a row. "Even in those early days," he recalled, "George was different from the other three. For example, just before going onstage at Shea Stadium, Paul asked me, 'What's going to happen here?' George wouldn't verbalize his concerns like that. He would simply study what was going on. Some people might look at him and think he was disassociated, that his head was somewhere else, but he struck me as even more present than the others, watching from within and absorbing and thinking about what was going on. He was very aware of his surroundings, planning ahead. He just wasn't verbal about it.

"I remember interviewing them," Morrow said, "and in those days, honestly, George wasn't the most exciting Beatle. As a journalist, you'd go after John or Paul or Ringo. George's introspection made us afraid of getting too much of the mortal sin for a broadcaster, namely dead air. But in retrospect, that was very wrong. I think now that if we had given George the courtesy and respect he deserved, his whole persona might have changed. But none of us did that. It was the other three who got 90 percent of the action.

"When he was interviewed, George was always direct," Morrow said, "never flowery with his words. He answered succinctly. If he could answer in two sentences, he never made it into a paragraph. He had kind eyes. When you spoke with him, he looked directly at you. You knew there was sensitivity at work. I remember talking to George in one Beatles interview, and McCartney butts in and asks John, 'Hey, John, why don't you tell him who you're sleeping with now?' First of all, in those days, you didn't make those kinds of references on the air.

But I remember George looking down. He didn't say anything, but he looked down as if he was embarrassed or disapproved. I don't know whether it was for me or for what McCartney said, but it did seem that he felt the comment out of line. Maybe their success in America had hit them so quickly that they didn't always know how to handle it and would sometimes react with nervous energy and get occasionally snippy. But Harrison never was."

George once described himself as someone who climbed to the top of the material wall, meeting along the way everyone worth meeting and doing everything worth doing only to discover how much more there was on the other side. Few people have had as dramatic a climb or as elevated a perch for assessing the world. It is difficult to calculate how successful he became. The numbers keep escalating. As early as their Shea Stadium concert, sales of Beatles records internationally had already surpassed £50 million, nearly $250 million in today's money. Everything they touched turned to gold. At Hollywood Bowl the year before, the group was given towels to dry their sweat. An enterprising businessman bought the towels for $100 and cut them into thousands of half-inch squares. The entire lot sold out in less than a day at $5 each—more than $100,000 earned off of Beatles body sweat. An American firm wrote to Brian Epstein asking if they could market Beatles bathwater. He politely declined.

Despite his good intentions, Epstein did not know how to defend the Beatles' financial interests. Perhaps feeling lucky that Parlophone agreed to take them on at all, he had agreed to a pitiable royalty of one penny for each single sold. Even for an unknown band, it was a ludicrous contract. Once the Beatles began their accelerated climb up the charts, Epstein compounded his financial offenses by accepting merchandise licenses for pennies on the dollar.

In fairness, few managers in 1963 had ever handled a group successful enough to warrant offers for personal endorsements or merchandising. Still, an inquiry would have revealed that Elvis Presley licenses in 1957 alone had grossed more than $20 million. By failing to read contracts and underestimating his boys' worth, Epstein had literally given away millions of dollars in revenues. More than one million Beatles shirts had been sold in three days during their first visit to New York by a company that paid a mere $48,000 for exclusive rights. His negotiations for their music publishing and movie contracts were even worse, netting the group a small fraction of what their creations earned. Once the extent of his errors became clear, Epstein was devastated, but nothing could be done. By age twenty-two, George Harrison had helped create the gold standard by which entertainment careers would forever be measured, but only a fraction of the money his hard labor generated would ever find its way into his pocket.

George wanted to see his own compositions produced, but the Lennon-McCartney monopoly left little room for that. "Because they had such a lot of tunes," he explained in 1969, "they automatically thought theirs should be priority. . . . I'd always have to wade through ten of their songs before they would even listen to one of mine." He managed to get only two original songs on each of the Beatles' two 1965 albums. For the sound track to their second movie, *Help!*, he composed "I Need You," dedicated to then girlfriend Pattie Boyd, and a throwaway love song called "You Like Me Too Much." For *Rubber Soul* he composed "Think for Yourself," which warned listeners not to heed lies, and another lightweight number for Pattie called "If I Needed Someone." Clearly there was talent at work, but it lacked direction. How could he grow as an artist? What should the subject matter of his songs be? Even if he wrote more songs, where could he go with them? He discussed these questions about the future and how to get there in conversations with others.

"George is a very nitty-gritty person," American disc jockey Murray "the K" Kaufman said that year. "When you say something to George, he'd say, 'Okay, now what do you mean?' He wants to be very specific. He's very upfront. He's very truthful. He will not allow something to go by that he doesn't know exactly."

By age twenty-two, George had begun pushing up against the limitations of material success and grown tired of its predictability. He observed, analyzed, and processed experiences with uncanny speed and had a voracious appetite for more. His next meal came from an unexpected source.

The first time George took LSD was an accident. It happened in the spring of 1965 at a dinner party for the Beatles and their wives given by George's dentist, who spiked their coffee with the drug. Suspecting that the dentist was hoping to involve them in an orgy, the couples left and headed for London's popular Ad Lib Club. Why not? It was just a drug. By this time, they were smoking marijuana for breakfast; how much worse could LSD be? They arrived at the club, and the LSD took effect. To their horror, the elevator, dance floor—the entire club—seemed engulfed in flames. Their table appeared to elongate before their eyes. The group left and somehow managed to find George's car. Even though George drove the group home at a safe eighteen miles an hour, John later said it seemed like a thousand.

The sensation of altered reality was life changing—"It was terrifying, but it was fantastic," John said—and that first experience with the hallucinogenic drug led to others. When describing what a trip on the drug was like, George would evoke images such as "living a thousand years in ten minutes" or "an astronaut in a spaceship looking back on Earth." To a reporter from *Rolling Stone* magazine he said, "Up until LSD I never realized that there was anything beyond this everyday state of consciousness. . . . The first time I took it, it just blew everything away. I had such an overwhelming feeling of well-being, that there was a God, and I could see him in every blade of grass. It was like gaining hundreds of years of experience in twelve hours." It was, he said, as though he had never tasted or smelled or heard anything before. "From that moment on, I wanted to have that depth and clarity of perception."

It was fairly common knowledge in the sixties that lysergic acid diethylamide came from a fungus that grew on rye and other grains. The "depth and clarity of perception" led users to believe they were seeing objects move, shapes warp, and colors change. Music sounded different: notes seemed to fluctuate and rhythms change in midstream. LSD made the skin tingle. Smells seemed stronger. The drug exaggerated thoughts and connected ideas in strange ways. In a decade obsessed with spectacle, the way LSD exaggerated colors was made to order.

Like many other drugs, LSD altered brain chemistry; there was nothing inherently spiritual about its effects. But that did not stop advocates in the sixties from praising it as a tool of enlightenment. George read an endorsement of hallucinogens such as LSD in *Doors of Perception* by philosopher Aldous Huxley: "To be shaken out of the ruts of ordinary perception, to be shown for a few timeless hours the outer and inner world, not as they appear to an animal obsessed with survival or to a human being obsessed with words and notions, but as they are apprehended, directly and unconditionally, by Mind at Large—this is an experience of inestimable value to everyone and especially to the intellectual."

He never considered himself an intellectual, but George was indeed shaken from his ordinary perceptions by the drug and assumed at first that others were having the same insights as he. Then they'd open their mouths, and he found out users "were just as stupid as they'd been before" and concluded that chemicals did not provide a path to enlightenment. "You can take it and take it as many times as you like," he told a reporter a few years later, "but you get to a point that you can't get any farther unless you *stop* taking it."

Where, then, should he turn to decipher his intuitions about deeper truths? Few people could understand his dilemma much less advise him what to do about it. Who knew where to go after conquering the world? Who else possessed all that life had to offer?

"There was only one person in the United States that we really wanted to meet," John told the press in August 1965, "and that was Elvis. It was difficult to describe how we felt about him. We just idolized the guy so much."

* * *

It took Brian Epstein three days of negotiations with Elvis's manager Colonel Tom Parker, but in the end he succeeded in scheduling a meeting for his boys with their hero. From childhood in Liverpool to that day in August 1965, George had worshiped Elvis Presley as much as John or Paul or Ringo. They all credited Elvis with sparking their desire to be musicians, and approaching his Beverly Hills home, everyone was nervous. Beatles road manager Mal Evans doubled as an officer in the Elvis Presley Fan Club of England. Anticipation over meeting his hero shook him so badly he had to be carried from the car to the door. Word had somehow leaked out that they would be visiting that evening, and thousands of people had gathered outside the gates.

George hustled to the front porch with his bandmates, Brian Epstein, Evans, and chauffeur Alf Bicknell. The door opened and a burly figure escorted them into a huge, circular room filled with a snooker table, craps table, roulette wheel, guitars on metal stands, and a plush horseshoe couch in the center of the room. There sat Elvis wearing a bright red shirt, skin-tight black slacks, and a close-fitting black jerkin with a high Napoleonic collar rimming his handsome face. Next to him sat his wife, Priscilla, her black bouffant hair rising up like a Chinese lacquer bowl, her eyes lined midnight blue, her lips painted pink. On her head shone a jeweled tiara. George looked around at a room full of people, Elvis's Memphis Mafia.

"Ah, zere you are," John quipped in his best imitation of Peter Sellers's Inspector Clouseau.

"Sit down," Elvis told his guests. "We'll talk."

George sat on the floor. The others followed suit, crosslegged in a semicircle, staring up at their guru. "They just looked up at him, and I'm telling you their jaws dropped," said Larry Geller, Elvis's stylist and friend who was there that evening. "This went on for a while, no one saying a word. The silence was palpable. All of a sudden, Elvis got up and said, 'Well, if you guys don't want talk to me, I'm going to bed.' That broke the ice. They started talking and didn't stop."

John looked over at the guitars. "Do you mind if I play one?"

Elvis handed him a guitar. Paul picked up a guitar, Elvis picked up a guitar, and they jammed for the next half hour, "Johnny Be Good," "Memphis," a few other songs, no voices, just instrumental.

"So, John, are you guys having a good time?" Elvis asked.

"Elvis," John said, "the crowds are crazy wherever we go. It's dangerous. Sometimes it scares the hell out of us."

Elvis smiled. "John, if you're scared of crowds, you're in the wrong business."

The banter flowed. Drinks were served. Ringo played pool with Elvis's crew. Epstein talked shop with the colonel, John and Paul jammed with the king. It was then that Geller noticed George had left the room.

"He wasn't in the bathroom or the kitchen, and I'm wondering what the hell is going on here. This was about ten o'clock at night. There was a door that led to the backyard. I opened the door and knew right away that George was there because the smell of pot was wafting over everything. At first I couldn't see him in the dark; then I saw someone standing by himself under a tree. I walked up, and this arm came out at me, offering me a joint like it was like a peace pipe. I took a hit, and we started talking about this and that."

Geller told George that he had been studying the teachings of kriya-yoga master Paramahansa Yogananda since 1960 and often discussed them with Elvis. "That really surprised George," Geller said. "He wasn't expecting that from Elvis. You need to remember the times. When the Beatles came on the scene in 1964, it was the middle of a cultural explosion, not a spiritual one. Nobody was talking about yoga. Elvis was getting into it, but he didn't talk about it publicly because whenever I'd take him to Yogananda's Self-Realization Fellowship center, his guys would laugh and make remarks. 'Uh-oh, here comes Geller. He's going to tear Elvis's head open again.'"

Geller's impression then was that George knew very little about gurus and teachers and that "he was a man who did his own thing. Everybody else was in the house with Elvis and when the conversation first started, they were telling him, 'Oh, Elvis, we're here because of you. You started the whole thing, man. If it wasn't for you, we wouldn't even be in music.' George stayed in the room for maybe twenty minutes—then he left. Why did he leave? It seemed to me he was distancing himself from the fame and the adulation. This was in 1965, just as his career was spiking, and I remember thinking, 'Interesting. This guy's an ascetic.'"

George had wanted to meet the king because there was no greater material frame of reference for understanding his own situation. No one came near Elvis in music or renown. His name transcended cultural barriers. Seeing firsthand how he looked, hearing how he sounded—maybe something would reveal a clue about what one found on reaching the mountaintop. Then the moment arrived, and when George came face-to-face with the summit, it turned out to be a costlier, more garish version of the same peak he lived on: a mansion with its own casino, a wife in a jeweled tiara, an audience outside his gates. Nothing happened, no flash of insight or even a hint that arriving at the top of the world had anything to do with knowing where one was. An estate in Beverly Hills—was that the end of the road? So he separated himself from the display and took a breather in the backyard. The others might enjoy rubbing elbows with the king; George preferred a moment of quiet under the night sky.

George and Geller sauntered back inside just as Elvis put down his guitar and said, "Hey, come on out here. I want to show you something." The group followed him out to a car compound to ogle his latest purchase. George loved cars, too, but coming at a moment of introspection, he found Elvis's ostentation disappointing. Just beyond the compound, a screaming crowd reached out to them through the bars of Elvis's gates.

"It was like Baghdad," Geller said, "screaming, thunderous, cameras flashing, people in trees—and then this mantra started. Half the crowd was shouting 'Elvis! Elvis! We love Elvis!' And the other half of the crowd was shouting 'Beatles! Beatles! We love you, Beatles!'" At about ten-thirty, the band said good night and headed back to their hotel.

"Man, I gotta tell you," Elvis said to Geller after their departure, "I like those boys. Those are good boys." Then he thought for a moment and added, "But just remember something. There's four of them. There's just one of me."

Elvis's words could have been George's own.

4

A Father to His Spirit

Music is the highest form of education.

—*Rig-Veda*

In October 1965, on the set of the Beatles' second movie, *Help!,* George came across a sitar and couldn't stop staring at it. He picked it up and was intrigued by its unusual shape and dozens of strings. He strummed it, taken by its unusual sound.

Back in London a few days later, in a little import shop at the northern end of Oxford Street, he purchased an inexpensive model and brought it to Abbey Road Studios. The group had been looking for something to enhance their song "Norwegian Wood," and when George improvised on the new instrument, the bizarre sound fit right in. "We were open to anything when George introduced the sitar," said Ringo. "You could walk in with an elephant as long as it was going to make a musical note."

Some of George's musician friends had been following the career of sitarist Ravi Shankar and urged George to hear what a real master of the instrument could do. George bought a few albums. He listened.

Life was never quite the same after that.

"Nothing was giving me a buzz anymore," he told *CBS This Morning.* "I just thought, well, I'm looking for something really, really beyond just the ordinary, the mundane. . . . I wanted somebody to impress me. I didn't expect it to be this little Indian man. But, you know, good things come in small packages."

One of Shankar's most popular albums in 1965 was *Raga*, which featured duets with childhood friend and sarod master Ali Akbar Khan. The opening track, "Raga Palas Kafi," began with a tambura's drone. Five long stainless steel strings, plucked in slow, hypnotic repetition, sent solitary notes resonating deep within the instrument's hollow base. Against this neutral, contemplative background, Shankar played a yearning, bending, dreamlike series of notes, more suggestions than statements of sound. Edges of music ebbed and flowed like waves lapping a beach, tempting listeners to wade into deeper waters. Describing the moment years later, George said the music felt familiar, not intellectually but emotionally, as though calling him back to a place he already knew.

Ever since he was a boy, Ravi Shankar had felt an almost missionary desire to increase the world's appreciation of India's classical music. From an early age, studying under his music guru Allauddin Khan, he had cultivated an appreciation for music as a channel to one's eternal soul. Shankar approached his art as a spiritual discipline that could raise a person to peacefulness and bliss and eventually to knowledge of God, and he was constantly exploring new styles, trying out new ways of making "God in sound," as it was called, accessible to people.

Shankar wanted to touch the hearts of listeners but faced the formidable task of finding a new musical language with which to do so. If he relied on his own subjective imagination, he might create interesting compositions but with little connection to tradition, compromising the power of God in sound. Yet if he limited himself to traditional forms of music, he might not reach a non-Indian audience. He needed a way to present pure spiritual music to a generation enmeshed in popular culture.

By mid-1965, Shankar had not yet broken through to mainstream audiences. His biggest fans were fellow musicians, particularly jazz artists attracted to the music's improvisational quality and its implicit message of peace and spirituality. John Coltrane, often credited with having built the bridge between jazz and India, came to see Shankar earlier that year. Coltrane had given up drugs and alcohol with the help of meditation. His practices had also led him to vegetarianism and books on Indian philosophy. To honor the culture that had done so much for him, he had named his recent albums *A Love Supreme*, *Om*, and *Meditations*. At their meeting, Shankar taught him the basics of ragas, and Coltrane expressed a desire to study the music in greater depth. A short time later, before further lessons could take place, Coltrane died of liver cancer.

When "Norwegian Wood" appeared on record store shelves, Shankar's niece and nephew bought a copy and played it for their uncle. Hearing George diddle on the sitar may have been mind-expanding for his young family members, but to his seasoned ear the sound was distressing. "Just imagine some Indian villager trying to play the violin," he said, "when you know what it *should* sound like."

In June 1965, George met Shankar for the first time at the home of a mutual friend, the founder of London's Asian Music Circle. George expressed appreciation for the master sitarist's recordings and admitted his ignorance of how to play the sitar properly. Impressed by the young man's humility, Shankar offered to give him lessons, and they agreed to meet later that week at George's home in Esher.

"Do you read music?" Ravi asked, settling in at George's home in Esher for their first lesson.

"No," George said, thinking he really shouldn't waste this man's time.

"Good," Ravi said. "It will only confuse you anyway."

George's first sitar lesson covered basics. Ravi showed him how to sit properly with one leg draped over the other in a half-lotus position. He demonstrated how to hold the large gourd against the instep of the left foot. He showed George how to play micronotes by stretching a string out to different tensions. He defined ragas, the fundamental form of Hindustani and Carnatic classical music. There were thousands of ragas, each with its own movement and theme and corresponding time of day. When played correctly, a raga would evoke in listeners a particular emotion such as happiness, sadness, joy, or wonder. Ravi told George that despite having given so many years of his life to the sitar, in his heart he knew he still had a long way to go before he mastered it. Then he played again, conjuring an alchemical mixture of notes and sounds and subtle bending of strings.

For the past four years, George had been in and out of the company of presidents, kings, luminaries of stage and screen, captains of industry—celebrities of every stripe. No one had affected him like this humble sitar player with wavy black hair and an unaffected smile who talked about soothing the world with a balm of sacred music.

Ravi embodied something new for the young musician, something that went far beyond fame and wealth. Ravi was inviting George to examine life through a lens that revealed something extraordinary: that the talent behind his unprecedented success had a higher purpose. God is all around us but hidden. If George made the right sound, he could bring God out of hiding.

Ravi finished the piece and set his sitar to the side. "There is more to it than exciting the senses of the listeners with virtuosity and loud crash-bang effects," he said. "My goal has always been to take the audience along with me deep inside, as in meditation, to feel the sweet pain of trying to reach out for the Supreme, to bring tears to the eyes, and to feel totally peaceful and cleansed."

The impact of this description on a young man who at age twenty-two had scaled the material mountain was dramatic, transforming, and permanent.

"I felt I wanted to walk out of my home that day and take a one-way ticket to Calcutta," George said. "I would even have left Pattie behind in that moment." Not that he had ever been indifferent to loved ones, but loved ones only knew him for what he had been, not what he could become. All his life he had wanted things he couldn't afford—fast cars, fancy clothes, a big house, a beautiful wife—and yet none of it had ever really satisfied him. Here was a greater treasure, something that could not be purchased.

He felt himself venturing into surreal territory where beauty took on otherworldly dimensions and where completeness had more to do with divestment than acquisition. Wife, career, and the people who enveloped him constituted an old world, dimming as it reached the end of its course. This new world as described by Ravi shone brightly. LSD had offered a hint of a more colorful reality, but what was opening up to him now through sacred music rendered such chemically induced visions shallow and crude.

That first lesson led to others, and with their excursion into the making of sacred sound came discussion of the philosophy behind it.

Shortly after George's first meeting with Ravi, television satirist Kenney Everett, who was a close friend of the Beatles at the time, told reporters, "George is getting deeper and deeper every day and will, probably, end up being a bald, recluse monk. . . . He's trying to figure out life, but don't let this sound mocking. He is very serious."

Ever since the Beatles had formed, George had been one-fourth of a musical package, an artist obliged to suppress his talents in deference to the Lennon-McCartney phenomenon. Ravi was introducing him to a new universe of sound and a new purpose that George could make his own.

Three dramatic events were about to unfold that would solidify George's determination to move away from life as a Beatle. In Japan, less than two weeks after Ravi's first visit, concert organizers, anticipating huge crowds, had booked the Beatles at Tokyo's Budokan Hall, a national monument to Japan's war dead. Right-wing factions were outraged at what they perceived as a desecration of their sacred shrine. Death threats were issued, resulting in deployment of thirty thousand uniformed police who lined the Beatles' route from the airport to the hotel to the stadium. The Tokyo Hilton was transformed into an armed camp with sharpshooters positioned on the roof, and George never left his room except to perform. Imprisonment inside his career had become unbearable.

In July, when the band arrived in Manila, Imelda Marcos and her husband announced that the Beatles would attend a three-hundred-person VIP luncheon in the palace. Unfortunately, no one bothered informing Brian Epstein, and the Marcos family took their failure to attend as an insult. By the morning of their departure, security had been withdrawn, and the Beatles were forced to board their plane by running a gauntlet of spitting, punching protesters. To the prison of George's professional life had been added a frightening reminder of its dangers.

The third event took place during the group's final tour of the United States. In a U.K. interview, John had commented, intending no disrespect, that the Beatles were more popular now than Jesus. "I don't know which will go first—rock 'n' roll or Christianity," he told the *Evening Standard*'s pop writer Maureen Cleave. "Jesus was all right, but his disciples were thick and ordinary."

Datebook magazine in the United States carried the quote out of context, and religious zealots, misconstruing his meaning, burned Beatles records and boycotted their concerts. Church rallies were held in states across the South to collect and destroy Beatles memorabilia. Within a week of the article's publication, dozens of radio stations had banned airplay of all Beatles music. The pastor of a Cleveland Baptist church promised to excommunicate any congregant who dared attend a Beatles concert. Members of the Ku Klux Klan in white robes paraded outside the auditorium before the Beatles' show in Washington D.C. A few days later in Memphis, waiting to go onstage, the band received an anonymous call threatening that one or all of them would be assassinated. During their performance, someone in the audience threw firecrackers. George nearly fell over from fright, and all four quickly looked at one another to see if anyone had been shot. Reaction to John's statement intensified. Beatles music was banned in South Africa; the Vatican newspaper *L'Osservatore Romano* warned that "some subjects must not be profaned, even in the world of beatniks." The market value of Northern Songs, which held publishing rights in the Beatles' music, dropped 25 percent in just one week.

It was with the knowledge in mind that his life as one of the world's most successful pop music artists was about to change forever that George walked across the lawn of San Francisco's

Candlestick Park for what would be their final concert performance. The date was August 29, 1966. The night was foggy and a cold wind blew across the ballpark. As always, frenzied fans threatened bedlam, and a six-foot-high wire fence had been erected around the stage. Less than four years before, as a teenager struggling to gain a foothold in music, George would have done anything to be standing here, playing to a crowd of adoring, screaming fans. Now he would have done anything to be anywhere else. An armored truck idled nearby, ready to whisk the band away after their last number. The Beatles finished a desultory performance, left the park, and boarded a plane home. To George, nothing mattered anymore, what day it was, where he was. It had all merged together, a gray blur obscuring the once colorful canvas of his life. It was obvious to him now, although he could not have anticipated it before: he had loved the image of success, but the reality of it made him ill.

Once on board their plane, George settled himself in a seat, took a sip of a drink, turned to his bandmates, and said, "Well, that's it. I'm finished. I'm not a Beatle anymore." As far as live performances were concerned, his statement would hold true. The Beatles never again played together in concert.

Epstein knew that despite their growing popularity, this would be the Beatles' final show. He had declined to attend, preferring to stay in his Beverly Hills hotel room and agonize about what he should do now that the most exciting time of his life was ending.

George, John, Paul, and Ringo had no regrets. They had had enough of touring and wanted to get on with their lives. John would start a film career. Paul would ask Epstein to find him a movie score to write. Ringo would spend quiet time with his family.

When a reporter asked George "What is your personal goal?" he answered, "To do as well as I can do, whatever I attempt. And someday to die with a peaceful mind."

Two weeks after Candlestick Park, almost six years to the day since beginning his career as a Beatle, George and his wife, Pattie, were on their way to India in search of a peaceful mind.

5

Rebirth

At last I've found somebody who makes some sense.

—*George, 1967*

From the window of their suite on the top floor of Bombay's Taj Hotel, George and Pattie looked out onto a traffic jam of beeping cars, rumbling bullock carts, bleating elephants, and ringing bicycles. Ravi Shankar and an assistant arrived at the hotel. Windows were closed against the noise. George's sitar lessons picked up where they had left off in England. When George developed back pains from sitting so long in unfamiliar positions, Ravi called in a yoga instructor who tutored George in postures and breath control, and with the addition of these simple daily exercises he was able to practice comfortably as his lessons progressed.

At first no one in the hotel recognized him. But after a few days, overconfident of his anonymity, he took an elevator down to the lobby, intending to do some shopping, and drew the attention of a teenage elevator operator. Could it be? The next morning, George and Pattie awoke to crowds of Indian Beatlemaniacs outside their window shouting, "We want George!"

"Oh, no," he said with a sigh. "Foxes have holes and birds have nests, but Beatles have nowhere to lay their heads."

Learning that a Beatle had come to India, the press chased him down and he agreed to an interview with a BBC correspondent. Even after so short a time as a student of Indian thought, he felt comfortable making the declaration, "I believe much more in the religions of India than in anything I ever learned from Christianity. The difference over here is that their religion is every second and every minute of their lives—and it is them, how they act, how they conduct themselves, and how they think."

To find some privacy, George, Pattie, Ravi, and Ravi's partner Kamala took a train north to the province of Kashmir, a lake-filled state bordered by Pakistan to the west and China to the north. Kashmir was the retreat of royalty, an idyllic land of fruit orchards and flowering gardens. They arrived at the city of Srinagar, nestled at the foot of the Himalayan mountains.

Golden saffron fields glowed in the morning sun, and flowers from the fabled Shalimar Gardens filled the air with their sweet fragrance. The group took up residence in a large wooden houseboat on the largest of the city's many lakes. Each evening the boat's owner stoked its heavy cast-iron stove with apple wood and placed hot water bottles between the blankets of their beds. Each morning he folded napkins into the shape of mosque domes and balanced them in crystal goblets on their breakfast table. Vases of freshly picked saffron flowers colored the deck of their houseboat. Through carved wood windows, George looked out on the Himalayas rising in the distance and savored freedom from life as a Beatle. Each morning, he breathed in the bracing mountain air and performed yoga exercises, then practiced on the sitar, eyes shut, his fingers familiarizing themselves with notes along the instrument's long wooden neck. When his exercises ended, he read books on self-realization and in the peace and calm of an ancient land discovered teachings that would permanently change the course of his life.

Among the books that Ravi had brought for George was *Raja-Yoga* by Swami Vivekananda. A tall, urbane Bengali, Vivekananda had made a dramatic impact at the 1893 World's Parliament of Religions Conference in Chicago, the first Hindu ever to address such a gathering of religious leaders in America. Before that speech, British missionaries had depicted Hinduism as a "heathen" religion. Liberal Unitarians were looking to reverse that impression by stimulating interfaith dialogue, and in Vivekananda, who held degrees in science and philosophy, they found an ideal spokesperson.

In *Raja-Yoga* George learned Vivekananda's central message: all people possess innate and eternal perfection. "*Tat tvam asi*— That thou art," Vivekananda declared. "You are that which you seek. There is nothing to do but realize it."

One passage in particular held George's attention: "What right has a man to say that he has a soul if he does not feel it, or that there is a God if he does not see Him? If there is a God we must see Him . . . otherwise it is better not to believe." Better to be an outspoken atheist, Vivekananda advised, than a hypocrite. *Raja-Yoga* was not a big book—a small paperback with a simple red cover—but its contents were vast.

George discovered that the word "yoga" meant "to link," as in the English words "yoke" or "union." In its early stages, George read, yoga involved physical exercises, but its goal was to link the soul with the Supreme Soul or God. To reach that goal a yogi must also practice *yama* or self-restraint, which included no killing and, by inference, a vegetarian diet; no lying; and no stealing or taking more than needed. Along with qualities such as cleanliness, austerity, and dependence on God, these formed the basics "without which no practice of yoga will succeed."

True yoga, Vivekananda wrote, did not depend on being Christian, Jew, Buddhist, atheist, or theist. The benefits of yoga were available to every human being through daily practice. Try to practice mornings and evenings, Vivekananda advised. Try not to eat before morning yoga is done. And try to control the sex drive. When contained, sexual energy transforms into nourishment for the brain. Without chastity, one loses stamina and mental strength. He wrote that the spiritual giants all knew this secret. Above all, never produce pain in any living being by thought, word, or deed. "There is no virtue," Vivekananda wrote, "higher than this."

From their houseboat, George and Pattie could hear the muezzin of a nearby mosque calling the faithful to prayer. A small wooden ferry tied to the dock bumped gently against its moorings. Sunlight glistened off lake water, creating veils of mist that grew into thick clouds. The clouds hovered over the Himalayas in the distance, pouring a gentle rain that snaked down the mountainside to nourish farmlands and fill reservoirs in an endless, perfect cycle.

Where was his childhood now, his career? What sense did the history of this one short life make compared to the eternity opening up before him? However exciting his achievements looked from the outside, something grand and majestic was transporting him beyond the minutiae of that world. What other people perceived of him—a working-class Liverpool boy who became part of history's most successful rock group, who married a top model and had more fans than Elvis—dwindled to mere facts. What he was finding in India spoke to the quintessence of experience, to the meaning and significance of his life. He had come for this without knowing its name or shape or depth.

Among the books stacked in George's room on the houseboat was another, *Autobiography of a Yogi*. The cover featured a photo of the author, Paramahansa Yogananda. Long black hair framed Yogananda's youthful face. His aquiline nose flared slightly and his mouth offered a Mona Lisa smile, as if he were amused by the fuss of being photographed. His eyes were startling white with deep pools for pupils. "The moment I looked at that picture of Yogananda," George later said, "his eyes went right through me."

Many seekers read Yogananda's book in the fifties and sixties. Published in 1946, it offered Westerners one of the few available portraits of mystic India. The book described Yogananda's search for spiritual masters and accounts of the supernatural events he witnessed in remote mountain retreats.

Empowered beings and mystic powers fascinated George. "I'd heard stories about men in caves up in the Himalayas who are very old and wise," he explained years later, "and about people who could levitate . . . mystic stories that had permeated my curiosity for years."

In his autobiography, Yogananda described meeting recluses such as the Levitating Saint. This yogi had mastered the circulation of "life airs" that govern physical and mental functions. By manipulating these airs, the Levitating Saint was said to raise himself off the ground and hover in midair for hours. The book also described Trailanga Swami, a giant of a man reputed to be more than two hundred years old and weighing nearly three hundred pounds. Trailanga lived in Benares and had a habit of sitting stark naked in the middle of busy streets, chanting the names of God, and disrupting traffic. Police tried locking him away from time to time, but rumor had it that by exercising yogic ability Trailanga reduced himself to the size of a pea, sneaked out under the door of his cell, and went back to chanting in the streets.

Other books George read described other popular mystics, such as Swami Haridas and his disciple Mian Tansen. By playing particular ragas, these fifteenth-century musicians were known to ignite fires, cause rain showers, bring flowers to blossom, and calm wild animals.

Yogananda's book talked about the *Yoga Sutras*, India's classical yogic text. The author, Sage Patanjali, described eight kinds of mystic powers a yogi could acquire by controlling breath and manipulating energies circulating in the body, by which masters of these techniques could make their bodies smaller or lighter or even invisible. They could generate as many as eight bodies identical to their own, make new physical worlds appear in the sky, and materialize objects from thin air.

Such feats, George read, occurred when the soul's unlimited energy was stimulated. The texts described the soul as small, "one ten-thousandth part of the tip of a hair," but as powerful as "ten thousand suns" that filled the body with consciousness. Even a little of the soul's energy could produce startling results. In his *Yoga Sutras* Sage Patanjali minimized such events, calling mystic displays "incidental flowers" along the sacred path. Advanced yogis never confused such power with yoga's true purpose: to reawaken love for God, and through that relationship, love for all creatures.

Mystical yoga in these stories seemed to George a lot like LSD. Was what yogis saw in meditation perhaps something like what he had seen on the drug? Did people who attain cosmic consciousness see under the earth, like Superman, and watch spiritual energy flow up through roots to nourish plants and flowers? Did they feel energy pulsating around them and realize they were one with that energy?

The books George read in Kashmir kept him enthralled with their descriptions of powers lying dormant within the soul. He discovered the Indian explanation for why pure souls would fall into the material world to be born into physical bodies and how they reincarnated from one species to another. He read essays on how meditation could lower metabolic levels, increase spiritual awareness, and eventually help the soul escape further reincarnations. As a child, George had little taste for reading—he had felt smothered in school and grown impatient with lessons and skipped classes. In Kashmir, he was rarely without a book in his hands.

He was twenty-three years old and as far back as memory allowed his sense of himself had been guided by what others told him, by childhood and family, by fame, and by caricatures in the press. If, as he now read, he had nothing to do with any of those Georges, then who was he? If after this life ended, *he* did not end but moved on, precisely *who* moved on? His body would fall away and with it the accumulations of a lifetime, but he, the soul within, would remain. The books explained that the person he thought himself to be, the George whom others saw and judged, was real but temporary, a gross body built from five elements—earth, air, water, fire, and space—and a subtle body consisting of mind, intelligence, and ego. It was his true self, the soul inside those coverings, that provided the energy to make them work. At death, when the temporal coverings fell away, earth again merging with earth, water with water, air with air, that inner self would move on to some other destination.

The way for him to reach his inner self, it seemed, was the same way he had reached his outer self—through music. "Our tradition teaches us that musical sound and the musical experience are steps to the realization of the self," Ravi explained. "The highest aim of our music is to reveal the essence of the universe it reflects, and ragas are among the means by which this essence can be apprehended."

To play a raga properly, he said, could take a lifetime of practice, and Ravi made sure George understood how deep the commitment had to be. Ravi's music guru, Allauddin Khan—Baba, as he was called by disciples—had practiced twenty hours a day for twelve years, just learning basic vocalization, scales, and études. Baba was nearly seventy when he finally agreed to accept Ravi, then only eighteen, as a disciple. "Taking a guru," Ravi said, "was the biggest decision of my life. Baba demanded absolute surrender, years of fanatical dedication and discipline. At least twenty years of such work and practice are necessary to reach maturity in performing ragas," he told George.

What good fortune, George thought, to know a man like Ravi who had been through the disciplines and could point him in the direction of wisdom. As George's respect and admiration for Ravi grew, he came to see the elder musician as more than a mentor. It seemed that he had found in the mannerly Bengali with penetrating eyes a second father, a spiritual father.

"Throughout the Beatle experience," George said years later, "we'd grown so many years within a short period of time . . . but I wanted something better, and I remember thinking, 'I'd love to meet somebody who will really impress me,' and that's when I met Ravi—which is funny, because he's this little fellow with this obscure instrument, from our point of view, and yet it led me into such depths. . . . I mean, I met Elvis—Elvis impressed me when I was a kid and impressed me when I met him because of the buzz of meeting Elvis—but you couldn't later on go round to him and say, 'Elvis, what's happening in the universe?'"

After Kashmir, George and Pattie traveled to Benares, an ancient city built on the banks of the Ganges River. Thousands of pilgrims had assembled there to hear a month-long recitation of *Ramayan*, the story of Rama, God incarnate and ideal king who, according to Indian scholars, walked the Earth around 3500 B.C.E. As far as the eye could see, thick burlap tents filled the Benares festival grounds. Colorful flags and banners waved in a brisk wind blowing off the river. From thousands of campfires drifted the scent of burning wood, incense, and camphor. The Raja of Benares arrived, riding an elephant. Descending by the riverbank, the king knelt down and offered prayers. Behind him, a brilliant orange sunset filled the evening sky. Legions of shaven-headed priests chanted in unison. Musicians playing brass shenai horns and beating large copper kettledrums launched a volley of sound over the plain. George and Pattie gazed out on the colorful tent city while around them a universe of music mingled in the air.

George began to look more kindly on the price he had paid to be a Beatle. Was this glimpse into his soul's immortality not the real reward for years of hard work as a rock and roller? Not fleeting moments of celebrity—that was only temporary and illusory—but the privilege of waking up and looking out to see what sages had seen for centuries, sacred mountains and rivers and hints of an eternal existence beyond this one life. Here was the real payoff for whatever good karma they had accrued.

He had to share this knowledge with his mates. Pattie seemed happy to be there with him, but what about John or Paul or Ringo? Would they agree to spend time in India? And if they did, would they catch spiritual fire the way he had? There was no guarantee that they would find those discoveries as meaningful as he did, and he would soon see that answering a spiritual call involved tough choices and a willingness to break free of old bonds.

After six weeks, George and Pattie returned to England. To reporters gathered at the airport to cover their arrival George said, "Too many people have the wrong idea about India. Everyone immediately associates India with poverty, suffering, and starvation. But there's much more than that. There's the spirit of the people, the beauty, and the goodness. The people there have a tremendous spiritual strength, which I don't think is found elsewhere. That's what I've been trying to learn about." Ravi arrived from India a few days later wearing a Western suit. George greeted him at the airport dressed in an Indian kurta shirt and yoga pants.

6

In the Land of Gods

At last, a chance to do straight drama! To deal with conflict,
with inner truth. . . . Of course, I think we should add a little
music.

—The Producers

George felt awkward being back in London. He didn't want
to be a fab Beatle again. The band was his job, and as a responsible member he would continue to play lead guitar and sing
harmony, but meditation was revealing to him an inner person
with creative energies and original ideas straining to be expressed.

One such idea was to play compositions backward. "He
would play the solos normal," recalled former Beatles engineer
Richard Lush, "then we'd flip the tapes and he'd listen to them
backward, just to see how they sounded. This would go on for
maybe seventy takes, turning the tape over, listening, turning it
back again—it would take literally hours to accomplish." Once
John and Paul realized that George had found new ways of max-
imizing sound, they started coming to him with rough sketches
of their songs and asked that he embellish them in the studio as
he saw fit. The results were often revelatory.

"You listen to a song like 'Dear Prudence,'" said singer-
songwriter Ian Hammond, "and you realize that they did it all
without the aid of an orchestra—even though the closing climac-
tic section is a natural candidate for brass and/or strings. How?

They relied heavily on Harrison, who came up with these great moving inner lines in the last verse and chorus."

At the time, George's contribution to Beatles music was not widely acknowledged. "Everybody talks about Lennon and McCartney and what a great songwriting team they were," noted Beatles historian Andy Babiuk, "but when you listen to some of the original rough demos, they're just okay. Had they left them like that, would they still have become these great songs that we've come to know and love? That's where George played such an important part."

Despite a growing sense of his artistic ability, in the words of biographer Alan Clayson, upon his return from that first trip to India in 1966, "George could still be made to do as he was told." Old habits would die hard.

In January 1967, George sat in the sound room of EMI Studios working with the other Beatles on their eighth album, *Sergeant Pepper's Lonely Hearts Club Band*, wishing it were done. He had hardly spent a day together with John, Paul, or Ringo since returning to London. Other things filled his mind. He was smitten with spirituality like a young man in love, and even commonplace events reminded him of India. Someone riding a bicycle recalled a street scene in Delhi. A walk through a park brought back images of Kashmir. Only his sensible nature stopped him from abandoning the studio and boarding the next plane back to Bombay.

"I'd give up everything if I could be a monk who walks from one side of India to another," he told artist Peter Max. George wanted to know who he was and who God was, and anything unrelated, however innovative, failed to hold his interest. Paul had come up with an innovative idea for their current album. The Beatles would pretend to be someone else, a make-believe group called Sergeant Pepper's Lonely Hearts Club Band, and every time one of the Beatles sang, he would pretend to be someone in the made-up band. The idea left George cold and bored. They had been working on the album since November, and there was still no end in sight.

To keep up his spirits, he added little bits and pieces of India whenever possible. Using a technique he had seen musicians use in Bombay, he imitated John's voice on guitar during "Lucy in the Sky with Diamonds." On March 10, in a session that ran until 4:00 A.M., he overdubbed a tambura's drone on "Getting Better." And when the group turned its attention to designing the album's historic cover, he brought in images of revered gurus. To photos of Albert Einstein, Marilyn Monroe, Bob Dylan, Marlon Brando, Laurel and Hardy, and other twentieth-century icons, he added Yogananda, Yogananda's grand guru Lahiri Mahasaya, and Mahasaya's guru Sri Mahavatara Babaji. The photos, he would explain in later years, were "clues to the spiritual aspect of me," but such moments merely made bearable a job he no longer cared to do.

He loved John, Paul, and Ringo, yet he wanted to wean himself from them. Professionally he still stood outside the Lennon-McCartney songwriting circle, something Paul in particular would not let him forget by correcting his guitar playing and issuing directions on what to do differently. "George was having to put up with an awful lot," said recording engineer Norman Smith. "As far as Paul was concerned, George could do no right. . . . I take my hat off to George that he swallowed what he had to swallow in terms of criticism."

Finally John and Paul invited George to contribute a song to *Sergeant Pepper*. One night after dinner with Pattie at the London home of Hamburg artist-musician Klaus Voormann, George walked into an adjoining room, sat down at a pedal harmonium, and summoned up not a song but a universe.

"Within You Without You," a remarkable microcosm of Indian music and philosophy, became many people's first meaningful contact with meditative sound. On the album, the song played just after "Being for the Benefit of Mr. Kite," a throwaway John had written to fill in the LP's running time. Compared with Mr. Kite's hackneyed calliopes and merry-go-rounds, "Within You Without You" flowed like music from another world.

George opened the song in classical Indian form: a tambura's drone invited listeners to shut the door and sit quietly. Tablas followed, setting a quick, quiet pulse. George entered singing a *sargam*, an atonal melody like those he often practiced with Ravi. A wall of illusion separates us from each other, he sang. We believe the illusion real, which only turns our love for one another cold. Peace will come when we learn to see past the illusion of differences and come to know that we are one—life is everywhere, within and without. A santoor, a zitherlike instrument played with two metal forks, echoed the melody. Cellos made their entrance, then violins, drawing listeners through a forest of vibrating strings. The music paused for two beats, then listeners were off on a series of toe-tapping musical dialogues. One instrument offered a brief statement, which was echoed by a second and then by a third—sitar then santoor, violins then cello, back and forth, truth, illusion, truth, illusion. The song faded out at the end, but not before offering a surprise coda: a few seconds of George laughing, his way of reminding listeners not to take his pontificating seriously—search for God but don't lose your sense of humor, he seemed to admonish himself as much as his listeners.

"When I first met George in 1963, he was Mister Fun, Mister Stay-Out-All-Night," said Apple employee Tony King, who attended Voormann's dinner that night. "Then all of a sudden, he found LSD and Indian religion and he became very serious. Things went from jolly weekends where we'd have steak and kidney pie and sit around giggling, to these rather serious weekends where everyone walked around blissed out and talked about the meaning of the universe."

"Within You Without You" was the longest track on the *Sergeant Pepper* album. It was the most complex, involving three changes of time signature, something never done before on a Beatles song. It was also the only song on the album in which only one Beatle performed; this was George's accomplishment and his alone. Juan Mascaro, a professor of Sanskrit teaching at Cambridge University, heard the track and wrote George to say, "it is a moving song and may it move the souls of millions; and there is more to come," Mascaro predicted, "as you are only beginning on the great journey."

Sergeant Pepper was released in June 1967 and, despite George's lack of enthusiasm over its creation, quickly earned a reputation as the most remarkable album of the decade—possibly of all time. Music critic William Mann hailed *Sergeant Pepper* as more genuinely creative than anything else in pop music. The album staked its place at number one on the U.S. charts and did not budge for fifteen weeks, and in the United Kingdom it stayed number one for twenty-two weeks.

Paul visited Bob Dylan in a London hotel and played a tape of some of the tracks for him. Dylan smiled and said, "Oh, I get it. You don't want to be cute anymore."

Journalists feasted on every move George made. His fascination with India provided fodder for a new round of interviews, and the aspiring yogi did his best to explain a theology that has baffled scholars for generations. "The realization of human love reciprocated is such a gas," he told the *International Times* that year. "It's a good vibration which makes you feel good. These vibrations that you get through yoga, cosmic chants, and things like that—I mean, it's such a buzz. It buzzes you out of everywhere. It's nothing to do with pills. It's just in your own head, the realization. It's such a buzz. It buzzes you right into the astral plane." Like someone learning a foreign language, George explained sophisticated concepts with the vocabulary he knew. "The only thing which is important in life is karma. That means roughly actions," he ventured. "Everything that's done has a reaction, like dropping this cushion down. See? There's a dent in it."

To promote their new album, Brian Epstein hosted a dinner party for selected journalists at his Belgravia, London, home. Music journalist Ray Coleman asked George about his turn to Indian music. "I don't fancy myself as the next Ravi Shankar," George said, "but I still prefer Indian music to any other form of music. It has taken over 100 percent in my musical life. . . . Just learning the sitar has inspired me."

He wanted to say more, to substantiate for the writer something that still eluded him, and he groped for the words. "You know how God is a, sort of, untouchable thing?" George asked.

"Well, that's how it is with Indian music. It's a very spiritual thing, so subtle and related to philosophy and life. It's not easy to understand the music at first, but it's beautiful when you get it.

"I've taken the time to learn about many religions," he said. "Religion is a day-to-day experience. You'll find it all around. You live it. Religion is here and now, not just something that comes on Sundays."

Sergeant Pepper had absorbed nearly six grueling months of studio work, nearly seven hundred hours. The intensity of production had put a strain on relations among George, John, Paul, and Ringo. In July 1967 they decided to celebrate the album's completion and renew their friendship by taking a trip to Greece. Despite Epstein's mismanagement of certain contracts, money still flowed their way, and John had proposed that they look for an island to buy. Designed properly, such a place might show the world how to lead a utopian life.

Utopia was hardly a new idea. By 1967, hippie communes dotted the American landscape, and England's Summerhill, an experiment in unstructured childhood education, was celebrating forty-six years of operation. John proposed that Beatle families and friends find an island where they could live in a circular arrangement of houses connected by tree-lined avenues. At the hub would be a central glass-enclosed arena, a biodome that would serve as stadium and playground. "They've tried everything else," he said, "wars, nationalism, fascism, communism, capitalism, nastiness, religion—none of it works. So why not this?" The entourage arrived in Athens, rented a boat, and sailed up the Greek coast looking for an island to renovate.

Before leaving for Greece, George purchased an album of Sanskrit prayers. One prayer in particular became the group's theme song while on the boat. "Attention all eternal wayfarers on the shores of earth," declared the album's back-cover notes. "Swami A. C. Bhaktivedanta leads his devotees in an authentic rendition of the Vedic mantra Hare Krishna, better known in India as the maha-mantra, sung on the banks of the Ganges for more than five thousand years." The cover notes went on to explain that the Swami had been a successful businessman when in 1922 he met spiritual master Bhaktisiddhanta Saraswati and became his disciple. Bhaktisiddhanta urged him to spread the chanting to English-speaking countries, and in 1965, at age seventy, Bhaktivedanta sailed to the West with the message entrusted to him nearly three decades earlier. The Swami arrived in New York without funds and barely survived that first winter. Soon, though, he attracted the interest of young idealists wandering the streets of the East Village, an immigrant neighborhood turned hippie-bohemian quarter. By the summer of 1966 the Swami had acquired a small group of followers and with their help opened a tiny storefront temple.

The album consisted of the Swami leading American disciples in a rousing chant to the rhythm of clay drums and the clang of brass hand cymbals. A liner quote from beat poet Allen Ginsberg explained, "chanting brings a state of ecstasy." Sailing a smooth Aegean Sea under a brilliant clear sky, George and John perched on the prow of their boat, played ukulele banjos, and chanted "Hare Krishna, Hare Krishna, Krishna Krishna, Hare Hare, Hare Rama, Hare Rama, Rama Rama, Hare Hare."

"Six hours we sang," George recalled, "because we couldn't stop once we got going. As soon as we stopped, it was like the lights went out. It went on to the point where our jaws were aching, singing the mantra over and over and over and over and over. We felt exalted. It was a very happy time for us."

George and friends sang into the night. The boat's captain held a steady course along a highway of moonlight rippling off the surface of the sea. "It seemed as if we were sailing up through the heavens, right up to the moon," remembered Epstein's assistant Alistair Taylor. "It was a wonderfully relaxing night as George picked out the notes of the Hare Krishna chorus on his ukulele, and John, Mal and I quietly chanted the words. Beatlemania seemed to have finally been left behind."

The next day, the boat docked at a small island just as a light rain began to fall. George stepped onto a pebbled beach, looking like a vagabond on the road to Damascus, a twenty-four-year-old man in white kurta shirt and drawstring cotton pants, wandering the shore for the good of his soul. Seagulls cawed overhead; rain dripped from his long hair.

George was becoming cleansed of the world, and he yearned for the others to understand his passion. Were they not best friends? Despite a few squabbles now and then, had they not always looked after each other's interests? After all they had been through, becoming self-realized together would make their partnership perfect. Surely they would see that all they had done so far was only a moment in cosmic time. The possibilities that lay ahead were infinite.

The rain stopped, and the young men and their companions boarded the boat and sailed away. The idea of creating heaven on earth was short-lived. "We were great at going on holiday with big ideas," Ringo said, "but we never carried them out. It was safer making records, because once they let us out we'd just go barmy."

Some time later, John did buy an island, a small outpost off the coast of Ireland used by farmers to graze goats. He spent only a short time there. Eventually he leased the land to a hippie community and never went there again. Sharing Utopia together as a group was a dream that never came true.

According to astrological calculation, by 1967 Earth was supposed to be emerging from a thousand years of confusion under the sign of Pisces—two fish swimming in opposite directions—and entering a golden age under the sign of Aquarius. Writers and poets prophesied that this new age would be one of harmony and understanding, and underground newspapers depicted San Francisco's Haight-Ashbury district as its epicenter, the home of LSD consciousness, filled with beautiful people in colorful costumes, dancing to psychedelic music and living the dream of the Aquarian Age. LSD had played a significant part in George's awakening, and he was excited to see what kind of culture the drug had inspired.

After returning from Greece, George and Pattie flew to San Francisco to visit Pattie's sister Jenny and her husband, drummer Mick Fleetwood, who lived near Haight-Ashbury. Together with a group of friends who included road manager Neil Aspinall and press agent Derek Taylor, they set out to explore the fabled capital of love. They parked their limo a block away from a corner of Haight-Ashbury and walked along the street like natives. George had dressed in psychedelic pants, tassled moccasins, and heart-shaped sunglasses, expecting to be part of something beautiful "with groovy people having spiritual awakenings and being artistic." What he found left him dismayed. Garbage littered the streets. Hippies lay sprawled on benches and sidewalks. Panhandlers—"horrible, spotty dropout kids on drugs," George called them—haunted the streets begging for coins in the name of love and peace.

Once they recognized who he was, hippies ran up and hugged him. "You're our leader, man," one enthused.

"No, you're wrong," George said.

"Oh, yes, man," the hippie insisted. "You know where it's at, man."

Others approached him with offerings of LSD. George turned them down, swearing to himself then and there that he would never take "the dreaded lysergic" again. The hippies were "hypocrites," he told a reporter from *Creem* magazine. "I don't mind anybody dropping out of anything, but it's the imposition on somebody else I don't like. I've just realized that it doesn't matter what you are as long as you work. In fact if you drop out, you put yourself further away from the goal of life than if you were to keep working."

George had grown up in a postwar culture that respected work. He may not have wished for himself the kind of manual labor his brothers had chosen, but he did not have a lazy bone in his body, and the sight of so many young people wasting their lives was a turning point for him. As their car pulled away, George took from his pocket a picture of Paramahansa Yogananda and held it up for the hippies outside to see.

"This is still it," he told friends in the car. "Ravi and all them are still right. *This* is where it is." After that visit, he became even more serious about meditation.

On a Learjet flying out of San Francisco, George sat behind the pilots. Shortly after take-off the plane stalled, lurched, and went into a dive. From his seat, George could see lights in the cockpit flashing UNSAFE. "Well, that's it," he thought and started chanting "Hare Krishna, Hare Krishna" and "Om, Christ, Om." Former Beatles press agent Derek Taylor, sitting next to him, took the hint and also began chanting "Hare Krishna, Hare Krishna." After a few harrowing moments, the plane pulled out of its stall and landed safely in Monterey. To recover from their ordeal, the group made a beeline for the nearest beach.

George's visit to the Haight-Ashbury neighborhood had been big news for San Francisco locals. A few days later, an interview published in the underground paper the *Oracle* quoted him as saying that spiritual music helped people reawaken their eternal selves and that mantras were the starting point. "Through the musical you reach the spiritual," George told the reporter.

In a storefront Hare Krishna temple just two blocks from Haight-Ashbury, temple leader Michael Grant read the article, thinking that was not quite right. A former pianist for saxophone legend Pharoah Sanders, Grant knew something about music. He also knew something about mantras from his teacher Bhaktivedanta Swami, an authority on the subject. Bhaktivedanta Swami had recently initiated Grant into the practice of bhakti, or devotional yoga, and awarded him the spiritual name Mukunda, "servant of Krishna the giver of liberation from birth and death." Mukunda had no way of knowing that his guru's album had provided George and John with their theme song while sailing around the Greek islands.

He took out a sheet of paper and wrote, "Dear George Harrison. What is important is not the musical, which can change according to time and culture. It is the mantra, the name of God that is spiritual and stimulates consciousness."

Mukunda and an old college buddy, Sam Speerstra, had helped Bhaktivedanta Swami open his Haight-Ashbury temple a year earlier. They called their teacher "Prabhupada," a term of respect that meant a master *(prabhu)* at whose feet *(pada)* other masters gathered. To raise funds, Sam had conceived of a mantra rock concert, held at the city's famous Avalon Ballroom. The concert, which took place a few weeks before George's visit, featured Big Brother and the Holding Company, Moby Grape, and other big-name bands from the area. When Prabhupada arrived at the ballroom, thousands of hippies respectfully stood to receive him with applause and cheers. He climbed to the stage and seated himself on a cushion next to Allen Ginsberg, an admirer who had come from New York.

To an enraptured audience Ginsberg described his experiences with chanting and recounted how the Swami had opened a small storefront temple in New York's East Village in 1965, where they met. He invited everyone to the new Haight-Ashbury temple. "I especially recommend the early-morning kirtans [group chanting]," he said, "for those coming down from LSD who want to stabilize their consciousness upon reentry." He started playing a harmonium and chanting while projectors flashed fifty-foot-high images of Krishna on the walls. People played drums and flutes and blew conch shells. Then Prabhupada stood up, lifted his arms, and began to dance, swaying back and forth, gesturing for everyone to join him. The audience rose to their feet, held hands, and danced in circles.

It was, in the words of historian Robert Ellwood, "perhaps the ultimate high of that era." Ginsberg called it "the height of Haight-Ashbury spiritual enthusiasm, the first time that there had been a music scene in San Francisco where everybody could be part of it and participate."

When a visitor to the temple asked Prabhupada if he was Allen Ginsberg's guru, the seventy-year-old teacher said, "I am nobody's guru. I am everybody's servant." His response was not intended to be clever. It reflected humility that George would later deeply admire.

Prabhupada's disciple Mukunda sealed his letter to George Harrison, addressed it in care of the underground newspaper, and sent it off. "Waste of time," he thought, never really expecting his point about mantras to reach one of the Fab Four.

After returning to England, George encountered a teacher who was to have a lasting influence on his daily practices, the Maharishi Mahesh Yogi, who had earned a degree in physics from Allahabad University before turning to the study of meditation. In 1958, at age forty-two, he moved to the United Kingdom and founded the Spiritual Regeneration Movement, which taught fundamentals of yoga, breathing, and mantra meditation. When George was a boy, he had seen the bearded teacher on Granada Television's current-affairs show *People and Places*. He didn't know much about him, but by 1967 George had reached a point in his studies where he wanted to meditate and knew he would need a mantra—"a password to get through into the other world."

In August, Pattie urged George to come with her to a lecture the Maharishi was scheduled to give in London. The press reported that the Maharishi had initiated more than ten thousand people into a technique he called Transcendental Meditation, and this would be his last lecture before leaving on a retreat with students to North Wales. George bought tickets to the lecture and, still hoping his mates would join him in this new dream, invited John and Paul to come along. Ringo, caring for his wife, Maureen, who had just given birth to their second son, was unable to attend.

On the evening of August 24, the fifty-one-year-old teacher took his seat on a raised platform in a conference room of the London Hilton. His bright eyes and ready smile greeted the assembly. He wore white silk robes, and a garland of marigolds hung from his neck and was entwined in his long hair and gray beard. Those sitting closest to him caught a faint scent of sandalwood oil. In a high voice accompanied by gentle chuckles, he proposed a simple program to his audience: meditate on a mantra twenty minutes in the morning and twenty minutes in the evening. The rewards, he promised, would be improved quality of life and relief from mental stress. The word "mantra," he said, is comprised of two parts: *man* (mind) and *traya* (liberation), and repeating a mantra calms the mind and brings inner peace. Wars, epidemics, famines, and earthquakes were all symptoms of tension, he said, as contagious as any other disease. If even one percent of the world's population followed this easy method of meditation, it would be enough to reduce tension and dispel the clouds of war for thousands of years.

After his lecture, the Maharishi invited George and his friends to join him for his ten-day course in North Wales, where they could learn Transcendental Meditation. The group accepted his invitation and placed a call to Brian Epstein, hoping he would also come along. For five years the boys had never gone anywhere without their manager or someone appointed by him to look out for them. "It's like going somewhere without your trousers on," John said. Epstein declined, suggesting he might drive up toward the end of the retreat.

The following Saturday, reporters and fans crowded into London's Euston Station to watch the Beatles embark on what the *Daily Mirror* described as a "Mystical Special"—the 3:05 local to Bangor. As the train departed, the Maharishi sat cross-legged in his compartment looking out at the crowds, appearing amused by all the attention. George, John, and Paul entered his compartment, and the Maharishi explained they would find his meditation technique quite convenient, like funds in a bank. "You don't have to carry money around with you," he said, "just make a withdrawal when needed."

What if you're greedy, asked John, and want another meditation after lunch and another after tea? His question sent the Maharishi into fits of laughter. "He was laughing all the time," said Ringo, who had managed to join them on the retreat. "That really struck home. This man is really happy, and he's having a great time in life."

The train pulled in to Bangor, a small seaport town on Wales's northern coast, and George looked out onto a crowd of three hundred students assembled to greet their teacher with offerings of flowers. Classes began the following day in the auditorium of a local school. In his course, the Maharishi gave students a word or syllable. Over time, he added more words or syllables until the pieces fit together to form one of India's traditional mantras. He took George aside, then his mates, and whispered a mantra in their ears.

"The Maharishi provided us with a device that allowed us to look at our own thoughts," explained singer Donovan Leitch, who also attended the Bangor program. Donovan's popular song "Mellow Yellow" had brought him into contact with George, and George had suggested that Donovan start sitar lessons. At a public program years later, Donovan explained that the Maharishi divided mantras into smaller syllables to make repeating them easier and acceptable to students with no interest in religion. "He said our thoughts were like bubbles in the ocean, some of hope, others of fear. You could see the thoughts passing if you set yourself apart to look at them. To do that, you chanted the mantra inside, breathing in, breathing out. The mantra he gave the Beatles was 'EE-ng'—just a sound to help follow the thoughts, which pass before you like a movie."

On the first day of the Bangor retreat, a telephone rang in one of the university offices. Paul, with typical Beatles levity, told a reporter, "I'll have to go and see who it is." He picked up the receiver and listened. "Oh, no," he said. "Oh, God, no." It was an assistant from Brian Epstein's office, reporting that Epstein had been found dead in his home. Later it was determined that their manager had died from an accidental overdose of sleeping pills, but at that moment no one knew what had happened.

George felt the irony of their friend and manager dying while they were on a retreat to explore life's meaning.

When word of what had occurred circulated, classes were halted. George and his friends approached the Maharishi and asked what they should do. You are a powerful force, he told them. If you hold on to Brian it will stop his soul from going to its next evolution. "You know you have to grieve for him and love him. Now you send him on his way."

George had lost only one person close to him before, Stuart Sutcliffe, and Brian was as close to George as anyone had ever been. All Brian had ever wanted for George was his success and happiness. Brian did well for himself, too, and if he owned a Bentley, a Rolls, an Austin Mini, and enough fine clothes to be selected as one of England's ten best-dressed men, he had earned that privilege. When the Beatles had been honored as MBEs, Members of the British Empire, George liked to say that MBE stood for Mr. Brian Epstein. But when the Beatles retired from live performances to work exclusively on studio recordings, Brian's involvement in their lives dwindled.

"What is it you fear most in life?" a reporter from *Melody Maker* magazine had asked him only two weeks before his death. "Loneliness," Epstein answered. "I hope I'll never be lonely, although, actually, one inflicts loneliness on oneself to a certain extent."

Just before leaving for Bangor, George had talked with Brian about India. It was their first and only serious discussion about spiritual interests. "I felt with Brian that he was interested in India and in what I was thinking and feeling," George said. "Maybe he would have liked to meet the Maharishi, but unfortunately it didn't work out like that." George's reflections were tinged with regret, as though admitting that he had failed to help someone he loved.

Wanting to keep media coverage to a minimum, the Beatles did not attend Brian's Liverpool funeral. Instead, on October 17, 1967, they gathered at New London Synagogue in St. John's Wood for a memorial service. George sat with the others, dressed in a suit and wearing a black paper yarmulke. They were only three blocks from the spot where Epstein had cabled them in Hamburg five years before, bursting with the news that EMI had offered the Beatles a recording test.

Shortly after Epstein's death, the Maharishi announced that he would conduct a retreat at his academy in Rishikesh, India. George invited a group of friends to join Pattie and him on the retreat. The group included John and his wife, Cynthia; Paul and his fiancée, actress Jane Asher; Ringo and his wife, Maureen; Beatles road manager Mal Evans; and musician friend Donovan Leitch. Prompted partly by a desire to put sadness over Epstein's death behind them, partly by their natural spirit of adventure, and partly by a curiosity to better understand George's fascination with meditation, they agreed.

"George himself is no mystery," John said. "But the mystery inside George is immense. It's watching him uncover it all little by little that's so damn interesting."

George hoped the trip would give his friends what his previous visit to India had given him: an intuition of immortality. Hiking up the sides of primordial mountains, breathing in air that had once filled the lungs of avatars or divine incarnations, plunging into crystal river water that locals swore flowed to Earth from Heaven—what better way to distance themselves from the sadness of Brian's death and from the shackles of their career as Beatles? If ever John and Paul and Ringo were to join him on his spiritual journey, shared time in the land of gods would tell.

"I am very excited that the Beatles will shortly follow me to Indian shores in order to further study Transcendental Meditation," the Maharishi told reporters at Madison Square Garden prior to a lecture in January 1968. "Because of the conscious mind expansion brought on by meditation, the Beatles' records will show changes in the future, which I feel will bring out the depths in their talents that even they haven't reached yet."

The group arrived in Delhi at three o'clock one morning in February 1968. Rishikesh lay at the end of a bumpy ride over crumbling bridges and 150 miles of open country. By noon their hired cars—battle-weary Ambassadors without springs or suspension—were weaving down Rishikesh's dusty streets crowded with cows and bullock carts. The caravan passed by open-air markets filled with mounds of red mangoes, jackfruit, ripe bananas, and green coconuts. Vendors draped in wool chadors smoked pungent beedies, hand-rolled cigarettes, while stirring vegetable fritters in woks of oil simmering over wood fires with long wooden ladles. The air was thick with spices. A dirt road hooded by arched trees led down an embankment to the edge of the Ganges. Their cars jumbled down the incline, the noise of busy markets fading behind them. Ten minutes later the group stopped, got out, and climbed a path leading to a bluff above the river's eastern bank.

Before them, stone huts and wooden bungalows mushroomed out from groves of teak and guava trees. Looking out over the bluff, the group traced the Ganges up the mountains. Over the centuries, schools for meditation and the study of sacred texts had been built along the banks of the river, and carved domes peeked out from forested hillsides. The group unpacked, wandered the grounds, and watched as day faded into evening and a blue horizon turned pink, indigo, and orange. Across the Ganges, flocks of bright green parrots settled for the night in flowering trees. Peacocks' cries echoed in the stillness.

The Maharishi's bungalow perched on the edge of a cliff overlooking the swiftly flowing river. Shortly after their arrival, the London party took off their shoes and entered a twenty-foot-long meditation hall inside the teacher's bungalow. A handful of other students were already seated inside, and the London guests joined them on white futons arranged before a slightly raised dais. George had recently composed the sound track for a film titled *Wonderwall*, and he carried the results into the meeting on a portable tape player. The film told the story of a man who loses hope and of a mystical woman who saves him by entering his life through a magical "wonderwall." It was less than inspired filmmaking, but the project gave George his first chance to create music independent of the Beatles. The album comprised several short pieces played on a variety of instruments in different Indian styles.

The Maharishi entered the room and pointed with a smile to the tape recorder. "Is it a new song, George," he asked, "or shall I recite verses from the Vedas?"

"A new song," George replied. He pushed the play button and "The Inner Light" wafted through the hall. Never one to limit his interests, George had written lyrics inspired by the

Chinese wisdom text *Tao Te Ching*. In soft, simple tones he sang of meditation and how it permitted him to know all things and understand the meaning of Heaven. A high-pitched bamboo bansari flute echoed his voice while a gentle tapping of tablas supported a melody as unassuming as a nursery rhyme. It was approachable, pleasant music anyone could appreciate.

Among the other students present at the meeting was Paul Saltzman, a twenty-three-year-old from Toronto who had arrived on assignment for the National Film Board of Canada. After hearing the Maharishi lecture at New Delhi University, he headed straight to Rishikesh. Like many young people in the sixties, Saltzman's first contact with mystical thoughts had come from the Beatles 1966 album *Revolver*, which included George's India-inspired "Love You, Too" and the sitar instrumentation on the Lennon/McCartney track "Tomorrow Never Knows," which urged listeners to abandon all thoughts and surrender to the shining self who dwells within.

"I knew the Beatles were telling me of a journey I had not yet made, of an internal place that held great love and knowing," Saltzman said. "Through their music and their interviews, I had already come to trust them."

Saltzman came upon the group sitting at an outdoor table.

"You're from the States, then?" John asked.

"No, Canada."

"Ah, one of the colonies."

They talked about meditation, and all nodded at Saltzman's description of how he heard voices while trying to still his mind, and how the only remedy that seemed to work was to again focus on his mantra.

"Not so easy, really," John confessed. "I often have music playing in my head."

George struck Saltzman as the most serious there about meditation, "a decent guy, warmhearted and unpretentious."

"How long have you played the sitar?" he asked George.

"A little over two years," George said. "We were filming and there was a sitar around. I was curious, but the first time I really listened to sitar music was off a Ravi Shankar album—" A baby monkey dropped onto their table, grabbed a crust of bread, and scampered off. "I'm going to play for a while," George said. "Would you like to listen?"

Sunlight filtered through the window of George's bungalow. He lifted his sitar and secured its large gourd against his left foot. They closed their eyes and George played, reaching deep to evoke his soul's yearning for God as he had learned from Ravi. Twenty minutes later, sympathetic strings echoed the final strains of his exercises.

"You can have everything in life," George told Saltzman. "Like we're the Beatles, aren't we? We can have anything that money can buy and all the fame we could dream of, but then what? It isn't love. It isn't health. It isn't peace inside." Meditation and the Maharishi, he said, had enriched his inner life.

George's days in Rishikesh consisted of a casual breakfast, morning meditation classes until lunch, leisure time in the afternoons, and sometimes as many as three more hours of meditation in the evenings. Some days the pattern varied, and students sunbathed or shopped for clothes in nearby villages. There were perhaps two hundred students and teachers present for the retreat.

Actress Mia Farrow had come with her younger sister Prudence, and though they had never met George before, they talked like old friends, as if picking up a conversation in midstream. Introductions were unnecessary in Rishikesh: theirs was a generation of perpetual dialogue. Having come halfway around the world in 1968, just being together in that spot overlooking India's most sacred river was all the introduction anyone needed. They were advance scouts reconnoitering the terrain of consciousness for their generation, and where you were born or when or to whom were mere details.

"We didn't need to say a lot about our past because we all shared the same past," one student recalled, "and knew we were there to do something about it. Reaching out to something higher was the next step for our generation, since there were no answers coming from parents or the government, and we were truly afraid the world might destroy itself. Looking for God was in the air. It was the only thing that mattered, and the people who understood that recognized one another, at least in a place like Rishikesh."

There was something else George discovered in Rishikesh, something that did not immediately announce its presence. After a while, once his eyes adjusted to the clarity of the air and the timbre of things, he saw it: *Nature.* Perfected creation. Ecology, flawless as fresh cloth, washed and ironed and uncorrupted, whole and healthy, a partnership of earth and air and water and sky. Flowering herbs opened their leaves each morning. Medicinal plants such as *primula*, *sausaurea*, and *aconitum* grew green and yellow with the rising sun. Purple ipomea, blue and yellow Himalayan poppies, and downy white thistle colored his view of steep gorges, overhanging cliffs, and vast stretches of forests and meadows. The area abounded with wildlife, and every so often a musk deer or Indian porcupine would poke out its snout from under a bush or from behind a tree.

Whatever other gods there were, however many more he would meet on this magical journey, this goddess of nature spoke to him in commanding tones, a goddess of magnificent things as large as a mountain and small as a leaf. She was called by many names: Bhumi, goddess of the Earth; Maha-Shakti, the divine mother; Kali-Ma, the personified universal energy. Everyone in Rishikesh, from the Maharishi to the truck driver who delivered the daily produce, paid her homage. They wore garlands made of her flowers; thin strands of bright orange marigolds; and, for special occasions, thick strands of puffy white carnations. They burned incense made of her fragrant woods and distilled oils. They lit candles in her honor, offering back to her a bit of herself, the way old people who bathed each morning in the Ganges cupped their hands to offer a taste of water back to the river. The goddess of nature cared for them with her food: chickpeas mixed with cumin seeds and toasted in clarified butter for breakfast, thick rounds of whole wheat dough rolled and baked over wood flames and spiced eggplant and potatoes harvested in nearby fields and served up for lunch. And these, too, were offered back with prayers and hymns before eating, a simple courtesy, a gesture of thanks, a gift of love.

At day's end, John, Paul, Ringo, and Donovan joined George on the roof of his bungalow. Back in London at this time of evening there would be a rush of traffic, a rattle of buses and trucks heading home, and a chatter from evening crowds escaping the drudgeries of offices and factories. Here, in their Himalayan retreat, George and his friends sat quietly listening to the swoosh of Ganges water as it blended with a whisper of wind blowing through gnarled trees and across ancient valleys in the distance.

In Rishikesh, John and Paul composed more than forty songs. Many were recorded on the *White Album*, and others would appear on the Beatles' final LP, *Abbey Road*. Too much time spent writing, though, struck George as a distraction from their purpose in coming to India, and he said as much. "We're not here to talk music. We're here to meditate."

"Calm down, man," Paul said. "Sense of humor needed here, you know."

George argued that they needed to make best use of their time. This is a land of yogis and saints, he said, and people hundreds of years old. "There's one somewhere around who was born before Christ—and is still living now." He went looking, climbing paths that snaked high into the mountains.

George's commitment to communing with these mystic beings impressed his friends. "The way George is going," John said with admiration, "he'll be flying a magic carpet by the time he's forty."

One of the classes led participants into a meditative state deeper and longer than they had attempted before. George felt himself traveling along subtle paths of consciousness. "It's hard to actually explain it," he said, "but it was just the feeling of consciousness traveling. I don't know where to. It wasn't up, down,

left, right—but there was no 'body' there. You don't feel as
though you're missing anything, but at the same time the consciousness is complete."

Prudence Farrow had similar experiences in meditation. Having taught yoga in Boston before accepting the Maharishi as her
guru, she was proficient in its techniques and would on occasion
spend so many hours in deep trance that it worried George and
John, who lived in bungalows next to hers. One of these pro-
longed absences prompted John to pick up his guitar and write
an invitation for her to come out. Dear Prudence, he sang, the
day is beautiful and so are you. Won't you come out and play?

George saw his friendship with John, Paul, and Ringo as a
continuation from past births. He quoted a lecture by Paramahansa Yogananda in which the kriya-yoga master described as-
sociations in this life as a carryover from previous lives. "There's
more to friendship than meets the eye," George said. Still, the
others had their own reasons for accepting his invitation to India.
Ringo went for the fun of it and stayed only two weeks. His
childhood peritonitis had left him sensitive to spicy foods, and
the ashram's abundance of houseflies made him and his wife,
Maureen, uncomfortable. "It was a good experience," he said.
"It just didn't last as long for me as it did for them."

Paul wanted to see how far the Maharishi could take him in
knowing himself spiritually. "Did you transcend?" he asked the
others after hours of private meditation. "I think I transcended."
No one seemed to have achieved blinding enlightenment, and
one month into the three-month program Paul decided, "This
will do me." That suited his fiancée, Jane Asher, just fine. Asher
was outspoken—if she disagreed with something, she said so.
She had little interest in the Maharishi and told Paul they would
achieve enlightenment on their own.

John had come with stronger ambitions. If they mastered
Transcendental Meditation, then they could help others do more
than groove to good music. Popular media insisted on enshrin-
ing the Beatles as youth leaders; why not be spiritual leaders,
too? "Within three months," the Maharishi told press shortly

after the retreat started, "I promise to turn [the Beatles] into fully qualified teachers or semigurus of Hindu meditation. George and John have progressed fantastically in the few days since they arrived here."

Promises of turning them into qualified teachers could not compete with rumors alleging that the Maharishi had acted inappropriately toward women disciples. When the rumors reached John, he packed his bags. What sort of teacher is this? Where is *his* renunciation? Where is *his* freedom from ego and the senses?

George could not confirm the rumors, but neither could he deny them. He knew women who had given themselves to gurus but hesitated to judge anyone else's way to God. If someone saw the divine manifested in a teacher's human body, who was he to say no? He felt so ill equipped to judge other people's inner workings and so unwilling to try that all he could do was urge John to see the positive side of their stay. "All [the] Maharishi ever gave me was good advice and the technique of meditation, which is really wonderful," George said. "I admire him for being able in spite of all the ridicule to just keep going."

John had wanted to return to London to rejoin his new love, avant-garde artist Yoko Ono, and his disenchantment with the Maharishi provided a convenient excuse. It also reinforced a personal philosophy that bordered on existential despair. "I haven't met anybody full of joy," he said later that year, "neither the Maharishi nor any swami or Hare Krishna singer. There is no constant. There's this dream of constant joy—it's bullshit as far as I'm concerned." Rishikesh ended John's interest in spiritual masters. "There is no guru," he said. "You have to believe in yourself. You've got to get down to your own God in your own temple. It's all down to you, mate."

Shortly after their return, John appeared on the *Tonight Show* and said of his time with the Maharishi, "We made a mistake. He's human like the rest of us."

By contrast, George credited the Maharishi with orchestrating one of the greatest experiences of his life. He never shared John's pessimism over accepting help from teachers or his friend's disbelief in a dream of constant joy. Still, a dream did take work, and a dictum of Vivekananda's, one George often quoted, said, "Each soul is potentially divine. Our job is to manifest that divinity."

The trip affected each of the Beatles differently. The fact that they had taken it at all affected the entire world. Their pilgrimage to Rishikesh was reported by press in every country and added impetus to a spiritual culture that had been gathering momentum for several years. By the end of 1968, courses on yoga and vegetarian cooking were flourishing, meditation centers had opened across the United States and Europe, and Ravi Shankar was a celebrity in his own right. The Beatles' film *Yellow Submarine*, released that July, confirmed George's new role as the mystic Beatle by depicting him in the lotus position, wearing wooden beads and veiled in a cloud of incense. Predictably, other bands followed his example by adding Indian instrumentation to their records, and a new category of programming, soon to be known as world music, appeared on radio stations. "We are now setting ourselves the highest possible goal: a development of consciousness where the whole of humanity is at stake," avant-garde composer Karlheinz Stockhausen wrote that year. "If we comprehend that, we will also produce the right music, making people aware of the whole."

Life magazine dubbed 1968 "The Year of the Guru," and *Look* magazine concluded that John, Paul, George, and Ringo were "the great scribes of our era."

George remained completely indifferent to the group's rising status. "He's found something stronger than the Beatles," his wife, Pattie, told the Beatles biographer Hunter Davies, "though he still wants them to share it."

That stronger something—a palpable sense of spiritual purpose—was providing George with extraordinary musical inspiration, and original compositions flowed. His *White Album* song "Long, Long, Long" conveyed a simple message of love for God lost and then found, set to chords borrowed from Bob Dylan's ode "Sad-Eyed Lady of the Low Land." George framed the hushed message in a dreamy tempo built with Indian instruments and folk guitar phrasing. He was unapologetic, even in this early solo composition, about amalgamating elements that pleased him from a variety of sources and cultures.

From Rishikesh, too, was born a very different tune, "Piggies," a raucous send-up of establishment types: little piggies in dirt and bigger piggies in white shirts, so filled with self-importance that they failed to see the cannibalism in their bacon dinner. Grandiose harpsichord flourishes underlined the absurdity of their predicament. George was stuck for a line in the middle that would rhyme with "lacking," and it was his mother who suggested "a damn good whacking," a practice she herself never employed in parenting.

Donning an advertiser's persona to promote the benefits of meditation, George transformed aphorisms from the Sanskrit text *Visvasara Tantra* into another tune penned in Rishikesh: a heavy rock number called "Sour Milk Sea." Is life getting you down? Not getting the breaks you want? Try illumination. He wanted to express a simple rule of thumb and chose a hard-driving, blues guitar medium to do so: If you're in the shit, don't go around moaning. Do something about it.

The pilgrimage to Rishikesh unleashed the most productive period of George's career, a phenomenon he attributed to having awakened to his higher purpose. "The more aware I've become," he told *Look* magazine that year, "the more I realize that all we are doing is acting out an incarnation. . . . not for yourself particularly but for everyone else, for whoever wants it."

Rishikesh also made clear to George that his bandmates were not interested in fulfilling their incarnation in quite the same way. To the contrary, it seemed they could hardly wait to get home and pick up where they had left off bickering.

By July 1968, recording sessions had become so tense that EMI engineer Geoff Emerick quit, no longer able to tolerate the lost tempers and frequent swearing. When it came to illuminating others, George concluded, it was up for grabs as to who would get turned on and who wouldn't, a thought he put into a new song, "Not Guilty," recorded in August 1968 at Abbey Road Studios. "Even though [the song] was [about] me getting pissed off with Lennon and McCartney for the grief I was catching," he explained, "it said I wasn't guilty of getting in the way of their careers or of leading them astray in our all going to Rishikesh to see the Maharishi. I was sticking up for myself."

In public he continued to respect the group's interests, telling *Time* magazine in September, "We haven't really started yet. We have only just discovered what we can do as musicians, what thresholds we can cross. The future stretches out beyond our imagination."

In private, though, his life as a Beatle was drawing to a close. Rishikesh turned out to be the last time George traveled together with John, Paul, and Ringo. George was for the moment alone in his spiritual interests and, despite Pattie's companionship, without friends with whom to share his life-transforming discoveries.

7

Devotees

None of us is God. We're just his servants.

—George, 1969

The Beatles had made their headquarters in a five-story Georgian town house nestled between fashion design offices and exclusive boutiques on London's posh Savile Row. Apple Corp., as they called their company, was Paul's idea, a way of channeling the group's impressive record revenues into new projects. Apple advertised in newspapers and magazines, encouraging creative people to send in whatever songs, movie scripts, or other materials needed a home. Noble motives inspired the company—to help artists avoid the clutches of greedy agents and domineering studios—but like many ideas that emerged after Brian Epstein's death, Apple was turning out to be a money-losing disaster, a haven for oddballs with impractical notions and wildly expensive schemes.

The company did some real business, signing recording artists such as James Taylor, Mary Hopkin, Jackie Lomax, the Modern Jazz Quartet, and Billy Preston. By November 1969, though, Apple had begun to spin out of control, adding fuel to the fire of George's discontent as a Beatle.

That month, George saw a photo in the *Times* of London of three shaven-headed American Krishna devotees and their sari-clad wives playing drums and chanting mantras on Oxford Street.

The article quoted one of the men, Gurudas, as saying, "Hare Krishna is a chant that sets God dancing on your tongue. Try chanting 'Queen Elizabeth, Queen Elizabeth' and see the difference." The article added that they next intended to chant in front of the London Stock Exchange. "What effect that will have," the reporter concluded, "Krishna only knows."

Another eye-catching group arrived in London that month: members of San Francisco's Hell's Angels. George had spoken briefly with the Hell's Angels during his visit to Haight-Asbury and had casually mentioned that if they ever made it to London they should look him up. Now here they were, Harley Davidson motorbikes in tow. When he found out the group had taken him seriously and planned on paying a visit, George circulated a memo to the Apple staff: "They may look as though they are going to do you in but are very straight and do good things, so don't fear them or uptight them. Try to assist them without neglecting your Apple business and without letting them take control."

On Christmas Eve, a winter rain fell on London. Outside the Apple building, photographers and a dozen or so Apple Scruffs, as the young women Beatles fans were known, stood around as they did every day, waiting for their heroes to make an appearance. A tall, shaven-headed Krishna devotee approached the building. An Apple Scruff looked at him and giggled. A black-suited guard with big shoulders waved him off and barred the entrance, flashing a sympathetic smile. "Just doing my job."

Just then, Yoko Ono pulled up in a white Rolls-Royce. The guard hopped down the stairs and opened the door for John's famous partner. Yoko stepped out, looked at the shaven-headed devotee, and said, "You must be one of George's. Come on in." Flashbulbs popped behind them.

Yoko and the devotee walked up a flight of stairs and into a spacious lounge outfitted with armchairs, sofas, little tables, and lamps. A Christmas tree winked in a corner. Fifty or so people stood about, drinking and talking. A few were recognizable musicians; others were elegantly dressed women, Carnaby Street mods, and men in Edwardian suits. Interspersed among them were the San Francisco Hell's Angels.

George was ensconced behind closed doors, reviewing yet more unpleasant business matters with his bandmates. Their meeting finally ended and one by one John, Paul, and Ringo peeked out and then quickly bolted for the exit, not pausing to speak with anyone. A few minutes later, George poked his head into the room. His intense dark eyes scanned the crowd and alighted on the devotee. As though spotting an old friend, he shot out from behind the door, crossed the room, and came straight up to the shaven-headed man in a white robe.

"Hare Krishna," he said, smiling at the stunned American. "Where have you been? I've been waiting to meet you." George sat and the devotee introduced himself by his spiritual name, Shyamsundar, which he said meant a servant of Krishna who has a dark complexion (*shyama*) and is very beautiful (*sundar*).

George motioned toward the guests milling around the room. "Do you know these people?" he asked.

Shyamsundar nodded at the Hell's Angels and said that he knew them from Haight-Ashbury, where he had become a disciple of Swami Prabhupada along with a number of other "ex-freaks like me."

George laughed and said he knew about Prabhupada from the teacher's recording of the Krishna chanting. He was even sure, he said, that once his life had been saved on a flight out of San Francisco by chanting the Hare Krishna mantra.

The American explained that he, his wife, and two other couples were living for the time being in an empty warehouse but that their plan was someday to start a temple for Krishna in London.

George wanted to know more about their guru, and the American explained that Prabhupada represented a line of teachers going back to the beginning of creation when Brahma, the first created being, received divine knowledge directly from Krishna.

"But what I don't get," George said, "is why just Krishna? I mean, you've got Shiva, Ganesh, Brahma," and he named other deities in India's pantheon. At least from what he had read and heard so far, Krishna was one manifestation among many of a formless higher energy. "They're all the same, aren't they?" he asked. "Why don't you chant 'Hare Shiva' or something?"

Devotees worshiped Krishna as God's original personal form, Shyamsundar said, the source from which all other divine beings came. Shiva, Ganesh, Brahma, and other personalities were honored as demigods, God's assistants, but devotees accepted Krishna as the fountainhead. Krishna was uniquely beautiful, he said, and in India's bhakti or devotional tradition God's impersonal energy took a backseat to this all-attractive personal form.

Guests at the gathering circulated, feigning indifference to the exotic encounter, gawking from the corner of their eyes.

"Just like now, which would I prefer," Shyamsundar said, "to sit in my pad stoned out on your music, or to be here with you personally, sharing some laughs? Your music's great, but I'd rather be here yakking with you in person."

George nodded, intrigued. "If you're free, we'll talk again Sunday at my place." He scrawled a map on a napkin, leaped up, and waved farewell, leaving Shyamsundar staring at the napkin in amazement.

The following Sunday, George and his wife, Pattie, greeted the shaven-headed American at their home in the suburb of Esher. Shyamsundar pulled up in a rickety pickup truck—a donation, he said, from a sympathetic Indian. The three retired to the den where sunshine streamed in through floor-to-ceiling windows. Sandalwood incense permeated the room. They sat on cushions and engaged in small talk for a while. The twenty-three-year-old American said that he had been a Fulbright scholar and professional skier but had felt unfulfilled by academia and the slopes. He had been living in a watchtower overlooking the forests of central Oregon, reading books on Eastern mysticism and wondering what was next, when an old college buddy arrived and convinced him to visit Prabhupada in Haight-Ashbury. Hearing Prabhupada explain about chanting and the Bhagavad Gita, he said, convinced him that everything in his life up to that time had been a preparation for Krishna consciousness.

George was hungry for just this kind of philosophical discussion. "I want to know what it's all about," he said, "and meeting you and hearing about Krishna and Prabhupada has come at the perfect time in my life. A lot of changes are going down. All these bits and pieces are running around in my head, but the pieces seem to fit together into the big picture the way you're saying it."

Shyamsundar quoted a Sanskrit text that said when one sincerely seeks God, that's when God sends a teacher to make introductions. He told George about his own meeting with Prabhupada and how it had changed his life.

Pattie poured tea from a tray, assessing the exchange.

George asked how devotees see their destiny after death. By serving Krishna with devotion, Shyamsundar said, at death their soul would be liberated from further births and go back to Krishna in the spiritual world.

Pattie stood. "You do it by chanting," she said to the American, making her way toward the kitchen. "Other people do it by meditating or some other kind of yoga."

Pattie prepared snacks while George asked one question after another. They talked about India and Hinduism, about the Beatles, and about George's desire for a more perfect life. Not until an hour and several plates of vegetarian treats later did the conversation wind down.

George admired the American's penchant for looking back on life with a laugh, and he needed no prodding to laugh along. He put on a Bob Dylan record and recounted a few anecdotes of their time together. Shyamsundar prepared to leave and invited George to come meet the other devotees in their temple-in-a-warehouse. George accepted with enthusiasm. Being a Beatle, he said, had proved to him there was some greater magic out there and had given him the freedom and the courage to seek it out. It was an opportunity earned after a million lifetimes and he felt a responsibility, especially after seeing Haight-Ashbury, to set a good example for others.

"If I don't use this opportunity," he said, "then I've wasted my life, haven't I?"

*   *   *

At five o'clock on a chilly winter afternoon, George drove his black Porsche to the devotees' temple-in-a-warehouse. Wearing jeans and a black fleecy Afghani jacket, he stepped out of the car and looked up. Devotees waved down from an open window on the second floor. Shyamsundar arrived at the front door and escorted George up the stairs.

Approaching the loft, George smelled the scent of marigolds mixed with an aroma of cumin and mustard seeds. He slipped off his shoes and entered a large, open space where five Americans crowded around.

Shyamsundar introduced his wife, Malati, and their infant daughter, Saraswati. With her free hand, Malati slipped a garland of marigolds around George's neck.

George joined his palms in thanks, as he had seen done so often in India.

A woman with soulful eyes, her hands covered in flour, emerged from a kitchen area at the back of the loft. Shyamsundar introduced Yamuna, who offered George a warm smile and slight bow, then returned to frying vegetables in a wok of oil. Batter popped like distant firecrackers as she dropped in the fritters. Other devotees stepped forward one by one. George shook hands with Mukunda and then squinted, trying to place the name.

"Didn't you send me a letter sometime back?" he asked. "About mantras, I think."

Mukunda appeared stunned. His letter had actually arrived, and George remembered it. He nodded and a grin burst over his face.

Gurudas, a tall devotee with apple cheeks, introduced himself. He had been on freedom marches in Alabama with Dr. Martin Luther King Jr. for five years, he said, and then relocated to San Francisco to work for the city's slum communities.

George spread his hands to indicate the group. "I saw a photo of you all in the *Times* last Sunday—with the baby chewing on your beads," he said, motioning to Saraswati. "You looked so, well, transcendental." He knew the effect he had on people and kept his voice light, as though reassuring them he wasn't there to judge or seem privileged or different but to enjoy their company and maybe learn something. Years later, the devotees would remember something almost self-effacing about George at that first meeting.

"Come in and see our altar," Gurudas said.

Mounted on a far wall of the loft, a cloth-covered shelf displayed pocket-size photos of shaven-headed men in robes. Incense and candles burned in small brass holders. On the altar stood eight-inch brass figures, one male and one female, in elaborate miniature gowns decorated with sequins and colored stones. Gurudas described that the Krishna tradition acknowledged God as both male and female. Devotees, he said, honored Radha—God's feminine feature—with even greater reverence than Krishna himself.

"Hare is another name for Radha," he said. "The mantra Hare Krishna asks Radha to engage us in service to Krishna. And if Radha asks Krishna to accept someone," he said with a grin, "Krishna can't possibly refuse."

George had seen larger versions of the Radha and Krishna deities in India. The deity of Radha was smiling, her right hand poised waist-high, her palm outward, blessing onlookers. Her left hand held a tiny brass lotus flower. The deity of Krishna stood with one foot draped casually over the other. A miniature brass flute rested in his hands near his lips, as though he were about to play. Tiny garlands hung from their necks, and candlelight flickered on their brass faces.

On the altar was a small painting of a golden figure, his hands raised in ecstasy. "That's Chaitanya, the 'golden avatar,'" Gurudas said. "Chaitanya started the street chanting in Bengal in the sixteenth century. One day in San Francisco, we moved our chanting outdoors, the way Chaitanya had done it. When Prabhupada heard about it, he said, 'Lord Chaitanya has inspired you,' and he asked us to continue street chanting every day. So when we got to London, we just did what we had been doing in the States. It may have had some historic significance, but we did it mostly because it made us feel good and people on the street liked it."

George bent down to look closer at photographs arranged in a line on the altar. "These must be your gurus, then?" Mukunda nodded and named each guru in historical order.

A few devotees came in from the loft's small kitchen bearing trays of food portioned out into stainless steel dishes and placed them on the altar. Yamuna bowed down to offer the food with prayers, lowering herself gracefully and leaning her head to the floor. There was no embarrassment in her prostrating herself, no awkwardness over performing such a humble gesture before someone she had just met. George watched in silent appreciation. After fifteen years in the company of egotistical musicians and self-important dealmakers—"soft-shoe shufflers," as he called them—he was unaccustomed to such unabashed devotion.

Mukunda picked up a double-headed mridanga drum. "Let's have a kirtan—a chant—while Krishna eats." Pillows were circulated and all sat cross-legged in a circle before the altar. Gurudas opened a rectangular wooden box and lifted up a keyboard nestled inside. He slid the box over to George. "Do you know how to play one of these?"

"Harmonium," George said with a nod to the instrument he knew well from his *Wonderwall* sound track sessions in India. He unlatched a bellows behind the keyboard and started pumping, sending a current of air through the valves, and ran his fingers over the instrument's ivory keys, tapping out a few Indian scales.

Shyamsundar opened another box and pulled out an esraj, a long-necked stringed instrument with a bulbous end. He placed the instrument upright in his lap and bowed a few sliding notes while other devotees grabbed hand cymbals. One by one they joined forces playing and chanting the mantra that George knew well: "Hare Krishna, Hare Krishna, Krishna Krishna, Hare Hare, Hare Rama. Hare Rama, Rama Rama, Hare Hare." Minutes raced by, the drumbeat quickened, and the kirtan ended in a blazing crescendo of instruments and song. The devotees bent down. George followed suit while Yamuna offered closing prayers.

The group sat up, flush with the energy and pleasure of chanting. "That was really divine," George said, wiping hair away from his eyes. He felt like a different man among these people. There had been nowhere for him to turn for fellowship until now, no one who shared the depth of his growing passion for spiritual philosophy.

In many ways the devotees were like him, in age and life experiences and awareness of their moments in history. They had followed parallel tracks in their journeys to God, through childhood in the postwar years, then rock and roll, LSD, and now mystic India. At ease in their company, George ate with gusto, asking the name of each dish and identifying the ones he knew from his time in Rishikesh: split-pea dahl soup, basmati rice, and vegetable-stuffed samosa fritters.

Prabhupada taught "kitchen religion," the devotees joked—how to eat one's way back to God. By meal's end, everyone was sprawled out on the floor, stuffed and giggling like children.

Gurudas walked George to a sink, where they washed their hands. "Washing is like chanting," Gurudas said. "They're both a cleansing process."

It was incredible. Here were educated Americans from well-to-do families. From what George knew of them, they had grown up with every prospect of becoming mature, full-fledged consumers. It was in their blood, that American appetite for ownership, a world-renowned personality trait. Yet here they were, sleeping on the floor, living on next to nothing, animated by faith, and truly happy. Maybe the happiest people he'd ever met. While he basked in the limelight of the world and spent money without any longer thinking about it, happiness often seemed to him a very elusive luxury. These people worked in anonymity and clearly had few resources, yet they beamed. In the scheme of things, was their simple, happy life of dedication to God not more meaningful than selling millions of records?

"I'm inspired here," he said to Gurudas with a smile, and they returned to the main room. "You guys have got everything," George said, "beautiful music, beautiful things all around you, great things to read and talk about, families—it's a whole way of life, isn't it?" He excused himself, said he had to get to a recording session, turned at the door, and invited them to visit his home sometime soon: maybe a little of this lifestyle could rub off on him and Pattie. He got in his car, waved good-bye to the couples standing by their loft window, and motored down the street into a wintry London night.

He could hardly wait to see them again.

The more George tried to separate from being a Beatle, the more events conspired to keep him locked in. Shortly before his visit to the devotees' loft, Martin Luther King Jr. was assassinated in Memphis, provoking riots across America. Two months later, Robert Kennedy was assassinated in Los Angeles. Soviet troops were massing on the Czech border, U.S. forces had increased the frequency and intensity of their bombing of Vietnamese villages, and demonstrations of one kind or another were ending in tragedy almost every day. In September 1968 alone, the American press reported more than two hundred demonstrations, most of which had led to fatalities.

Anger that year took absurd and tragic turns, as when madman Charles Manson claimed that George's song "Piggies" compelled him to order a series of brutal murders. *Time* magazine summarized the year with an article titled "Wilting Flowers." It felt to many as though the world had gone insane, and Beatles music represented one of the few positive inspirations left.

George recorded a lament for humanity in his *White Album* song "While My Guitar Gently Weeps," which he had composed during a visit to his parents' house earlier that year. From his vantage point on the periphery of the Lennon-McCartney creative circle, it was clear to George that inspiration for a song could come from anywhere.

Brian Epstein's assistant Alistair Taylor had once told Paul how much he admired his songwriting skills. Paul insisted that anyone could write a song. He marched Taylor into his dining room, where he kept an old hand-carved harmonium, then sat himself at the low end and Taylor at the high end and said, "You hit any note you like on the keyboard . . . and I'll do the same. Now, whenever I shout out a word, you shout out the opposite. That's all, and I'll make up a tune. You watch."

"Black," Paul said.

"White," Taylor replied.

"Yes."

"No."

"Good."

"Bad."

And on they went for a few minutes until they ran out of pairs of opposites. Later that week, Paul arrived at the Apple offices with a demo of the Beatles' hit song "Hello, Good-bye."

George, too, had no musical plan when he started to write "While My Guitar Gently Weeps." He did have an idea, though, inspired by the *I Ching* (*Book of Changes*), the widely read Chinese classic book of divinations. The book encouraged accepting every event as now, neither past nor future, and as completely relevant to now. In that spirit, George rummaged around his parents' house until he found a book. Whatever he saw in that book, he decided, would become his song. He opened the book, and the first words his eyes saw were "gently weeps."

The song that emerged began with a series of minor chords working their way down the scale as though musically tracing humanity's decline. George distanced himself from those victimized by the decline, singing that he grieved for them. But his regret was passive, and the song ended with a slow fade, suggesting that if people didn't take action, their misery would merely go on and on.

As sober as it was, the public loved this new brand of Beatles music, deeming it socially relevant and intellectually challenging. Record sales soared. By year's end, the *White Album* had sold more than four million copies. Despite his growing distaste for fame, Beatle George was becoming more famous by the minute.

"This group by itself," wrote critic Carl Pelz in 1968, "has generated more public enthusiasm and more activity in the music industry than any individual or group in rock history, even more than Elvis Presley generated when he appeared in 1956." But backlash against the Beatles also had increased. The controversy that followed John's statement about Jesus never fully disappeared, and recently Paul added a controversy of his own by admitting to reporters that the Beatles had taken LSD. In an interview with the United Kingdom's *Queen* magazine, he went so far as to comment that it had made him "a better, more honest, more tolerant member of society."

To these concerns was now added George's preoccupation with India.

"What's happened to the Beatles?" an editorial in the *Daily Mail* complained. "It's now around four years since the Beatles happened, and . . . [they] have changed completely. They rose as heroes of a social revolution. They were everybody's next-door neighbors. . . . Now they have isolated themselves, not only personally but also musically. They have become contemplative, secretive, exclusive."

Did the public love them? Hate them? Without Brian Epstein's guidance, the band members could no longer figure out how to interpret or manage their image and career. Still, they had commitments to fulfill as a group, including another movie. After much debate they at last agreed on a concept for the movie. They would film themselves at work, writing songs, rehearsing for a show, and then end the movie with a live performance. Shooting on *Let It Be* began in January at Twickenham Studios, where much of *Help!* and *A Hard Day's Night* had been filmed.

The concept proved disastrous. They had never had much privacy, but now even their petty tiffs were being taped for posterity, including harsh words between George and Paul.

"I'm just saying you could try playing it like this," Paul instructed, assuming once again the role of leader.

"I'll play whatever you want me to play," George replied submissively, "or I won't play at all if you don't want. Whatever it is that will please you, I'll do it." The days were long and the satisfactions meager.

George thought he was quite capable of being relatively happy on his own. Even so, he was not cut out to be a loner. It was better company he wanted, not isolation.

George and Pattie spent the last few months of 1968 at Bob Dylan's home in Woodstock, New York, where members of Dylan's backup group, the Band, gathered for spontaneous jams. It was a happy time spent making good music and communing with friends and their families.

When the Band played, they created tight vocal harmonies and rarely indulged in instrumental solos. George liked that natural modesty among musicians. Nothing could have been more satisfying—or more unlike the headaches of life as a Beatle.

George had been a teenager when he first saw Bob Dylan in Liverpool on a Granada television program about New York's beat poets. While appearing in Paris in 1964, the Beatles picked up two of Bob Dylan's albums at a radio station and were so mesmerized by his wise lyrics and simple chords that they played the albums constantly in their Hôtel George V suite.

The admiration was mutual. Dylan drove cross-country from Denver to New York in 1963 with friend and photographer Barry Feinstein, playing the radio nonstop, and by midjourney it was clear to Dylan that the Beatles were "doing things nobody was doing. Their chords were outrageous and their harmonies made it all valid, but I kept it to myself that I really dug them," he told biographer Anthony Scaduto. "Everybody else thought they were for the teenyboppers, that they were going to pass right away, but it was obvious to me that they had staying power."

On August 28, 1964, journalist Al Aronowitz introduced Dylan to the Beatles at a New York hotel. "I'd hate to think that putting Bob together with the Beatles is the only thing I'll ever be remembered for," Aronowitz later said, "but I think it certainly was the right thing to do. Hasn't the whole world benefited? Look at all the beautiful music that we have as a result. The Beatles' magic was in their sound. Bob's magic was in his words. After they met, the Beatles' words got grittier and Bob invented folk-rock."

Over the years, George attended a number of Dylan's concerts and was present at London's Royal Albert Hall in May 1965 when Dylan walked onstage with an electric guitar, prompting boos from fans who viewed the switch from acoustic as a betrayal of his folk purity. George called those who walked out of the concert "idiots" and argued "it was all still pure Dylan, and he has to find out his own directions. If he felt he wanted electrification, that's the way he has to do it. Who's laying down the rules?"

Dylan had started his career with folk songs and protest music but by 1966 had moved away from pointing fingers at others and begun examining himself. His introspection culminated in the album *John Wesley Harding,* acclaimed as one of the great musical compositions of the period. To everyone's surprise, Dylan chose that moment of success to walk away from complex themes and to revert to the simplest, most unpretentious of all musical styles: country.

Like Dylan, George was beginning to see that his next step needed to be away from everything he had done up to that moment.

Watching Dylan over Thanksgiving in Woodstock in 1968 showed George how happy someone could be following his own direction and making his own rules. If Dylan walked away at *his* moment of triumph to be his own man, why could George not do the same?

"Even his stuff which people loathe, I like," George said, "because every single thing he does represents something that's him."

One of the people who dropped by for the 1968 Thanksgiving gathering was artist Judith Jamison, a Woodstock resident. "What was interesting about that day was that not one Beatle song was sung," she recalled. "There was lots of other music being played. George even asked me what I'd like to hear. I said 'Over the Rainbow,' and he kindly played it—but not one song from his Beatles past. It was music like in the movie *De-Lovely*—classic, American, a mix of everything, but no rock 'n' roll, no Beatles."

"Dylan's influence was incredible," noted Barry Feinstein, who was a friend of both George and Dylan. "You couldn't be with Dylan and not be influenced, not think about everything that you've done and see it simply as bullshit by comparison. I was with Dylan at a party when he said to Mick Jagger, 'Are you *serious* about what you write and play and sing? You can't be *serious* about your music.' Mick said, 'Of course I am.' 'No, man,' Bob said. 'That kind of music's not serious.' That gave me a handle on what happened to George. People who knew Bob would get this feeling, 'Take everything I've done and throw it out and let me start over again. *This* is where it's *at*. Let me see if I can get on the same trip.'

"One thing that was really important for Dylan," Feinstein added, "was that he believed once you've done something, you don't go back to fix it. Move on. That was an important lesson for George. If you write a song or take a picture, then later you don't think it was that good—leave it, let it go, and get on with the next thing. That's what made Dylan great, and that's what Bob's influence was on George."

With excitement over the prospect of moving on with his career and not looking back on the past, George returned to London from Woodstock on January 1, 1969. But as soon as he came together with John and Paul and Ringo at Twickenham Studios to complete work on their *Let It Be* project, the bickering started all over again: what to do with the Apple company, how to finish their next album, who should make the decisions.

On the evening of January 7 after another day of disputes, George sat down and wrote a song he called "I, Me, Mine." "There are two 'i's," he said, "the little i—when people say, '*I* am this'—and the big I, that is, Om, the complete whole universal consciousness that is void of the relatively and ego. There is nothing that isn't part of the complete whole. When the little i merges into the big I, then you are really smiling."

Nobody was smiling at Twickenham Studios, where little i's were going at it tooth and nail.

A few days into the sessions, as the group spent yet another morning arguing, Paul insisted that to salvage the band they ought to return to touring and television. That anyone should even consider resuscitating that painful period from their past was more than George could bear.

On Friday, January 10, 1969, he walked up to the others after lunch, told them, "See you 'round the clubs," got into his car, and left. He drove away and didn't look back.

Driving north to Esher, back home in the bright light of day, he may have silently thanked Paul for liberating him to do what he had not done before: move past the frustration and bitterness to become his own man.

It was a stunning departure, the first time he had ever done anything like it, and after the initial unreality had worn off John, Paul, and Ringo took stock of it and saw that he commanded their respect. "George had to leave because he thought Paul was dominating him," Ringo said. "Well, he was."

Character, George's exit said, not career should govern their behavior. After standing to the side for years, he was too much in control of his destiny now and too sure of his life's higher purpose to waste any more time on petty squabbles.

George explained to Pattie what had happened, told her he had decided to spend a few days at home with his folks, and packed a bag.

Before leaving Esher for Liverpool, he penned a musical response to the bickering. "Wah-Wah" was a hard-driving tune whose title referred to the stopperlike sound created on a guitar's mute pedal, symbolizing the band's musical success, and also a headache. The Beatles had given him both, yet unlike the others, he refused to fight anymore—life was too short—so he wrote a song. The emerging George Harrison was someone who could master hostility and channel the energy to creative ends. He was, according to childhood friend Bill Harry, "completely different. He wasn't under the domination of the others. He wasn't a passenger anymore." Nor was he now a backup guitarist or an economy Beatle who hovered on the side and allowed himself to be placated with a track or two on an album. From the adolescent uncertainty of his first song, "Don't Bother Me," to the mature confidence of "Wah-Wah," a strong and assertive artist had surfaced.

It felt good to put those difficult years behind him. Some of George's self-assurance sprang from natural growth and experience but he knew that yoga and meditation were also making a contribution. He felt himself evolving, reshaping to fit an ideal he had found among the saints of India. From meditating on that ideal came a recollection: here, too, in his declaration of independence, there was a right way and a wrong way of doing things. Once he might have considered striking back the true measure of a man—certainly that had been so as a boy in grammar school who saw no hope for a brighter future and who "would punch people out just to get it out of your system." But he held himself up to a different standard now. Controlling anger, forgiving those who hurt him, would be the enlightened response.

Five days after his dramatic departure, he returned from Liverpool and made the others an intelligent, yogilike offer. Provided there was no more talk about touring or television, he would rejoin the group. Two days after that, they were back recording.

Soon after, the frictions had returned. Hoping to calm things down, George called the temple-in-a-warehouse. Shyamsundar answered the phone.

"I'd like you to come out and talk to the boys," George said. "We're about an hour from London. Can you make it—today?"

Outside the Twickenham Studio gates, police held back crowds of girls clutching flowers and autograph books. Shyamsundar arrived and watched from the sidelines. Police were allowing no one to enter. A white Rolls-Royce limousine with tinted windows drove up and was quickly waved through. Shyamsundar bent down and duckwalked by the side of the limo, out of sight. Yoko grinned down at him through a crack in the window.

Inside the compound, actors in costume strolled across the grounds. Dracula, stage blood oozing down his white tuxedo shirt, smiled at Shyamsundar, whose shaved head and yellow robes fit right in. Ignoring a red flashing NO ENTRY light, the American pushed open a heavy door marked "soundstage" and entered a cavernous room shrouded in darkness except for a spotlight at the far end.

George looked up soberly and nodded at his friend. "Hare Krishna," he said into a microphone. Then he turned back to Paul, who was saying something about playing notes in a different way. John stood nearby holding a guitar, Yoko sitting beside him with her arm around his leg. Ringo perched silently at his drums on a platform behind the others. The floor was littered with wires and cables. Finally someone shouted, "Two hours, everyone."

George hopped down from the stage and waved to his friend. "We're having a little break. Can you come along? The boys all want to hear what you've got to say."

George introduced Shyamsundar to John, Paul, Ringo, road manager Mal Evans, and some others. The group walked down halls filled with mockups of castles and Jack the Ripper streets and entered a large furnished room. George sat the devotee on a chair in the center of the room. Everyone stretched out on couches and armchairs, and the door slammed shut.

"All right," said John. "What's it all about then?"

George knew bringing his friend to meet John and Paul and Ringo might fail to calm the waters. After the debacle of Rishikesh, it was a wonder they had even agreed to meet another of George's seeker friends at all. But he trusted Shyamsundar's native intelligence and natural warmth. If anyone could apply some healing glue to the cracks that were opening among them, it was the American.

Shyamsundar started from the top. He said that souls enter the material world and get caught up in a struggle of repeated birth and death, and a simple way to escape that cycle of reincarnation is to chant God's names.

"So what about music," Paul said, "as an expression of consciousness? How does that fit in?"

The right kind of music, the American replied, could link the soul to God. Spiritual music such as mantras penetrated consciousness to awaken the sleeping soul.

"What about peace then?" John asked. "I mean, you can't have all these people running around the world killing each other, can you?"

George had invited Shyamsundar to speak that day because they were friends and because the devotee could fairly represent the journey they shared. But John's question bordered on entrapment. No one knew how to put an end to violence and war.

It was January 1969, and war had been the decade's ultimate dilemma. Peace demonstrations in New York and Washington, D.C., were taking place to sound tracks of Lennon-McCartney songs. Protesters in Berkeley, California, were rousting navy recruiters with choruses of "We all live in a yellow submarine." John's soon-to-be-recorded "Give Peace a Chance" would become the antiwar movement's theme song. The political troubadour of his generation had put the devotee in a delicate position. If Shyamsundar talked about enlightened warriors such as Arjuna or about fighting for a righteous cause, he would rouse John's opposition to violence of any kind.

"The only way real peace can happen," Shyamsundar said, "is if people of the world recognize they are all part and parcel of the same one God. If you love the Father, you can love his children." We are all children of God, he said, animals as much as people. Don't animals also suffer? For peace to be widespread and real, it had to include all life. "Start at the root, with love of God," he said. "Then automatically peace will be there for all living creatures."

John seemed impressed, and George relaxed.

On and on the conversation went, late into the afternoon. The film producer's repeated calls to return for shooting went unanswered as the group plowed forward with their talks. They laughed a lot and made fun of Shyamsundar's dress.

"Hey, it was the only way I could get you to notice me," he shot back.

The conversation ranged from reminiscences of the Beatles' trip to India to their weeks with the Maharishi and the time George and John chanted "Hare Krishna" all day cruising the Adriatic.

"It made me high," John said. "It really did."

As they left the building, George mentioned to John that the devotees had no temple of their own, and John offered to let them stay at his new country estate in exchange for doing repairs. The meeting was a success.

George left the studio feeling comfortable, even elated. He had taken a risk inviting his friend at a delicate time, and it had paid off. The rest of the world was blowing up, but here, for the moment, there was peace among the Beatles.

In January 1957, at age thirteen, George practicing for his future career.

In 1961, Hamburg's red-light district provided seventeen-year-old George with ample doses of sex, drugs, and rock and roll.

Beginning in 1962, the Beatles played Liverpool's Cavern Club more than three hundred times.

In 1963, George taking time out from life as a Beatle to have breakfast with his dad at home in Liverpool.

In February 1964, for his
twenty-first birthday,
George received seven
truckloads of cards,
letters, and gifts.

In February 1964, back
from the Beatles' conquest
of America, George showing
his mom and dad a British
European Airways travel
bag labeled BEAtles.

George contemplating his wax image at Madame Tussaud's
Wax Museum in London.

In July 1964, Beatles manager Brian Epstein and the Beatles celebrating the opening of their film *A Hard Day's Night*.

Fans swooning
at a 1964 Beatles
concert.

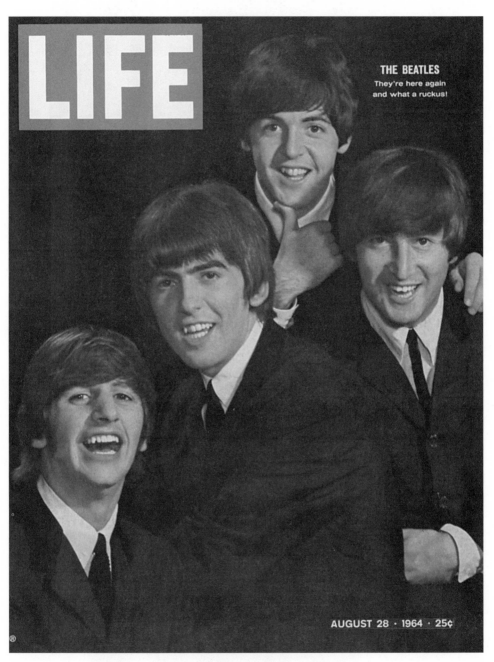

On August 28, 1964, *Life* magazine ran a cover story about the Beatles' second tour of America.

By June 1965, George had become enamored of the sitar and meditation. His growing dedication to spirituality contributed to the eventual dissolution of his marriage to model Pattie Boyd.

In 1966, George induced the other three Beatles to accompany him and Pattie on a yoga retreat with the Maharishi Mahesh Yogi. On the train to Bangor, Wales, George and the Maharishi enjoyed a quip from John Lennon about adding meditation to afternoon tea.

In September 1966, George and Pattie traveled with Ravi Shankar and his partner to Srinagar, Kashmir, where they stayed on this houseboat overlooking the Himalayas. George spent his time practicing sitar, reading the works of Paramahansa Yogananda and Swami Vivekananda, and contemplating his identity.

In 1967 on vacation in Los Angeles, George explained for reporters that his sitar studies under virtuoso Ravi Shankar had led him to the spiritual philosophy behind Indian music.

On August 7, 1967, George visited the San Francisco hippie community in Haight-Ashbury with his wife, Pattie, and friends. The visit soured his fascination with drugs and heightened his determination to pursue meditation.

In 1969, after the Beatles returned from Rishikesh, George met Shyamsundar, an American Krishna follower and one of the first to bring the chanting of Hare Krishna to London. The two became lifelong friends.

After meeting Krishna devotees and their guru Bhaktivedanta Swami, George made the chanting of Hare Krishna a part of his daily spiritual practice. From left, Prabhupada, Pattie, and George.

Among the most important books contributing to George's spiritual journey was the Sanskrit scripture Bhagavad Gita. This painting depicts Krishna delivering the Bhagavad Gita to his warrior-devotee Arjuna.

In 1969, John Lennon and Yoko Ono invited Krishna devotees to live with them while renovations continued on the London Krishna temple building off Oxford Street. Here, during a chanting session at the Lennon estate, American devotee Janaki Dasi demonstrated how to play brass kartal hand cymbals.

Apple Records released "Hare Krishna Mantra" in 1969 with no idea how the public would respond to a Sanskrit prayer set to a Ringo drumbeat. The single sold sixty thousand copies the first day and went to number one on charts across Europe. George and devotee friends held a press conference at a private estate in Sydenham.

George recording a fully orchestrated version of "Govinda," a prayer reputed to be the world's first poem. The session at EMI Studios included his devotee friend Mukunda on piano.

With two top-ten singles and a briskly selling album of Indian devotional music, the London Radha Krishna Temple combined sacred sound and popular appeal. I'm in the photo with my hands raised, standing behind George.

"One of the greatest thrills of my life," George said, seeing devotees chant "Hare Krishna Mantra" on England's popular TV show *Top Of The Pops* in 1970.

In 1970, George purchased an estate north of London for use as a Krishna retreat. Bhaktivedanta Manor has become England's most popular Hindu temple.

The August 1971 Concert for Bangladesh set a precedent for all charity rock concerts to come and brought Bob Dylan onstage for the first time in two years. Leon Russell (right) was part of the backup band.

Some fans and press reacted with mixed feelings to George's use of his 1974 Dark Horse tour to promote a spiritual message through music. He took the criticism to heart and did not tour again for twenty years. Left to right: Billy Preston on organ, Willie Weeks on bass, Andy Newmark on drums, George, and Robben Ford on guitar.

In September 1987, George pausing before a statue of the demigod Shiva installed on the grounds of Friar Park. George had purchased the statue from Krishna devotee sculptors in Los Angeles.

In 1989, George posing with wife, Olivia, and their ten-year-old son, Dhani, at home in Friar Park.

In 1985, George with his friend Eric Clapton in a salute to singer-songwriter Carl Perkins.

In 1996, on pilgrimage to Mayapur, West Bengal, George receiving sanctified vegetarian food from a temple monk.

At the wedding of friend and fellow musician Joe Brown in 2000, George, in one of the last photos taken of him, appears calm and peaceful despite his worsening health.

By the second day after George's death on November 29, 2001, memorial candles and messages of affection lined Hollywood's Walk of Fame.

8

Looking for Krishna

In this age, the only means of deliverance is the chanting of the holy names of God. There is no other way, no other way, no other way.

—*Brhan-naradiya Purana*
38.126

On January 20, 1969, recording of what would eventually be called the *Abbey Road* album moved from Twickenham Studios to Apple Studios. The Apple sessions came off with less arguing, in large measure thanks to the presence of Billy Preston, a young keyboardist who happened to be in the Apple Corp. reception area that week. George grabbed him and practically insisted he join the sessions downstairs. They had known each other since 1962 when, as a member of Little Richard's backing group, Preston shared a two-week gig with the Beatles at Hamburg's Star Club. Preston had learned to play as a young boy in Texas and by age ten was keyboardist for such gospel greats as Mahalia Jackson. His cheerful nature and easy demeanor during the *Abbey Road* sessions lifted everyone's spirits, and recording proceeded well.

Driving George to get the Beatles album done was a growing appetite to carry on with his own songs. The sooner his obligations to the band were met, the sooner he could return to what had him most passionate these days—writing and composing.

In February, George had a recurrence of his childhood tonsillitis and he had to be hospitalized. A week of confinement in bed at London's University College Hospital at a time when creative ideas were occurring to him almost daily was like prison. "You have to be IN to know how good it is OUT," he wrote to his friend Derek Taylor. He was finally discharged, and on February 26, 1969, as a twenty-sixth birthday present to himself, he booked EMI Studios and spent the evening recording new songs.

That night he recorded three demos. For the first, "Old Brown Shoe," he let his fingers wander over the keys of the studio's Steinway grand piano until he found a strong base line and a driving melody. He laid some basic tracks down on tape, then sang voice-over from a corner of the cavernous studio to simulate the echo of early blues recordings. He finished by overdubbing one of the most complex lead guitar solos on any Beatles song.

The second demo, "All Things Must Pass," had started taking shape three months earlier, at Bob Dylan's home in Woodstock. Inspiration for the lyrics came from a poem in Timothy Leary's book *Psychedelic Prayers after the Tao Te Ching*. A sunrise doesn't last forever, George sang, but neither does a rain cloud. All things pass away.

It was late when George began work on a third song he had also begun in Woodstock, a slow, passionate number about a man who meets the love of his life, feels overwhelmed by emotion, and is afraid of losing what he has found. The singer's uncertainty over the future suggested that his voice should sound tentative. George kept the melody within a small range of notes. He echoed the tension in an undulating guitar solo that bent notes up and down, as though asking which way to go. In the sound room, nineteen-year-old tape operator Alan Parsons sat pushing the stop-start button on the tape deck at George's signal.

"George was very meticulous when he worked on his own songs like 'Something,'" Parsons said. "He was very devoted to getting his solos right. He was a perfectionist. I wouldn't call it obsessive, but he shared common ground with the other Beatles in that he knew he could do what he wanted in the studio. He'd do take after take after take—and at the end of every take he'd say, 'Just one more time,' again and again. If he improvised something that wasn't quite right, he'd do it over as often as he wanted."

Listening to his work that evening, George felt dissatisfied. This is too easy, he thought. It sounds so simple.

The following day was crisp, bright, and clear. George had invited his Krishna friends to spend the day with him and Pattie at their home and greeted them with hugs—the three couples, men in shaved heads and robes, women in silk saris, and an energetic eight-month-old baby—as they disembarked from their rickety van. Inside, George introduced them to Billy Preston. The muscular young organist's huge Afro and striped bell-bottoms contrasted colorfully against the men's shaved heads and saffron robes. This was company George could relish without reservation, good people on a sunshiny day. God was smiling.

Everyone sat on large colorful cushions and commented on the beautiful oil paintings of Hindu deities that decorated the Harrisons' walls: dancing Shiva, elephant-headed Ganesh, goddess Saraswati playing her stringed vina, and framed photos of George's teachers: kriya-yoga master Yogananda, Yogananda's guru Sri Yukteshwar, and bhakti-yoga teacher Bhaktivedanta Swami Prabhupada. George put on a Ravi Shankar afternoon raga and everyone fell into a mellow mood. Mukunda spotted a big sit-down harmonium painted with psychedelic flowers, opened its top, and began pumping out a tune. George rustled among a dozen guitars lined up on a rack. He picked one out and plugged it into a small amp.

"There's a little song I've been working on. It's very simple," he said. "I call it 'Something.'" He cleared his throat, strummed an opening chord, and slowly worked his way into the arrangement he had completed the night before. He looked up and saw his guests sitting motionless, enraptured by what they were hearing. The song ended, and one by one they emerged from the music's magic hold.

"Do you think it'll sell?" George asked sheepishly. Pattie smiled, accustomed to his insecurities. As long as she had known him, he had been an enigma, sometimes exuding self-confidence, sometimes doubting whether he could do anything right. When they met, he had invoked in her, as he had in thousands of young women and men, the excitement of superstardom. It seemed unthinkable back then that beneath the glory there lived someone with such doubts about himself. The psychology of the human being was so much more complex than his image.

Guests sat silently around the room, moved by the eloquent simplicity of what they had heard. "Actually," George said, "it's about Krishna. But I couldn't say *he*, could I? I had to say *she*," adding with a twinkle in his eye, "or they'd think I'm a poof."

Apart from recollections by those who were there that evening, no notes exist verifying the spiritual meaning of "Something." George rarely elaborated on his work, preferring to let the music speak for itself. Still, in many songs he had begun equating love between a soul and God with love between a woman and a man—it was often hard to tell which he meant.

A reporter once noted his inability to tell if George was singing about Krishna or a woman. "That's good," George replied. "I like that. I think individual love is just a little of universal love. . . . Singing to the Lord or an individual is, in a way, the same. I've done that consciously in some songs."

George played a few closing notes and looked around. "Shall we have a kirtan?" he asked, referring to a group chant with instruments. Mukunda picked up a mridanga drum. Billy Preston sat down at the harmonium and loosened up with a Bach fugue and a few bars of ragtime. Shyamsundar unpacked his esraj and prepared the bow with rosin. Yamuna and Gurudas clanged brass kartal cymbals, Malati grabbed a tambourine, and the crew wove together a slow, melodic rendition of the Hare Krishna mantra. Yamuna led with her deep, powerful voice. The tempo picked up. Some of the devotees stood and started to dance. George switched from guitar to sitar and back again, on and on for an hour until finally the kirtan ground to a halt and everyone crashed onto cushions, exhausted and exhilarated.

"We've got to make a record," George said, out of breath. "I can see it now—the first Sanskrit song in the top ten."

Taking their time devouring a sumptuous feast of vegetarian *prasadam*—sanctified food—they gossiped and told stories, joked about this and that, listened to records, and talked philosophy deep into the night. Eventually the devotees lined up at the door to leave, embracing the Harrisons and thanking them. Mukunda's wife, Janaki, remembered a gift and handed George an embroidered bag. George reached inside and pulled out a two-foot loop of wooden chanting beads. He had seen people chanting on *japa* beads in India and had always admired such private communing with God, a soft murmuring of holy names while slowly turning the beads between their fingers. He put the beads back in their bag and turned to Janaki with folded hands and a smile.

The next morning, George phoned the Covent Garden warehouse and invited the devotees to meet him at Abbey Road Studios that night. "You're going to make a record," he said. Rarely did George plan his moves out long in advance. Devotees joked about a Harrison Bat-Light: George would shine his signal into the night sky, and off they would go on another adventure.

As always, fans crowded around outside Abbey Road Studios that evening. Guards escorted the devotees into a huge room filled with equipment. Paul had recently married photographer Linda Eastman, and the couple waved to them from behind a glass control booth. Chris O'Dell, who served as Apple Corp.'s receptionist, road manager Mal Evans, and other Apple staff people had also come for the session. Yamuna applied clay tilak markings—sacred Ganges clay mixed with water—to the foreheads of the recording technicians while Malati unpacked a picnic basket and other devotees pinned pictures of Krishna around the studio and lit sticks of sandalwood incense.

Mukunda took his place behind a grand piano, then George worked with him on a melody line. George asked Yamuna to sing the verses, but one voice sounded weak against the large devotee chorus. He paired Yamuna with Shyamsundar, and their duet on lead worked well. George experimented to determine which instrument he would play, shifting from harmonium to guitar, then back, finally settling on the harmonium. Technicians moved microphones and wires.

Paul offered recommendations on positioning for the best sound quality. George moved Gurudas and others with hand cymbals farther back, away from the microphones, and then assembled the chorus behind a microphone of their own. Unlike twenty-first-century recording studios that dispose of hundreds of digital recording tracks, in April 1969 eight tracks and analog tape constituted top of the line. Everything had to be balanced manually.

An American devotee had brought a trumpet along, hoping to add horns to the mix. The loud sound overwhelmed everything, and George politely asked him to back up slightly—then slightly more, and slightly more again, until he had backed him into a bathroom at the far end of the studio. "That'll do!" George called out.

One take, two takes . . . on the third try everyone knew this was it. The maha-mantra flowed: "Hare Krishna, Hare Krishna." Yamuna's strong voice led the chorus, commanding and pure, slightly nasal, as Indian singing often tended to be. The music swelled, gained momentum, and spiraled for three and one-half minutes of pure transcendental sound until—*Bong!* Malati hit a gong and brought the show to a spontaneous and rousing end.

George and Paul went back to finishing work on the *Abbey Road* album, while the devotees crowded into their tiny van and drove off, wondering what would become of the recording.

Later that night, George returned to the studio to mix the "Hare Krishna Mantra." He dubbed in a bass guitar track, laid back the work to a master Ampex magnetic tape, and turned the finished product over to technicians to make ready for pressing.

This is going to be big, he thought.

Doing something big was important to him, even if it meant sacrificing his privacy and reputation to do it.

"Go away? I've thought about it for years," he told a reporter that month. "But I won't. I'll stay and stick it out here. ... They can nail me to the wall, but it doesn't matter because I'm secure. I don't mean secure with money. I mean knowing myself, having a good belief in what people call God. I would sacrifice everything I have to find the Truth."

The Truth was where everything began for him now and where he wanted everything to end. It didn't matter to him anymore if he ever wrote another song or if the world ever heard his name again. He wanted to do God's will, whatever it might be, and was ready to leave everything behind if that's what it would take to get it done. He had good role models. Dylan was also always ready to move on; so was John.

George had discovered singing God's glories through the Krishna mantra. It made him feel good; it was easy and musical. How wonderful to think that God played a flute, that he was a musician. Since first hearing the Hare Krishna mantra on Prabhupada's record prior to the Beatles' trip to Greece, George had maintained a deep respect for chanting, and by the time he recorded "Hare Krishna Mantra" in 1969, chanting had become a part of his daily routine. George would rise before dawn, perform yoga postures for half an hour or so, then sit quietly with his *japa* beads before pictures of his teachers and various deities. He focused on his chanting. He sat up straight, like a yogi, and listened to the sound of each word. If he allowed his mind to wander, it would change the quality of his prayer: he would produce sound but not divinity, fulfill a ritual but not evoke love. So he paid attention. Cares over business or tensions with friends might have distracted him from time to time, but as far as possible he would put all thoughts aside and focus on hearing the sound of each word of the mantra, reaching deep inside to nurture his devotion and to sense God's presence through sacred sound.

Chanting God's names steadied his mind, and George felt purified of anger and greed. Beyond wanting that peace for himself, he felt a calling to reach people who had no knowledge of spiritual life. Recording mantras would be his way of giving back something for all he had received. The world would acknowledge that gift or not; that was out of his hands. But at least he would see to it that as many people as possible heard the chanting.

In August 1969, Apple Records released "Hare Krishna Mantra" with no idea how the public would react to a Sanskrit prayer set to a rock drumbeat. Nearly a hundred reporters and photographers gathered at a press conference convened by Apple Corp. on the manicured lawn of an elegant country house in Sydenham.

George explained that "Hare Krishna Mantra" wasn't a pop song but actually an ancient mantra that awakened spiritual bliss. "I never stop chanting the Krishna mantra," he told reporters. "I chant for about three-quarters of an hour in the morning. To go to an ordinary church is okay, it's a nice feeling, but they don't show you the way to Christ consciousness."

Writers looking for simple sound bites scratched their heads, put away their pencils, and reached for the tasty feast of spicy potato samosas and sweet mango drinks.

The following day, "Hare Krishna Mantra" received favorable reviews in the British papers and constant airplay on U.K. radio. On the first day of its release, the record sold seventy thousand copies. Within two weeks it rose to the number one spot in the top ten. England's most popular television show, *Top Of The Pops,* twice broadcast devotees chanting "Hare Krishna" surrounded by go-go dancers and swirling clouds of dry-ice mist. Gurudas had convinced the show's producer to cover the scantily clad dancers in sarilike cloth and dance "the Swami step," arms raised, left foot over right, then right foot over left, as Prabhupada had done at the San Francisco mantra rock concert.

George watched the nationally televised show with glee. It was, he later remarked, "one of the greatest thrills in my life."

A few days later, George was crossing Wardour Street with Shyamsundar on their way to the Apple offices. Watching them amble along, gabbing and gesturing, passersby might have mistaken them for eccentric cousins cooking up some heady scheme for curing the world. Eyes turned, following the tall, shaven-headed American in flowing robes. George leaned over and whispered, "There's a first—more people looking at you than looking at me. I love it."

"Hare Krishna Mantra" continued to soar, climbing the charts in Holland, Germany, France, and Sweden, reaching the number one slot as far away as Yugoslavia, South Africa, and Australia. Devotees found themselves signing autographs and posing for photographers.

George had his staff book the Radha Krishna Temple at outdoor rock concerts, television shows, and nightclubs across Europe. Devotees toured, sang with Joe Cocker, and played with the band Deep Purple in Amsterdam and with the Moody Blues in Sheffield. They headlined at the Midnight Sun Festival in Stockholm and appeared at the Star Club in Hamburg, where the Beatles had begun their career.

The phrase "Hare Krishna" earned constant airplay on radio and television. It poured out of speakers in clubs and restaurants and found its way into newspapers, magazines, movies, and comedy routines. Other bands incorporated the mantra into their records and concerts.

The "key cultural artifact" of the sixties, according to historian Arthur Marwick, was the rock musical *Hair*, which opened on Broadway shortly after the Beatles' return from India and included a chanting scene. The London production, held in the Shaftsbury Theatre, offered theatergoers a special bonus. At the end of each show, ushers opened the doors and brought the London devotees onstage, where they joined the cast in a rousing finale of "Hare Krishna."

Sometimes in earnest, sometimes in jest, the chanting of "Hare Krishna" spread around the world.

When the Beatles had sung "All You Need Is Love" on a live satellite broadcast in June 1967, the worldwide transmission reached more than five hundred million television viewers, a feat that had required more than a hundred technicians. Now, barely two years later, George was reaching an even larger audience with a hit song he produced himself—and in doing so, he was also helping to fulfill a prophecy dating from the sixteenth century.

"One day," avatar Chaitanya had predicted, "the chanting of the holy names of God will be heard in every town and village of the world."

And so they were.

George demonstrated his appreciation for the devotees' dedication to a God-conscious life by offering to act as guarantor for lease of a small building near the British Museum. Once renovated, the building would be their long-dreamed-of Krishna temple in London.

While waiting to move in, devotees accepted John and Yoko's offer to stay at the Lennon estate in exchange for performing work on the grounds. To help them with repairs, the devotees invited a few new recruits to come along.

"Not the best move," Gurudas said, looking back, as some new faces turned out "just a hair short of lunatic." One wrapped himself in a bedsheet, climbed atop a studio where the Beatles were rehearsing, and crashed through the skylight onto the studio floor. John, strumming away as though nothing had happened, looked at the inert body, then up at George. "Must be one of yours," he said, and strummed on without missing a beat.

Devotees occupied servants' quarters two minutes' walk from the Lennons' main house. In another building, which had once been a recital hall, they created a makeshift temple. Mornings and evenings the hills of Ascot echoed with cymbals, drums, and bells.

Renovations at Bury Place had not yet been completed when Prabhupada arrived on September 11, 1969, anxious to rejoin his disciples and encourage their work in England. He emerged from the airplane looking as they remembered him from San Francisco, his head held high, his bronze skin glowing, his saffron robes neatly pressed, his head cleanly shaved, a garland of flowers around his neck, and two streaks of white clay rising from his nose to his forehead. For a few minutes Prabhupada answered questions from reporters who had gathered around.

"Swami, why have you come to England?"

"I have come here to teach you what you have forgotten—love of God. As we are sitting here face to face, you can see God face to face if you are sincere and if you are serious." Then, with a wave to his students, he slipped into a limousine that George had sent from Apple and set out for the Lennons' Tittenhurst estate.

John and Yoko's estate, Tittenhurst Manor, was the creation of a wealthy horticulturist who had adorned its seventy-two acres with nearly every tree that would grow in the British climate. The estate included a forest and fenced-in pasture grounds lined with trails and footpaths.

Soon after Prabhupada's arrival, George drove through the gates in his black Porsche, past a marble fountain, and a long row of trees in the last bloom of summer, and up to the front steps of the main house. John and Yoko met him at the door, and they walked together to an adjoining gatehouse where Prabhupada was staying.

George was excited to finally meet the Krishna guru, but he was also distracted. His mother, Louise, had recently been diagnosed with brain cancer and admitted to a hospital in Liverpool. Moreover, Pattie had declined to come with him to meet Prabhupada, and it was impossible to avoid seeing her absence as symbolic of a rift that had been opening between them. They had started out on a spiritual journey together, but George's passion for that journey had begun to consume him. His new devotee friends absorbed whatever free time he had, and they both knew there was little she could do about it. His spiritual renewal had changed the dynamic between them.

It was surprising to George that after John's falling out with the Maharishi, John of all people would invite Prabhupada to stay in his home. But then, George knew this was a difficult time: John was now struggling with heroin addiction. Perhaps John saw a spiritual presence in his home as conducive to rehabilitation.

It was early afternoon when they entered Prabhupada's room. The elderly teacher greeted them with palms joined together in salutation. He signaled an assistant to offer them flower garlands and invited them to sit on cushions across from him. They took their places. Shyamsundar pressed the start button on a reel-to-reel tape recorder.

"There is a verse in Bhagavad Gita," Prabhupada said, "that says anything accepted by leading persons, ordinary persons follow them. If the leading person says, 'It is nice, it is all right,' then others also accept it. By the grace of God, Krishna, you are leaders. Thousands of young people follow you. If you give them something actually nice, the face of the world will change."

Prabhupada said that he had come to America at the behest of his spiritual master to teach the Bhagavad Gita and to urge people to chant God's names. If people would simply chant, there could be peace in the world.

"John and Yoko recently made a very popular record called 'Give Peace a Chance,'" Shyamsundar said. "It's chanted like a mantra for peace, over and over." Prabhupada nodded appreciatively but cautioned that few people understood what constituted real peace. Peace could only be lasting, he said, if one accepted God as proprietor of all creation and knowledge of God as the goal of human life.

George must have wondered how John was responding to Prabhupada's depiction of a God-centered creation. For more than fifteen years, George had witnessed John's brilliant but painful growth from a petulant boy furious over the death of his mother to a precocious adolescent who poked fun at deformity and ugliness to an inspired songwriter grappling with addiction. The world seen through John Lennon's glasses was neither pretty nor divinely managed.

"Everything is there in the Bhagavad Gita," Prabhupada said to John. He motioned to a book on the table. "You have read our *Bhagavad Gita As It Is*?"

"I've read bits of the Bhagavad Gita," John said. "I don't know which version it was—there're so many different translations."

"Therefore I have called this edition *As It Is*," Prabhupada said. "Interpretation is required when things are not clear, but the Bhagavad Gita is so clear. It is just like sunlight. Sunlight does not require any other lamp." The real purpose of the Bhagavad Gita, he said, was to know Krishna as the Supreme Godhead and oneself as his servant. This knowledge, he said, would allow the soul at death to return to the spiritual world. "We can go there," he said emphatically. "We can join Krishna and dance happily. Through musical vibration we can approach the Supreme."

This was the message George had first received from Ravi Shankar and then from the writings of Vivekananda and Yogananda. Now Prabhupada was confirming the power of sacred sound to reveal God.

Prabhupada closed his eyes and sang a verse of the Bhagavad Gita. His voice rang out deep and thick. To George's mind the whole of Indian theology distilled in that moment to a devoted soul singing to his beloved Lord.

After a pause, the teacher opened his eyes and looked at John. "What kind of philosophy are you following, may I ask?"

"'Following'?" John said.

"We don't follow anything," Yoko said. We're just living." They had received mantras, John said, from the Maharishi, although they were secret mantras and not to be chanted out loud.

"If a mantra has power, why it should be secret?" Prabhupada asked. "It should be distributed. People are suffering." George had read a similar message in Vivekananda's book *Raja-Yoga*: "Anything that is secret and mysterious in this system of yoga should at once be rejected," Vivekananda wrote. "So far as it is true, it ought to be preached in the public streets in broad daylight."

Yoko asked whether there was any need to chant other mantras if Hare Krishna was so strong. Prabhupada acknowledged that other mantras were also authorized, "but the Hare Krishna mantra is especially recommended for this age. And the mantras are chanted with music," he said, again intimating a service his guests could perform. "Chanting with musical instruments does not introduce anything new. It is from time immemorial."

"If all mantras are just the name of God," John said, "it doesn't really make much difference, does it, which one you sing?"

Prabhupada disagreed and compared mantras to medicines that cure different diseases. All may be potent, but to know which one to use requires the guidance of a qualified doctor. Mantras come from God, he said, and must be prescribed by a qualified guru.

"But how would you know, anyway?" John asked. "I mean, how are we to tell one master from the other? Maharishi said exactly the same thing about his mantra, that it is coming down with seemingly as much authority as you."

"If a mantra is coming down in that way," Prabhupada agreed, "then it is potent. The potency is there."

"But Hare Krishna is the best one?" John asked.

"Yes. You don't require to bother to say anything else," Prabhupada said. "The Hare Krishna mantra is sufficient for one's perfection."

George listened to the exchange carefully, troubled by the thought of exclusivity. Maybe he was underestimating Prabhupada, he thought, but the world seemed divisive enough. In this realm, among gurus looking to lead others to spiritual life, should there not be accommodation?

"Surely it's like flowers," George said. "Somebody may prefer roses and somebody may like carnations better. Isn't it really a matter for the person? One person may find Hare Krishna is more beneficial to his spiritual progress, and yet for somebody else some other mantra may be more beneficial. Isn't it a matter of taste?"

George knew that Prabhupada shared his hope for unity among all paths. The devotees had often told him how their teacher encouraged religious leaders to engage their congregations in chanting the names of God. "Whatever name you have," he would tell them. Still, Indian texts distinguished secondary names of God, such as "Lord" or "Almighty," which spoke to God's authority and power, from primary or personal names such as "Krishna" and "Govinda." Personal names stimulate love because they have greater potency.

Prabhupada said it was regrettable that so many people had presumed to interpret Krishna as merely one among many incarnations of an impersonal energy. That is why, he reiterated, his edition of the Bhagavad Gita was subtitled *As It Is*, meaning without interpretation.

"But Bhagavad Gita as it is, is Sanskrit," George said.

"We have made English," Prabhupada said.

"Everybody is translating from the original text," John said. "So what's the difference between one and the other? If somebody else translates, how are we to tell their version from your version?"

"If you are a serious student," Prabhupada said, "then you study the Sanskrit original."

"Study Sanskrit?" John balked. "Oh, now you're talking."

"Vivekananda said that books and rituals and temples are secondary details, anyway," George said. "He said they're not the most important thing. You don't have to read the book in order to have the perception."

Prabhupada agreed. "Actually, one who chants Hare Krishna regularly doesn't require to read any books. Just like Chaitanya Mahaprabhu," he said, referring to the sixteenth-century avatar who brought the chanting of Hare Krishna into the streets of Bengal. "He was simply chanting. But when he met stalwart scholars, he did not lag behind. The mantra is sufficient, but we should not be dumb. If someone comes to argue philosophy, we must be prepared."

"I'm not saying Krishna isn't the Supreme," George said. "I believe that. But there was a misunderstanding. We thought you were saying your translation was the authority and that the others were not. But we didn't really have any misunderstanding as to the identity of Krishna."

This was a gesture aimed at accommodating all concerned. The alternative was for George unconscionable. Throughout history, how much suffering had fanatics caused by believing they held an exclusive handle on truth? Not that he saw Prabhupada in such terms. But claiming only one way to God could never be George's way.

"That's all right," Prabhupada said, appreciating George's effort to create a place of harmony where all could live. Still, he said, if you believe Krishna is the Supreme Lord, then you should learn about him from those who have given themselves to him body and soul. Prabhupada looked around the room at young British and American disciples. "These people are twenty-four hours chanting 'Krishna.' But another person, who has not a single word to say about Krishna, who does not utter even the name of Krishna—how can he be Krishna's representative? Those who accept Krishna as authority, those who are directly *addicted* to Krishna—they are also authority."

It was not clear to George whether the teacher knew of John's addiction, but his choice of words echoed across the room.

For nearly two hours, each one offered his point of view. The guests shifted uncomfortably on their low cushions. "Let us have kirtan," Prabhupada suggested.

Shyamsundar handed George a pair of brass kartals and motioned for him to lead the singing. George closed his eyes, clanged the cymbals lightly together, and began singing, "Hare Krishna, Hare Krishna, Krishna Krishna, Hare Hare . . ." The group joined in, responding to his lead, clapping hands.

A few minutes later George stopped chanting, thinking of his ailing mother in Liverpool, and excused himself, explaining why he had to leave. Prabhupada offered prayers for her health and thanked his guests for coming. The group headed out the door.

Walking down the stairs, Yoko turned to John. "Look how simply he's living," she said, with a nod back at Prabhupada's room, at his meager belongings and rigorous daily regimen. "Could you live like that?"

George heard her question and may have wondered whether he, too, could live like that. If he were really serious about pursuing God, should he not live in a place where God lived? Should he move into a temple?

The trip to Liverpool afforded George time to reflect on his talk with Prabhupada. The elderly teacher had offered appreciation for George's and John's music and had expressed sincere interest in their ideas concerning peace. He acknowledged George's desire for harmony among the world's many faiths. He never asked for anything, although he seemed to encourage George and John to create more spiritual recordings.

George appreciated that Prabhupada had not hinted that he should move into a temple. That would have spoiled it. A choice like that had to come from George himself. But the teacher hadn't made George feel like an outsider. Most of all, George appreciated Prabhupada's humility.

"A lot of people say, 'I'm *it*. I'm the divine incarnation. I'm here, and let me hip you," George told his friend Mukunda. "But Prabhupada was never like that. . . . I always liked his humbleness and his simplicity: 'the servant of the servant of the servant' is really what it is, you know. None of us is God. We're just his servants."

At the Liverpool hospital, doctors informed George that the tumor in his mother's brain had grown too big to be removed. George had spent the past four years exploring the eternal nature of the soul, but this was his mother, and she was dying.

Like all mothers and sons, they had had their occasional differences. Fan mail, for instance. Why she had insisted on always answering fan letters was beyond him. It was naive. To her way of thinking, a letter from a stranger halfway around the world deserved a personalized response and maybe even a snippet of lining from one of her son's old coats. It never seemed to occur to her that the letter might have been sent by a stalker, or that someone had found their home address and chose to invade their privacy.

Then again, this was the woman who had taken on extra jobs at Christmas when George was a boy so that he and his siblings would have holiday gifts. It was Louise who had bought him his first guitar and who had urged his father to let him go to Germany despite their concerns for his safety. He wanted to play music, and that had been enough reason for her. Her love was unstinting.

Even George's journey into Hindu practices hadn't thrown her. His talk about spirit being inside each of us rang true for Louise, who found Krishna beliefs a perfectly acceptable way to be spiritual. "As long as no one is hurt" was her measuring stick. Would being spiritual have any meaning if he failed to be here now, in her time of need? Was the compassion of India's great teachers not rooted in their love for all God's children? And were parents not also children?

A short time later, George's brothers joined him at the hospital. Their mother was conscious that day, and they reminisced about this and that, silly stuff from childhood days, and laughed until she grew tired. After the others had gone, George sat by her side, reading to her and chanting on his beads until she fell asleep.

A few weeks after his visit, Louise's cancer went into remission.

Nineteen sixty-nine was the year that dreams of a peaceful Aquarian Age died a hard death. It was a year of extreme protests and deadly violence, with revolutionaries such as Cuba's Che Guevara and France's Danny the Red calling for armed overthrow of governments.

George called their brand of revolution superficial, a futile effort "to change the outward physical structure, when really that automatically changes if the internal structure is straight." Had his generation learned nothing from history? What the world needed was not political revolution but spiritual revolution. It wasn't governments that needed toppling, it was our own greed and anger and illusion.

"Christ said, 'Put your own house in order,'" he told the *International Times* that year. "If everybody just fixes themselves up first instead of trying to fix everybody else up like the Lone Ranger, then there isn't any problem."

Putting the Beatles' house in order, though, was more of an ordeal than George wished to undertake. The group now flatly refused to work together, a state of affairs that was reflected in a promotion for George's song "Something"—an unusual film clip produced by Neil Aspinall, formerly the Beatles' road manager and now head of their Apple Corp. enterprise. Each mem-

ber of the Beatles was filmed walking through lush country set-
tings with his respective wife, creating a poetic visual background
to George's hit love song. Those familiar with how the film was
produced knew its ironic undertone. Not once did any two of
the group appear together. The paean to love was constructed in
an edit room from footage of four men who could no longer
stand one another's company.

The company of devotees remained a pleasure for George,
and he enjoyed regaling them with stories from his Beatles
years. To Gurudas he recounted his visit to Haight-Ashbury
two years before, bobbing his head up and down, imitating the
hippies who had surrounded him. "Hey, man, want a joint,
man?" he mimicked. "Let me lay this peyote on you, man. I got
this record, man. This is my girlfriend, man."

George recounted another Beatles-era story, this one about a
gig in Texas. "We flew into Houston, and somehow the fans
broke through the security gates and were scampering all over
the airfield. I remember looking out of the plane window—and
there was a head, upside down, staring back at me. They had
climbed up on top of this huge jet plane and were holding one
another by the feet, just to get a look. They could have gotten
themselves killed."

Reports from devotees living at John and Yoko's estate included few such friendly exchanges with their hosts. John seemed
mostly indifferent to his robed houseguests, although the vegetarian cooking and daily chanting had their effects on him.

One morning John came into the kitchen where a devotee
was working, sat down at an upright piano, and entertained his
guest by playing "Hare Krishna Mantra" in one musical idiom
after another: bluegrass, classical, rock and roll. The music swelled
and John's voice sailed until Yoko, contending with a difficult
pregnancy, appeared in the doorway, complaining of a headache.

In December 1969, Prabhupada moved from the Lennons'
estate to the building off Oxford Street that would become London's Radha Krishna Temple. George's signature on the lease as
guarantor had allowed his six American friends to move in and

begin renovations, an act of generosity that prompted Prabhupada to begin calling him "Hari's son," Hari being another name
of Krishna. "Never mind he is not initiated," Prabhupada told
Shyamsundar. "That is a little awkward for him."

Initiation would have required that George follow basic rules
of devotional life. No eating meat, which posed no problem, since
George had already become vegetarian. No gambling, which never
interested George anyway. No sex except for procreation. And
no intoxicants, including coffee, tea, and cigarettes. George was
not prepared for that degree of austerity and made no effort to
hide his habits from those closest to him. "I have told him there
is no need to change name or shave head," Prabhupada said,
"just carry on serving Krishna. That is the perfection of life."

Shyamsundar mentioned that he would be seeing George the
following day. George and his friend David Wynne, Britain's
sculptor laureate, had offered to select a slab of marble for the
temple's altar.

Prabhupada nodded and contemplated a stack of papers on his
desk, his translation of the tenth division of *Srimad-Bhagavatam*,
the most intimate section of all Sanskrit devotional texts. Prabhupada considered this particular scripture critical for understanding God as a person. He called the work *KRSNA Book*,
using the transliterated spelling of the name Krishna. Prabhupada
took up the stack and handed it across the table.

Shyamsundar thumbed through the massive work and
blanched, intuiting what Prabhupada would say next.

"Kindly ask George to publish this book," Prabhupada said.
"It will cost nineteen thousand dollars to print five thousand
copies, with fifty-four color pages."

Shyamsundar's shoulders slumped and he stared at his hands.
Nineteen thousand dollars might not have been a lot of money
to someone as wealthy as George, but there was a higher princi-
ple involved. "Swamiji, we must be very careful with George.
We never ask him for anything. We just try to give to him, not
take anything from him. If he gives, it's something he offers on
his own."

Prabhupada nodded in appreciation. "I understand." From the outset of his mission in the West he had followed the same formula, giving people chanting and instruction and never asking for payment. Nor was he asking for any payment now from George. This was a unique opportunity to bring an important scripture to Western readers and he was extending a chance for George to take part.

"You may inform George that it is my personal request. You will see. Krishna will help you to say it."

The following night, rain pounded the roof of David Wynne's Wimbledon home while George, Shyamsundar, and the Wynne family finished a vegetarian dinner. The renowned designer, his wife, and two teenage children barraged their American guest with questions. Shyamsundar smiled and remained cordial, but George thought he noted an uncharacteristic discomfort in his friend that night.

Thunder echoed in the night sky. Wynne was regaling his guests with anecdotes about sculpting busts of the queen mother and the Beatles. Everyone agreed that luck had guided them earlier that day to a slab of flawless Sienna marble. The massive golden square would make a beautiful altar for the deities of Radha and Krishna.

More thunder. They would have to leave soon.

"George," Shyamsundar said abruptly, "do you remember I was telling you about that book Prabhupada wrote, *KRSNA Book?* He was saying that now everyone is hearing Krishna's name," he went on, "but no one knows anything about Krishna's pastimes or what he looks like. That's what *KRSNA Book* is about."

George tilted his head, wary that his friend might be turning out like so many who wanted something from him. Noting a change in mood, the Wynnes looked at one another in confusion.

"Prabhupada asked me to ask you something," Shyamsundar said. He took a breath and rushed ahead. "He wants you to publish *KRSNA Book,* nineteen thousand dollars for five thousand copies with lots of color paintings and—"

At that moment the houselights blazed hot, then exploded—like bursts from a strobe. The house shook. Lightning had hit the roof. Everything went black.

"My God," the Wynnes exclaimed.

"Wow," said their teenagers.

The darkness continued for several long moments. Then just as abruptly, power returned. George leaned back in his chair, eyes wide, grinning from ear to ear. "Well," he found himself admitting to the American, "there's no arguing with *that*, is there?"

Shyamsundar wiped his lips. "Prabhupada said Krishna would help me, but that was a little much," he said and chuckled in disbelief. The Wynnes and their guests talked and talked, giddy with excitement over the magical display.

Finally George and Shyamsundar said good night and set out for their separate homes, dazed, content, and reassured to know that guidance comes from unexpected places.

In May 1970, a copy of *KRSNA Book* arrived at George's home from Japan's Dai Nippon Printers. It was massive—a foot tall, weighing two pounds, and running almost four hundred pages long. A luminescent oil painting on its cover depicted Radha and Krishna entwined in loving embrace. The book was mysterious and beautiful.

As George turned the pages, he read an opening description of astrological signs that presaged Krishna's appearance and divine origins. As a child, the text continued, Krishna grew up in Vrindavan, a cowherd village on the banks of the Yamuna River. Soon malicious creatures disrupted his peaceful life. Giant ogres and animal-shaped spirits invaded the village, sent by a despotic king set on destroying Krishna before the divine child matured and could threaten the king's rule. Krishna found extraordinary and ingenious ways of dispatching the evildoers, in one instance even transforming a mile-long serpent's body into a playground for his cowherd friends.

George admired the full-color paintings that showed Krishna in various poses, standing medium height, a peacock feather adorning his long black hair. Krishna's eyes were tapered like petals of a lotus flower, his lips were colored slightly red from chewing betel nuts, and a garland of flowers hung from his neck. His complexion resembled a soothing rain cloud, dark blue, and he carried a flute wedged into a yellow silk cloth tied around his waist.

As Krishna grew to boyhood, George read, his beauty and playful nature inspired love in the Gopis or cowherd girls of Vrindavan. On full-moon nights he played his flute, and the notes wafted across the village, calling the Gopis to join him. Assembled together in the forest, Krishna and the Gopis danced in the moonlight. When pride over Krishna's attentions entered the Gopis' hearts, he disappeared from their sight and the Gopis went mad from separation. "Have you seen him?" they pleaded with bumblebees and shrubs.

Just after the book's title page was a big green apple—the Beatles' Apple Corp. logo—and beneath the apple was a foreword that George had written. In appreciation for providing funds, Prabhupada had invited him to write the book's opening remarks. It was an appropriate gesture but one that challenged George to express a faith still forming within him. He was still acclimating himself to this ancient universe of fabulous creatures and divine beings, and in writing about it he wanted to avoid sectarian overtones.

Writing the foreword had come at a difficult time in George's professional career. Rifts over legal and financial matters had split the Beatles even farther apart, with George and Ringo facing off against Paul and John on personal, business, and creative issues. Anticipating the release of the *Abbey Road* album, the public was mostly unaware of how far the Beatles' partnership had broken down. John had even declined to take part in a record session of George's song "I, Me, Mine." What could George write at such a time? What words would convey his feelings as a believer? How might he express a love that had emerged for his bandmates, for his devotee friends, for all living things as eternal beings, as divine, as part and parcel of the one universal Spirit?

What came to him was this:

Everybody is looking for Krishna. Some don't realize that
they are, but they are. Krishna is God, the Source of all that
exists, the Cause of all that is, was, or ever will be. As God is
unlimited, he has many Names. Allah-Buddha-Jehova-Rama:
All are Krishna, all are One. God is not abstract. He has both
the impersonal and the personal aspects to His personality,
which is supreme, eternal, blissful, and full of knowledge.

As a single drop of water has the same qualities as an ocean
of water, so has our consciousness the qualities of God's consciousness. But through our identification and attachment
with material energy (physical body, sense pleasures, material
possessions, ego, etc.) our true transcendental consciousness
has been polluted, and like a dirty mirror it is unable to reflect
a pure image. With many lives our association with the temporary has grown. This impermanent body, a bag of bones and
flesh, is mistaken for our true self, and we have accepted this
temporary condition to be final.

Through all ages great saints have remained as living proof
that this non-temporary, permanent state of God-Consciousness
can be revived in all living Souls. Each soul is potentially divine.
Krishna says in Bhagavad Gita: "Steady in the Self, being freed
from all material contamination, the yogi achieves the highest
perfectional stage of happiness in touch with the Supreme Consciousness." (VI. 28).

Yoga, a scientific method for God (Self) realization, is the
process by which we purify our consciousness, stop further
pollution, and arrive at the state of perfection, full knowledge,
full bliss. If there's a God, I want to see Him. It's pointless to believe in something without proof, and Krishna-Consciousness
and meditation are methods where you can actually obtain God
perception. You can actually see God and hear Him, play with
Him. It might sound crazy, but He is actually there, actually
with you.

There are many yogic Paths, Raja, Jnana, Hatha, Kriya,
Karma, Bhakti—which are all acclaimed by the masters of each

method. Swami Bhaktivedanta is as his title says, a Bhakti Yogi following the path of devotion. By serving God through each thought, word, and deed, and by chanting his holy names, the devotee quickly develops God-Consciousness. By chanting: Hare Krishna, Hare Krishna, Krishna Krishna, Hare Hare, Hare Rama, Hare Rama, Rama Rama, Hare Hare, one inevitably arrives at Krishna-Consciousness. (The proof of the pudding is in the eating!) I request that you take advantage of this book KRSNA, and enter into its understanding. I also request that you make an appointment to meet your God now, through the self-liberating process of yoga (union) and GIVE PEACE A CHANCE.

> All you need is love (Krishna),
> Hari Bol—George Harrison 31/3/70

Over the next thirty years, *KRSNA Book* would be translated into twenty languages and sell more than five million copies. In 1970, it seemed as if everything George touched turned to gold. Whether it was an ancient Sanskrit mantra that he transformed into a top ten hit or an esoteric devotional scripture that he helped make a best seller, the greater the challenge, the farther he advanced on his spiritual journey.

9

All Things Must Pass

I want to be God-conscious. . . . Everything else in life
is incidental.

—George, 1970

"Something" quickly rose to become one of the most successful singles ever written by a Beatle, garnering the Ivor Novello award for the best song musically and lyrically of the year and earning George his first top ten A side. It was "the most beautiful love song of the past fifty years," according to Frank Sinatra, and apart from Paul McCartney's "Yesterday," it would become the Beatles song most recorded by other artists around the world.

A floodgate of creative writing had opened, and each evening after Beatles duties ended, George composed and recorded more original songs.

Inspiration came in its own way, and George wanted a studio of his own where he could go whenever the impulse struck. The Harrison house in Esher was too small to accommodate a studio, so in January 1970 he phoned Shyamsundar to invite him to visit a place called Friar Park, which George was thinking about buying. Built by an eccentric aristocrat named Sir Frankie Crisp, the thirty-five-acre estate north of London had been left to the Catholic Church.

"There's only a couple of nuns and an old padre living there now," George said, "and they have to sell it."

The late Sir Frankie, a multimillionaire lawyer and adviser to England's Liberal Party, had been "a bit like Lewis Carroll," George said, "or Walt Disney." Around the grounds, Crisp had dug lakes, planted topiaries, and carved a river that flowed under the property. He had planted thousands of varieties of flowers and trees around the estate and excavated a complex of subterranean caves, some featuring skeletons and distorting mirrors. Dominating an alpine rock garden in the center of the estate was a hundred-foot-high replica of the Matterhorn built from tons of millstone grit.

"You can take a boat through all these grottoes and caves," George said enthusiastically. "There's carvings all over the place, and little signs with these, what do you call them, clever little sayings . . ."

"Homilies?" Shyamsundar offered.

"Yeah, homilies, like songs really, about the devil, about friendship, life. . . ."

A few days later, the American drove his red pickup through rusted metal gates and up a winding hard-dirt approach. Tall bushes hung down, neglected and overgrown with ivy, and even from a distance he could see a dark jungle of weeds marring what must have once been a beautiful estate. Shyamsundar encountered his first Frankie Crisp homily on a sign prominently posted: "DO NOT STAY OFF THE GRASS." A legend around the base of a stone sundial read, "SHADOWS WE ARE AND SHADOWS WE DEPART." At the top of the approach he pulled up to a four-story Gothic castle capped with gargoyle-encrusted towers.

George greeted his friend at the door and escorted him inside. The place was ultimate revenge for a boy from working-class Liverpool, a house of stone such as he could never have imagined with a fireplace as big as his boyhood Wavertree bedroom, fifteen-foot-high ceilings, intricately carved wood moldings, a wide entranceway, and an elegant curved staircase leading up to more rooms and more stairs leading to turrets and towers and a view of the rest of the world.

They crossed a long hallway. Through a window George pointed out a relief carved into the outside stone facade: a life-size statue of a priest holding up a frying pan riddled with holes. A small plaque at the statue's base read, "TWO HOLY FRIARS." Every room held a surprise: a carving of a monk that smiled when viewed from one side and frowned when viewed from the other; light switches and doorknobs cast in the shape of monks' heads. George showed his friend a large brick fireplace where he had placed a framed poster of four-armed Vishnu. In one hand, the majestic Vishnu form held a large club. In a second hand, he held a wheel of fire. His third hand cradled a conch shell, and between the fingers of his fourth hand Vishnu held a lotus flower.

Colorful images of Vishnu and other divinities were common adornments in Hindu homes. Housed in a Gothic English manor fireplace, the poster looked surreal.

"The nuns were really freaked out by that one," George said. "I told them, 'If God is unlimited, then he can appear in any form, whichever way he likes.' Shook them up a bit. But you know, they're not bad people, just uninformed. That's why no one joins up anymore." They continued on their tour of the mansion's many rooms.

"The place is too big for them," George said. "They can't pay the light bill and the grounds are a mess. If I get the place, I was hoping some of you could live out here and help me clean up a bit."

Shyamsundar wrote to Prabhupada about the idea. The teacher sent back his approval, provided George would allow one room to be used as a temple so that daily practices could be maintained. George decided to purchase Friar Park, and with so much work needed on the enormous property the American couples and a handful of new recruits soon moved into one of the building's wings. Their presence infused his rambling castle with scents of sandalwood and cumin, a perpetual murmur of *japa,* and fabulous images of four-armed deities dwelling on planets where rivers of milk and nectar flowed. For George, Krishna theology was exciting, sensual, and for a time provided all the satisfactions a newcomer to the spiritual journey could ever hope to find.

Pattie was cordial and tried to make friends with the devotees, but she found it hard to fit in with George's buddies. He wanted to pursue his path to its conclusion, and that was fine with her. But more and more, when he wasn't working on a new song it seemed he wanted to be with them, and theirs was a jargon and culture she just didn't share. So many people living in their home, with their own ways and habits—with her husband or without him, she did not want to be deprived of a life of her own.

Meanwhile, it was clear to music industry executives that George had tapped some hidden nerve in the public with his spiritual ideas. However much or little they appreciated his message, George's business associates had no cause to dispute the numbers.

"Dear George, I'm hooked on 'Hare Krishna,'" the president of EMI wrote him that year. The kids were coming out to buy George Harrison records now, even without the other Beatles, and provided nothing happened to change his appeal, the cash registers would keep ringing.

"Chaaarge!" A blast of high-octane fire gushed from George's flamethrower and consumed a clump of unsuspecting weeds.

"Banzai, treacherous nonbelievers!" Shyamsundar fired his flamethrower, and a patch of brambles went up in smoke. The World War II equipment was George's solution for dealing with wild blackberry bushes and rampant ivy that hoes and machetes had failed to clear away. In muddy boots and rain-soaked jeans, George turned off the flamethrower, blew a tendril of smoke from the barrel, pointed his finger at Shyamsundar, and laughed. He wasn't used to seeing the shaven-headed devotee in kamikaze gear.

Friar Park's cavernous Victorian tile kitchen, the only warm space in the castle, had become the focal point of their daily lives. Most mornings, Pattie came in briefly on her way out to chores or personal appointments. George frequently stayed out late, often spending all night in a recording studio and then driving home to grab a quick bite before dashing off again to London. He left Shyamsundar alone most of the time, scraping thick layers of paint from the manor's oak interior.

George roared up after one all-night session, parked by the back door to the kitchen, and clumped in with Billy Preston and bassist Klaus Voorman, boisterous and full of energy. Billy sat down at the organ and thumped out a wild gospel melody. George and Klaus grabbed guitars, plugged them in, and wailed out a tune they had been rehearsing earlier. "My sweet Lord, oooh my Lord, Hallelujah, my sweet Lord." George doubled as chorus, singing, "Hare Krishna, Hare Krishna." Shyamsundar had been finishing a bowl of porridge. He dropped his spoon and jumped into the fray, and pretty soon they were all dancing around, singing at the top of their lungs, the rising sun streaming through stained-glass windows and bathing them in light.

"That one's going to be on the new album," George said, flushed and smiling.

Affection and good humor governed his time with devotees, but he was also fond of reminding them that he was a Pisces, a man of opposites who sometimes lapsed into a different mood.

Anger still surfaced in him, and even small things could set it off. While in Nice, France, a few weeks earlier, he had attacked a photographer, damaging the man's knee and incurring a thousand-franc fine. Shortly after the kitchen sing-along, George drove up from an all-night session, grousing over some studio mishap; then, strained and exhausted and guitar case in hand, he was mumbling and bumping through the back door. There he found Shyamsundar standing atop a ladder, scraping paint from molding around the kitchen ceiling.

"I've been thinking about this," George said, pacing the floor, "and I don't believe Krishna in his human form is the highest manifestation of God. Vivekananda says . . ." Shyamsundar paused in midstroke and looked down. This early in the morning?

"So I think Prabhupada's got it all wrong. There's something beyond Krishna." Shyamsundar nodded, controlling himself, keeping in mind how frustrating all-night recording sessions can be.

"Well, George," he said, "then why does Krishna tell Arjuna in the Bhagavad Gita that there is nothing superior beyond this human form that he is seeing?"

George shook his head. "Prabhupada just doesn't have a clue about it."

That was more than a faithful disciple could handle. With his jaw clenched, Shyamsundar jumped off the ladder and turned toward George. Shyamsundar pushed him to the wall, then stopped, took a deep breath, exhaled slowly, turned, and walked toward the kitchen door.

"Hey, Shyamsundar," George called out.

The American looked back, and at that moment George grinned, seeing the effect his words had had on his friend. George was an innocent again, smiling with natural ease and neutrality over his own arguments.

"Just checking," George said.

Whatever issues George may have had with Krishna theology, he never doubted the power of its music. In December 1969, he invited his devotee friends to think of songs that could extend the "Hare Krishna Mantra" single into an entire album. Of the several choices George and the devotees made, one was reputed to be the world's first poem. Over a plate of vegetarian food, Gurudas regaled George with the story.

"In the beginning," Gurudas said, "there was Om, or God in the form of pure sound. From that original Om came time and space and matter, and everything was swirling in a vast cosmic ocean surrounded by darkness. Then a thousand-hooded serpent appeared on the ocean, coiled up like a gigantic couch, and Krishna in a four-armed form called Vishnu descended from the spiritual world and lay down on that couch. From Vishnu's navel a lotus flower sprouted, and from the whorl of the lotus Brahma, the first mortal being, was born. Brahma opened his eyes and stared into darkness. He had no idea who he was or where he was, so he started to meditate. After a thousand celestial years,

Brahma became a perfect yogi and was able to see the spiritual world. It was so beautiful that he put his vision into a poem called 'Govinda.'"

As he had done for "Hare Krishna Mantra," George now set himself the task of popularizing the world's first poem.

In January 1970, devotees gathered instruments and trays of vegetarian foods and arrived at Trident Studios in St. Anne's Alley. George greeted them with a smile of anticipation, positioned them at three microphones, then signaled his engineer Alan Parsons, and out of the studio's large speakers came an instrumental track of guitar and drums. George recorded the devotees singing verses of Brahma's prayer, with Yamuna once again taking the lead.

"You know," George told her after one of the takes, "with a voice like yours I could make you a famous rock star. I'm serious. Do you want to do it?" Yamuna politely declined.

Between takes, the devotees circulated around the studio distributing plates of rice and vegetables to technicians and guests. Billy Preston; Donovan; Mary Hopkin, whose song "Those Were the Days" had entered the charts in the fall of 1968; and others dropped by to listen or join in the chorus. After recording the main track, George created a musical introduction by pairing Shyamsundar on esraj with Harivilas, a new devotee from Tehran, on oud, a Middle Eastern instrument resembling a mandolin. Harivilas plucked notes rapid-fire on the oud, using a feather for a pick, a flighty musical bird doubling on top of the esraj's smooth bowed tones.

Once the vocals and introduction were done, George emptied the studio, preferring to finish the work on his own. To create an orchestral swell similar to the one the Beatles had used on "Hey Jude" the year before, he brought in musicians from the London Philharmonic Orchestra. Harps, strings, gongs, and timpani rose little by little, until the song's finale became a tidal wave of sound.

When he was satisfied with the mix of instruments and voices, George made a cassette copy of "Govinda" and Shyamsundar sent it to Prabhupada in Los Angeles.

Prabhupada entered the temple room the morning after the package arrived. He took his place to begin class, the recording playing over the temple room speakers. The teacher's body shivered and he moved his head from side to side. Tears streamed from his eyes. The recording ended.

"Is everyone all right?" he asked with a smile and then began his class.

Later he told his students, "Please play this recording every day when we greet the deities."

From then on, "Govinda" became an integral part of morning ceremonies in Prabhupada's growing number of Krishna temples around the world. Shortly after, Apple Records released the single, and "Govinda" started its climb up the charts.

"Where did the song come from?" a London reporter asked Gurudas.

"The song comes from the Satya Yuga or Golden Era of the universe and was passed down through the ages by a chain of self-realized gurus," Gurudas answered without irony.

"Oh," the reporter said and quickly walked away.

George never thought of himself as a missionary, but by year's end the world's first poem was part of a worldwide religious community's daily ritual—and a top-ten hit on pop charts across Europe.

Springtime 1970 arrived. Friar Park blossomed into a metaphor for George's exploration of the spirit: a place of discovery that was wild at first, then yielded its secrets one by one. Occasionally he would still come across a Frankie Crisp homily carved on a stone or on a rusty old plaque. "SCAN NOT A FRIEND WITH A MICROSCOPIC GLASS," one such aphorism ran. "YOU KNOW HIS FAULTS—NOW LET THE FOIBLES PASS." George savored Crisp's oddball bits of wisdom and incorporated them into his songs. Sometimes he would sit on a wall or on the steps to his house, guitar in hand, playing one of these new tunes.

"What's another word for 'contaminated?'" he called out.

"'Polluted'?" Shyamsundar ventured.

"Yeah, 'polluted,'" George said. He added the word to a verse he was composing and stretched his voice higher and higher until it cracked and he shook his head at his own silliness. Every so often he drove to a nearby nursery to purchase trees and plants.

The owner, Konrad Engbers, remembers the first time George came in.

"How are things going?" George asked.

"A little slow," Engbers said.

"I'll give it a little push for you," George replied and then bought almost every tree Engbers had in stock. From time to time, George walked down the hill from Friar Park to the market where Engbers had a stall. George would wait in the line and take his turn, not expecting any preferential treatment. Seeing his friend, Engbers would take a break and the two would sit in a nearby coffee shop in their dirty overalls and talk about herbs and plants.

"Such a kind man," Engbers recalled, "with no airs and graces—a man with a truly big heart."

At other times, George roamed the grounds of Friar Park, keeping his own company, singing to himself or chanting to God. Depending on his mood, he hoisted one of two flags over the tower: an Om symbol on good days, a skull-and-crossbones on others. He said little to his devotee guests about tensions with Pattie or about his perpetual sadness from living under the world's "microscopic glass." Devotees were his escape from such material trials, an innocent group who had no interest in fame or wealth or getting high, like other people in his life.

George had his rock and roll friends and he had his transcendental friends, and he liked to keep them separate.

"George talked about how being a rock star wasn't glamorous anymore," Gurudas remembered, "and how he didn't like hanging out with musicians because they were looking for 'unending pleasure.' He mentioned that really good friends like Eric Clapton and Bob Dylan were more in the mode of goodness, and so those were the people he surrounded himself with.

He did say how he was feeling empty and that 'that's what happens in material life,' and how he didn't want to make any 'nonsense records' anymore. We agreed that a soul without God is on the wheel of birth and death like a hamster going round and round, not getting anyplace."

While circulating in the material world, George wore around his neck a thin strand of beads carved from India's sacred *tulsi* bush. At every glance in the mirror, the discreet collar reminded him of the Self within himself and helped him maintain that awareness throughout the day. While beginners in the Krishna tradition wore one strand of *tulsi* beads, initiated disciples wore three. George wore two strands, positioning himself as serious about Krishna but not exclusively so. He was keeping his spiritual options open.

George's future wife, Olivia, would later elaborate on those options, noting that George could quote as easily from a Monty Python sketch or Mel Brooks's film *The Producers* as from the Bhagavad Gita. That easy navigation between wit and wisdom occasionally left more somber devotees puzzled, such as when a group visiting his former home in Esher discovered that between images of demigods Ganesh and Saraswati George had hung the famous poster of dogs sitting around a poker table, playing cards and smoking cigars.

George often walked around with his right hand in his bead bag, turning the wooden prayer beads and chanting quietly to himself. "Did you hurt your hand?" people would ask. The questioning became so frequent that he took to saying, "Yeah, yeah, I had an accident," which was easier than having to explain how he was chanting Sanskrit names of God on a strand of wooden beads.

George appreciated that the devotees did not misuse his friendship. Prabhupada's London group made no public announcements concerning their time with him and never exploited his affection. "We never even accepted taxi fare," one devotee explained. That discretion motivated George to focus the spotlight on them and lend a helping hand whenever possible.

Once renovations were completed in the new temple off
Oxford Street, George drove down to pay a visit.

Shyamsundar was just hanging up the phone and gave George
a perfunctory wave that did not fit his usually enthusiastic greet-
ing. A friend had just called from Paris, Shyamsundar said. French
police were giving devotees a hard time when they went out
chanting in the streets, confiscating their literature and throwing
them in jail.

George nodded, imagining the scene. "It's not like that here,
is it? I mean, you're celebrities here, aren't you? *Top Of The
Pops,* lots of publicity—people know you."

"There's no temple in Paris," Shyamsundar said, "only a
small flat, no money. People over there just don't know anything about us."

"Well, why don't we go over there and tell them?" George
asked, flashing a signature grin. "I'm still one of the Fab Four.
They'll listen to me, won't they?"

It was an astonishing offer. This was 1970. No Beatle had
been to Paris since the group performed there in April 1965. The
press would have a field day. To George's way of thinking it
could only serve a greater good.

"We'll hold a press conference, get all the reporters to come.
'Look here, Krishna is God, we're all his servants, why not help
out?'—all that bit." George picked up the phone receiver and
called the Apple offices. In minutes he arranged a press conference in Paris for the following night. Another Harrison Bat-
Light Special.

Maxim's, on the rue Royale, one of Europe's most exclusive restaurants, featured baroque furnishings, crystal chandeliers, and
museum-quality silverware. The restaurant's Grand Salon was
reserved for large gatherings and formal receptions. It was now
reserved for a press conference convened by a Beatle who wanted
to help build a temple for Krishna.

It was an important night for Maxim's. Richard Nixon had
been inaugurated as U.S. president the previous year and managed
to secure the South Vietnamese government's participation in

peace talks. That night delegates were scheduled to dine in Maxim's Imperial Room adjacent to the Grand Salon, where George's press conference would be held. Waiters scurried back and forth, assuring that every fork and goblet was properly positioned. The huge salon echoed with clatter and conversation. Photographers snapped candid shots of Brigitte Bardot; former Vietnamese first lady Madame Nhu; and Madame Sukarno, wife of the recently deposed president of Indonesia. Ignored were six Hare Krishnas huddled on a banquette along the far wall, waiting for George to arrive.

A white poodle in her lap, Madame Sukarno shared a small glass-topped table with Shyamsundar and eyed him suspiciously. The American's two-year-old daughter, Saraswati, capered nearby. Saraswati saw the white poodle and made a grab. The dog yipped and leaped, then Madame Sukarno leaped. The table upended, and champagne and canapés splashed across her Chanel gown. It was chaos.

George walked through the door and the room went silent. He looked around at the stunned assembly and called out, "Hare Krishna." There were shouts, screams, and a mad rush toward the lone Beatle. The devotees quickly guided him into a small room and slammed the door against flashing bulbs and grasping hands. George smiled and said, "Welcome to Beatlemania. I used to do that dash twice a day."

Shyamsundar took charge of organizing the interviews. "George, you sit here. Gurudas, you let in three reporters at a time." The husky Gurudas, who once ran interference for Martin Luther King Jr.'s freedom marches, positioned himself by the door. "They'll get five minutes each," Shyamsundar said, looking around the room. "Then they'll go out this other door, and Gurudas, you let three more come in."

Everyone sat, and Gurudas carefully opened the door. After a lot of shouting and pushing, he escorted three reporters in and shut the door quickly behind them.

"How did you begin the Beatle hairstyle?" asked a writer from *Elle* magazine.

George nodded toward the shaven-headed devotees. "Their hairstyle is more interesting. We're here to talk about—"

"Are the Beatles breaking up?" another reporter asked, poking a tape recorder under George's nose.

"This isn't about the Beatles," George replied. "This is about Krishna—"

"Are the other Beatles coming to Paris?" interrupted another. A loud clamor penetrated the closed door as reporters outside grew impatient for their turn. George raised his voice. "The International Society for Krishna Consciousness wants to start a new temple here and they need your—"

The door splintered off its hinges and crashed to the floor. Reporters and photographers landed in a pile. More reporters circled around back and began pressing against the other door, which groaned and bent inward in a U-shape.

George's purpose in convening the conference mattered not at all to a press corps with its own agenda, and there was no point in raising his voice any louder. They had no interest in what he had come to say. Looking for an exit, Shyamsundar spotted a small hatch in the wall and opened it. A laundry chute led down two floors to a mound of dirty linens.

"George! Through here!"

George jumped down the chute with no more hesitation than a child coasting down a playground slide. Shyamsundar hitched up his dhoti, took a deep breath, and followed him down just as the second door shattered and crashed to the floor. The two men landed on a mountain of used tablecloths and napkins as half a dozen astonished laundry maids stared in disbelief.

The Beatle and the monk sprinted through rooms filled with steaming pipes and clattering laundry machines, just ahead of reporters who followed their prey down the chute and were racing after them.

The two friends burst out the basement door into a cold winter street, as though filming a scene from *A Hard Day's Night*. A black Citroën taxi sat idling in the alley, its parking lights blinking. They whipped open the back door and jumped in. To George's amusement, the driver did not at first recognize his world-famous passenger and shook his head.

"Non, non, monsieur. Occupé! Occupé!"

Just then the mob hit the car with a thump. Shyamsundar jumped out, and George quickly locked the door behind him. The American pushed the photographers away, but a few threw themselves in front of the taxi, desperate to keep their celebrity victim from driving off. George watched as his friend, robes billowing in a rough evening wind, dragged them aside and then jumped back in the taxi.

"Allez! Let's go!" he yelled.

Finally realizing this was no ordinary fare, the driver floored the Citroën, screeched down the avenue past the Place de l'Opéra, and sped off while his two breathless passengers convulsed with laughter.

For the rest of England, 1970 was not so amusing. Race riots broke out in Notting Hill. A national dock strike paralyzed industry. The economy soured. Anarchists bombed BBC vans at anti–Vietnam War protests. Then an event was announced that CBS News deemed "so momentous historians may one day view it as a landmark in the decline of the British Empire." The rumors had been true: the Beatles *were* breaking up. After two years of squabbling and a flurry of lawsuits among themselves, Paul announced that he had no plans to ever work with the group again and filed suit to formally dissolve their partnership "because of personal, business, and musical differences."

George was flourishing as a solo artist, but he took no pleasure in seeing his partnership with John, Paul, and Ringo dissolve. They were his closest friends. The four of them had grown up together, discovered the world together. But they had declined to join him on his spiritual journey, and the fabric that bound them as a team had come undone. He would miss their company, though not their past as the world's greatest pop group. That phase was finally over.

If he were to continue creating music, he would do so from the solitude of his own home. Of course, they would remain close, communicate, see each other from time to time. How could it be otherwise? They'd built a rapport that was nearly "telepathic," as Ringo had once described it.

Of the three, George knew, Ringo could always be counted on for good humor and affection. Ringo would always be there for him. "For all I know," he said, "Ringo might be a yogi disguised as a drummer."

"I don't want to die as 'George Harrison record producer' or 'George Harrison lead guitarist' or even just a Beatle," George told *New Musical Express* in March 1970. "They're all me—but they're not really me. The moment people start typecasting, then it's time to move on. I'm unlimited. We're all unlimited."

Even unlimited beings must deal with material realities, and that year George's mother, Louise, was readmitted to a Liverpool hospital. Her cancer had returned. Shortly after, his father, Harold, was admitted to the same hospital, with ulcers. George found himself running back and forth between sickrooms, pretending to one parent that the other was doing fine and then commuting down to London, where he was recording his first solo album.

George's frustration over not being able to help those he loved came out in music. In "Deep Blue," he sang about having to watch "tired bodies" full of sickness and pain, and he prayed to God to help him and shine down His light. In July, Harold recovered sufficiently to go home, but Louise did not improve. George, his sister Louise, and their two brothers sat by their mother's side.

When the others left the room, George remained to read to her from the Bhagavad Gita. After some time, she could no longer recognize him and began losing consciousness. He put down the book and began chanting softly into her ear. With her son by her side, looking out for her soul, Louise passed away.

In the days following his mother's death, George invited his brother Harry to come live with him and assume responsibility as Friar Park's estate manager. He invited his other brother, Peter, to move in and oversee the property's team of gardeners and botanists. Turning to God had not turned him away from family, and shared loss prompted more time together than they had known since childhood.

Music industry regulations did not permit advance copies of a record to leave the pressing plant before its release date, so in order to approve the sound quality of his first solo album, *All Things Must Pass,* George flew to Los Angeles. Inside the record factory, he listened as hundreds of machines transferred his music onto acetate discs. Then he drove to a gathering at the home of Alan Pariser, a well-to-do aficionado of pop music who threw extravagant parties at his palatial Beverly Hills home.

"If there was an Olympics for groupies back then," described record producer Joel Dorn, "Alan would have a whole lot of gold medals. Whatever you needed, it was there at his house." Dorn remembered arriving at Pariser's home and hearing a noise that "sounded like a thousand engines going at one time." He moved toward someone standing by Pariser's stereo speakers and discovered it was George.

"I asked him what that noise was," Dorn said, "and he explained that he had gone to the factory to approve a pressing and was fascinated by the sound of all these machines going at once, so he recorded it. It was the kind of goofy, surreal stuff that I was into, and we had a conversation about what can be done with certain kinds of sounds. There was no formal introduction, just a casual discussion about what grabbed us musically.

"One of the things about people who are famous," Dorn said, "especially from the sixties and seventies, is that they tended to be, in my view, unbearable to be around. George didn't have that extreme star thing. He didn't have any of those silly trappings that a lot of people put on where they become, you know, so publicly spiritual that you want to push them down a flight of stairs. He wasn't wrapped up in himself. We had this conversation about how you have to follow your heart, follow your instincts, and at the same time serve people through the projects you're involved with. In that sense, he was unique in the circles

I ran with in those years. I didn't catch any false humility. He seemed to be into the core, the essence of it rather than proselytizing or preaching."

On their way back to England, George and Pattie took time out to visit their friend journalist Al Aronowitz and his wife and three children in New Jersey. It was Thanksgiving, and despite being in a losing, painful five-year battle with cancer, Al's wife had cooked them a turkey dinner, the least she could do to thank George for having "loaned" them the money to rent their home.

Al was uncertain whether George gave the money because his own mother had died of cancer earlier that year or because he was grateful that Aronowitz had introduced him to his hero, Bob Dylan. Whatever George's reason, Al said the house money was "an exhibition of saintliness unequaled by any rock superstar I knew."

George and Pattie grabbed chairs, set aside their vegetarian regimen for the evening, and accepted the hospitality of friends.

"Part of George's charm is that he always feels so inadequate to repay the world for what the world has given him," Aronowitz said. "Acts of kindness have become an art with him." George's sister, Louise, agreed with that assessment.

"An art, yes, that's how it was with him. He would pay people's hospital bills and do other random acts of kindness—not so that people would think well of him but simply because he believed kindness should be done in the world. Okay, he was on a spiritual search, but he was a good human being. Our mum always taught us to be careful about judging good or bad. Her criterion was, 'Does this harm anyone?' If so, then it was wrong, and George lived by that."

Later that month, George's *All Things Must Pass* reached record stores. In the history of popular music, there had never been anything like it.

"Of all the Beatles' solo albums to date," wrote the *Times* of London, "*All Things Must Pass* makes far and away the best listening. Harrison's light has been hidden under the egos of McCartney and Lennon, but from time to time there have been hints on several of their albums that he was more than he was allowed to be."

Melody Maker's Richard Williams wrote that hearing George's first solo album was "the rock equivalent of the shock felt by prewar moviegoers when Garbo first opened her mouth in a talkie: 'Garbo talks!—Harrison is free!'"

George was out of the shadows and creating a sound of his own.

Not only was this the first three-record pop music collection, it was also an intimately detailed account of a spiritual journey. The singer was a man convinced of his union with God ("Awaiting on You All") but uncertain that he deserved such divine favor ("What Is Life?"). He was a life-lover who admitted to sexual fantasies and pleaded with God to "burn out this desire" ("Hear Me, Lord"). He was an observer of the human condition who one moment grieved for the suffering of others ("Isn't It a Pity"), then celebrated love's victory over pain ("Behind That Locked Door"). He was a missionary, exhorting listeners to see Jesus by opening up their hearts ("Awaiting on You All") and also a repentant, begging God's forgiveness for ignoring him so long. He was an oracle, warning listeners to be alert against earthly pleasures masquerading as happiness ("Beware of Darkness"), yet also a skeptic suspicious of his own message ("Run of the Mill") who reminded listeners that they had free will and the right to decide how to live for themselves.

Along with the three-record collection came release of its most overtly spiritual single, "My Sweet Lord," inspired by the Edwin Hawkins Singers' "Oh, Happy Day," a two-hundred-year-old gospel classic that featured a chorus repeating the song's title over and over. George wrote a choral line using the word "Hallelujah" as the refrain, then switched midway through the song to the phrase "Hare Krishna."

"I wanted to show that 'Hallelujah' and 'Hare Krishna' are quite the same thing," he told his friend Mukunda. "I did the voices singing 'Hallelujah' and then the change to 'Hare Krishna' so that people would be chanting the maha-mantra before they knew what was going on." The song was meant to be "a Western pop equivalent of a mantra, which repeats over and over again the holy names."

The lyrics declared George's purpose in undertaking a spiritual quest. "I really want to see you," he sang. God was invisible to him but remained "sweet" despite the anguish of their separation. George ended the song with a Sanskrit prayer of thanks to those teachers who had helped him find his spiritual path:

> *gurur brahma, gurur vishnu, gurur deva maheshwara*
> *gurur sakshat, parabrahma, tasmai shri gurave namah.*

"I offer homage to my guru," the prayer said, "who is as great as the creator Brahma, the maintainer Vishnu, the destroyer Shiva, and who is the very energy of God." Devotees and scholars familiar with ancient mantras were stunned to find one serving as a choral refrain in a top-ten pop tune.

Ben Gerson in *Rolling Stone* described the sound of *All Things Must Pass* as "Wagnerian, Brucknerian, the music of mountaintops and vast horizons," and summed the album up as an "extravaganza of piety and sacrifice and joy, whose sheer magnitude and ambition may dub it the *War and Peace* of rock 'n' roll." Another music critic judged its hit single "My Sweet Lord" to be "among the boldest steps in the history of popular music" yet with the potential to be "a fatal career move." The boldness was the naked emotion of George's surrender to God. The gamble was whether fans would still accept him after realizing the depth of his devotion.

"At that time," George later explained, "nobody was committed to that type of music in the pop world. There was, I felt, a real need for that. So rather than sitting and waiting for somebody else, I decided to do it myself. A lot of times, we think, 'Well, I agree with you, but I'm not going to actually stand up and be counted—too risky.' Everybody is always trying to keep themselves covered, stay commercial. So I thought, 'Just do it.' Nobody else is, and I'm sick of all these young people just boogying around, wasting their lives, you know."

Once the record made it to radio, letters addressed to George Harrison started pouring into the London temple from all parts of the world. It seemed a lot of people had been waiting for someone to validate their own search for God, and from the day the record was released, thank you letters started coming and never stopped.

"I still get letters from people," he said in the 1980s, "so I know by the Lord's grace I am a small part in the cosmic play."

"My Sweet Lord" featured George's friend and organist Billy Preston. Scoring a Sanskrit mantra to Preston's gospel rhythms proved to be a musical inspiration—Hindu revivalism, the pop equivalent of interfaith prayer.

Response to the song was positive and strong, and "My Sweet Lord" became an international megahit. Elton John first heard it while riding in a taxi. "My God!" he thought and broke out in chills. The song commanded constant airplay.

"Every time I put the radio on," John Lennon said, "it's 'Oh, My Lord.' I'm beginning to think there *must* be a God."

In October 1970, John was recording at Abbey Road Studios at the same moment George was finishing "My Sweet Lord." John's message, though, was less devotional. "God is a concept by which we measure our pain," he sang for his album *Plastic Ono Band*.

All Things Must Pass launched George as a force in contemporary music, an inspired singer-composer who could make great music independent of the Beatles. Journalists dubbed him "the ex-Beatle most benefiting from the group's dissolution," although the title meant nothing to him. True, he had felt held back in the company of John and Paul, but he harbored no ambition to prove himself their better. He wanted only to promote music as a channel to God, and record-buyers, at least for the moment, were responding well.

"One thing you'd learn about George very early," said guitarist Joey Molland, "was that if you talked to him like he was a Beatle, he would close up and walk away. If you talked to him like he was a regular bloke, about your car breaking down or your guitar not working properly or something, then he'd be all ears and get right into it with you." Molland, who had grown up in Liverpool in the fifties, went on to become a founding member of the band Badfinger and a studio musician on *All Things Must Pass.*

"I remember only once when he did refer to the Beatles," Molland said. "Badfinger was going to represent Apple at a Capitol Records convention in Hawaii, and George said, 'You know, I went to Hawaii once. It's a fantastic, beautiful place. Of course, we couldn't go out. I had to look at it from the hotel room or the inside of a car.' The moment passed, and we went on to talk about other things, but you got this impression that he was very sad about the whole affair. Being a Beatle wasn't a great memory for him."

Within a month of their release, both *All Things Must Pass* and the "My Sweet Lord" single had climbed to the number one spot in America. When asked about his future ambitions, George said, "I want to be God-conscious. That's really my only ambition, and everything else in life is incidental." Success may have been incidental to God-consciousness and something that didn't stop him from being an ordinary bloke, but as his stature in the music world continued to rise, George would confront challenges he could never have imagined.

10

The Sky beneath
His Feet

When ten thousand men clash with arms and fire,
It is always a single man's actions that make the difference.
—*from the Tao Te Ching*

By the end of January 1971, George's career was flourishing.
"My Sweet Lord" was selling more than thirty thousand
copies a day, with total sales in America surpassing the 2 million
mark. In the United Kingdom George's triple album *All Things
Must Pass* had earned more than £10 million. In June, with his
work solidly in the number one spot on charts around the
world, he took time off from his own recordings to help Ravi
Shankar complete *Raga,* an autobiographical film. When he arrived at Ravi's Los Angeles home, he found the elder musician
distraught.

"George," Ravi said, laying out a sheaf of newspaper clippings, "can you help me?"

The clippings described a situation George knew only on its
surface, something that had not quite registered as he walked
past a television or radio. What he read shocked him. Two months
before, East Pakistan had declared independence from West
Pakistan and renamed itself Bangladesh. War between the two
states broke out and hundreds of thousands of civilians lay dead.

Millions more were fleeing into India, where lack of food and facilities had transformed refugee camps into infectious open-air graveyards. Among the refugees were members of Ravi's family.

"Something should be done," George said.

Ravi suggested mounting a benefit concert, hoping they could collect as much as $25,000 to purchase food and supplies for refugees.

"That's nothing," George said. "Let's do something bigger."

Judging by sales of his devotional records, the more George put his faith on the line, the more God rewarded him with success. He had always admired John for operating that way, just going for something if he felt strongly about it. John's recent work with Yoko Ono was proof of that: avant-garde recordings—music the Beatles used to call "avant-gotta clue"—and a cinema verité–style movie that featured a camera panning across dozens of bared bottoms. The work wasn't to George's taste, but he admired the guts John had to make it. Now, thanks to Ravi, he would embark on another adventure of his own, this one to even greater effect.

George rented a house in Los Angeles and began mounting the music industry's first charity rock concert. He spent the second half of June and the first half of July making phone calls, convincing some of the world's finest rock artists to join together in a humanitarian gesture unprecedented for the music industry. Ringo instantly agreed to take time off from filming the Western *Blindman* to come and play, although it would be his first appearance onstage in three years and he was, in George's words, "crazy with nerves beforehand."

George invited Paul to play. Paul said he would agree if George and the others dropped a countersuit they had brought against him for wanting to dissolve the Beatles. George could not agree to having one issue affect the other, and Paul declined to perform.

When George asked John to appear in the show, John stipulated that Yoko would also have to perform. That was not acceptable to George, who had handpicked world-class musicians for the concert, and heated words were exchanged. Just this once, for a worthy cause, he may have wondered, could his friends not set aside their personal demands?

George invited Mick Jagger, but Jagger couldn't come to New York due to visa complications.

George flew to London and asked the group Badfinger to excuse him for not honoring his promise to produce their record that month. Instead, he said, would they like to join him for the show?

If anyone could make this concert a success, it would be Bob Dylan, and George put in a call even though the odds of convincing his reclusive friend to appear onstage were slim. Dylan said they could talk about it, but he wouldn't commit to play.

The concert had to take place while events in Bangladesh still commanded front-page attention. Wanting all the help they could get, back in Los Angeles, George and Ravi consulted an astrologer, who advised that Sunday, August 1, would be a favorable day for the concert.

Of the many venues they considered, New York's Madison Square Garden was available that day, and George reserved the massive arena. This would be his first live show since the breakup of the Beatles, an uncomfortable position for someone striving to chip away at ego.

"George was very nervous, but he got this strength through his friends and his religion," said bassist Klaus Voormann. "His view was 'It's my gig, I have to do this. . . .' If it wasn't for the cause, he wouldn't have done it." George reserved a suite of rooms at the Plaza Hotel as offices, and then together with journalist Al Aronowitz he flew to New York to begin rehearsals.

On a short break with Aronowitz, George passed by the Central Park Zoo. Budget cuts and staff shortages had left the city-run sanctuary in sad shape, and George shook his head. "The squirrels look as if they're dying," he said. "The grass seems to be gasping for breath. The foliage is cancered—now I know what Dylan meant by 'haunted, frightened trees.'"

Aronowitz remembered the impression George made walking down Fifth Avenue, like some holy man with long hair flowing over his shoulders "like wisdom from a fountain." As they were finishing lunch at a sidewalk café, a man with a mustache gave George a quizzical look. He walked over and asked, "Are you George Harrison?"

"No," George said, deadpan.

The man skulked away, convinced he had been misled.

George turned to Aronowitz and laughed. "We've got to explain to them that we're not these bodies."

Back at the Plaza, George greeted arriving musicians with enthusiasm. They clapped each other on the back, stoked a boiler of excitement, and energized one other with a shared sense of mission. What he envisioned, he told them, was a dignified concert, spirit in action, a happy thing that would be very much worth the effort.

When George's philosophizing threatened to spill over, the musicians poked affectionate fun by calling him "Mr. Professor" or "Curly Toes," referring to the pointy plastic shoes that Indian gurus sometimes wore.

The ensemble acted as a unit, but it was George who was the engine, pacing the room, tossing out ideas, rallying the troops. When the lights went down and the curtains parted, everyone knew it would be his reputation on the line. He would bear the praise or scorn of the public, the press, and the world.

The ensemble had only had five days to rehearse. George booked rooms for musicians at the Essex House, down the street from the Plaza. Rehearsals took place in a rented studio near Carnegie Hall. "Ringo, Billy Preston, my band Badfinger, Klaus Voormann, and different musicians arrived during the week," explained guitarist Joey Molland, "and the band got bigger and bigger. We started by reviewing all the rhythm tracks. Then once we had that together the horn people came in, then the lead players showed up, and then the vocalists. Dylan and George went up onstage for a quick rehearsal. It was great because for about forty-five minutes in Madison Square Garden we had a private Bob Dylan concert." Despite the rehearsal, Dylan still hadn't committed to play.

As the day of the concert approached, people hustled in and out of elevators in the Plaza Hotel, rehearsed songs, talked on phones, arranged wardrobes, and checked equipment. George was seated at a desk reviewing the musical lineup when he looked up from his papers and found Shyamsundar smiling down at him. The two had not seen each other in months.

They embraced, and the American explained that he traveled around the world now as Prabhupada's assistant. They were passing through New York and had heard about the concert.

"It was Ravi's idea," George said. "You know, they've been hit by war—and now there are cyclones. They're in real bad shape over there. We've got Madison Square Garden booked for two shows. I'm trying to get John to play, Eric, even Bobby Dylan. But he hasn't done a concert in years so he's a bit—spooky." Dylan had not performed live since the Isle of Wight festival in August 1969. "I was thinking to have a kirtan in the show, get the whole crowd chanting Hare Krishna. But I don't know," he said. "That may not fit in."

Shyamsundar asked if he could help. George grinned and suggested the crew could use a healthy dose of *prasadam*. Shyamsundar made a quick count and headed out the door. The following afternoon he returned with a vanload of vegetarian delights: sacks of whole-wheat chapati bread rounds, tubs of fried milk curd in tomato sauce, mounds of saffron rice, pots brimming with hot dahl soup—enough to feed an army. George's floor at the Plaza swarmed with musicians and crew, and people fell on the feast with gusto.

Chords from a lone guitar filtered out from a room off to the side where Dylan sat in a chair playing "Like a Rolling Stone," glancing at notes scattered on a bed. The tall devotee deposited a heaping plate of *prasadam* on a nearby table and quietly closed the door behind him.

George worked his way through the crowd and went straight for a cup of hot lentil soup. His devotee friend started to leave. "Wait a minute," George said, tugging at Shyamsundar's yellow robe. "I want to show you something." He brought him to a closet, pulled out a pure white cotton suit, and showed him Om signs stitched to the lapels. "I had a tailor embroider the Hare Krishna mantra all around," he said, pointing to tiny embellishments on the collar. "On the cuffs, too. It's very small, but I'll know it's there." In India, George discovered the many ingenious ways Krishna worshipers surrounded themselves with the mantra. Sanskrit letters spelling out the sixteen-word prayer decorated shawls and shirts and rimmed the edges of photograph frames, book covers, doorways—God in the details. Some followers had the mantra tattooed on their bodies.

"I guess we can't have a kirtan onstage after all," George said. "Nobody seems to like the idea but me. We've got Ravi and his crew, and that's already too much Far East stuff for most people." Western crowds would not care that the musicians Ravi had assembled were among India's most gifted artists. It was rock and roll they wanted.

Tickets sold out instantly. Scalpers were collecting up to $600 for a single $7.50 seat. Sunday, August 1, arrived and George looked out from the wings of Madison Square Garden to see twenty thousand attendees filing in for the first of two concerts.

He would have liked more time to prepare. A show like this, at one of the most important venues in the world, with so many artists, so much attention in the press—he needed weeks but had had only days. There had been no choice, really. This was an emergency and something he felt duty bound to do.

The lights of the Garden dimmed.

What followed was one of the greatest rock spectacles of all time. George began the program by paying homage to his music guru. He brought out Ravi and company, bowing to the maestro respectfully. Ravi reciprocated with an energetic sitar performance.

Half an hour later, George returned to the stage and opened his set with a rousing rendition of original songs. There was a logical chronology to his choices, starting with "Wah Wah," which declared his independence from the Beatles; followed by "My Sweet Lord," which celebrated his internal discovery of God and spirit; and then "Awaiting on You All," which projected his message to the world. If you just open your heart, the song declared, you would see that you've been polluted. By chanting the names of the Lord, you'll be cleansed. You don't need a passport or visa to see Jesus. Just open your heart.

Aware that the concert demanded impeccable pacing, he remained onstage to introduce every one of the artists who followed. George encouraged them with a nod or a smile, his reassurance energizing their playing.

Billy Preston belted out a gospel rocker, "That's the Way God Planned It," with enough conviction to move even nonbelievers. His soulful organ, spontaneous dancing, and gospel chorus backup had the audience cheering.

Next, Ringo contributed a measure of good cheer and humor with a jaunty performance of his pop hit "It Don't Come Easy."

George's friend Eric Clapton wailed in a guitar duet with him on "While My Guitar Gently Weeps." After a number of other up-tempo numbers, George had a sound crew remove equipment from the stage and against a bare background shed a gentle rain over the thunderous concert with a quiet acoustic version of his ode to hope, "Here Comes the Sun." Musicians from the Apple band Badfinger provided flawless backup, and the audience's applause was full-hearted and warm.

George had had a piece of paper taped to the side of his guitar with the lineup on it. After "Here Comes the Sun," he had written the name Bob Dylan and a question mark. At the rehearsal the day before, the reclusive singer had given every indication of withdrawing from the show.

"Hey, man," Dylan had told George, "this isn't my scene. I can't make this."

"This isn't my scene either," George answered. "This is the first time I have ever done anything on my own. You at least have been a solo artist for years." George had begun feeling the pressure, not only from putting himself on the line for what he believed, but also from weeks of nonstop preparation. Dylan's hesitation pushed the show to the edge of an agonizing precipice.

"I've got to get back to Long Island," Dylan said. Then he walked out, leaving George in the dark as to his intentions.

Following "Here Comes the Sun," George waited for the applause to die down; then he turned around, not knowing what to expect. There was a bearded Bob Dylan, emerging from the wings, visibly nervous, his guitar in hand and a harmonica strapped to his neck. George faced the audience.

"Like to bring on a friend of us all," he said with a smile. *"Mister Bob Dylan."*

Madison Square Garden exploded in cheers and applause as Bob Dylan, in denim jacket and bluejeans, approached the microphone. George had managed the impossible, and in that moment he might have felt something like ecstasy. Like Dylan, George wanted to bring light into a dark world. Like him, too, he had been blessed with enough talent and opportunity to exercise that desire on a world stage. Now they were appearing onstage together, and the force of their combined presence was palpable.

For seventeen minutes, Dylan sang out his most popular songs: "A Hard Rain's Gonna Fall," "Blowin' in the Wind," "Mr. Tambourine Man," "Just Like a Woman." The applause that followed each offering was thunderous. Forty-four microphones captured every note on tape.

As the second show came to an end, the audience yelled and screamed and begged for more. The musicians crowded around center stage for final bows, cheers washed up in waves from the audience, and even Dylan was swept up in the euphoria.

Backstage, Dylan picked George up and squeezed him.

"God," Dylan said, "if only we'd done *three* shows."

George beamed like a schoolboy. For him, this was even better than the *Ed Sullivan Show* in 1964.

Nothing was of his creating, George reminded himself, certainly not the results of the concert. He wanted to work in a spirit of detachment, content to know that a wiser force guided the gears and cogs of his life. If he woke up tomorrow and found that the concert had changed nothing, so be it—he would have done his best. But he couldn't stand by and watch people killing each other. Where was the spirituality in that? That's what he'd told the artists, and thank God they'd responded, especially Dylan. They'd played, all of them, with compassion for people none of them knew, halfway around the world, purely because they were human beings in need of help.

With time, the Concert for Bangladesh would touch emotions around the globe. "It was a thrilling moment in the midst of all the sad news emanating from the battlefront," wrote one reviewer. "The warmth, care, and goodwill expressed at the Concert for Bangladesh were echoed all over the world." The concert was "rock reaching for its manhood," wrote *Rolling Stone* reporter Jon Landau. It was musicians acknowledging "in a deliberate, self-conscious, and professional way" that they had a responsibility to the world around them.

One disappointment marred the concert. While the artists had agreed to perform without fee, even waiving their film and sound-track royalties, the record company EMI proved to be less generous. Transfer of $400,000 in concert receipts to the people of Bangladesh was delayed as Bhaskar Menon, then head of Capitol EMI Music Worldwide, demanded costly fees for distributing what George had intended as a charity recording. George was outraged and threatened to take the recording to CBS, Capitol's competitor, if the funds were not released. When he appeared on America's popular Dick Cavett television show in November, he made his feelings public.

"I'll release the damn album myself," he told a startled Cavett. The audience laughed, amused by the display of a Beatle with talons. Few seemed to sense the sober purpose behind his defiance, the outrage over the fact that halfway around the world, people were dying of starvation and disease and money meant to help them was being held ransom.

"Sue me, Bhaskar!" George said to the camera.

The public bought enough copies of the concert record to earn it a Grammy award for Album of the Year. Eventually, film and record sales grossed more than $14 million.

"The money we raised was secondary," George told the press years later. "The main thing was, we spread the word and helped get the war ended. . . . What we did show was that musicians and people are more humane than politicians. Today, people accept the commitment rock 'n' roll musicians have when they perform for a charity. When I did it, they said things like, 'He's only doing this to be nice.' "

Triumphal as the Bangladesh concert had been, George hankered to return to composing music. Songwriting helped him "get rid of some subconscious burden," like "going to confession." In June 1972 he boarded a plane without Pattie, arrived in Portugal, and drove east along stretches of the golden coastal beach into France, contemplating what subconscious burden to dispose of next. In summer the Riviera offered an unobstructed view of brilliant green hills, ripe peach orchards, and an opalescent sea glowing with sunlight. He passed through towns and villages, stopped for meals of fresh bread and cheese, set out again when the impulse struck, and chanted to his heart's content.

"I drove for about twenty-three hours and chanted all the way," he described to a friend later. "The funny thing was that I didn't even know where I was going. I mean, I had bought a map, and I knew basically which way I was aiming, but I couldn't speak French, Spanish, or Portuguese. But none of that seemed to matter. You know, once you get chanting, then things start to happen transcendentally."

The preparation paid off. Back in London, he immersed himself in production at Abbey Road Studios and emerged three months later with his second album, *Living in the Material World*. The collection of original songs quickly rose to the number one spot on music charts worldwide and didn't come down for nine weeks. The album revealed a self-confident George, and contained many of the strongest compositions of his career.

Some of the songs distilled spiritual concepts into phrases so elegant they resembled Vedic *sutras*: short codes that contain volumes of meaning. In the album's opening number, "Give Me Love," he transformed the phrase "Oh, my Lord" into a commentary on the universality of faith with a simple device. By sustaining the first two words for a dozen bars, they became the sacred syllable Om: "Ohhmmmm my Lord."

In the album's title song, "Living in the Material World," he condensed a lengthy passage from the Bhagavad Gita into a dozen simple words. Desires, he sang, are never fulfilled in this world but swell like a tide that threatens to drown us. He set this to big, full-bodied rock and roll music. A raunchy Reeperbahn quality exploded from striking keyboard riffs, a wailing guitar, a heavy saxophone, and a driving percussion. Then he stopped the music and a gentle, tabla-filled interlude lifted the song to a meditative realm. I have sweet memories of the spiritual sky, he sang, and I pray to never again go astray—then *bang!* He brought listeners back into the material world, drums pounding out the price of insatiable desire. See how easy it is, the abrupt return declared, to forget and again get caught up in maya, in illusion? He ended with a statement as intimate as a page from a diary: I'm trying to get a message through, not just for others but for myself as well. I want out of here, too. By the Lord's grace maybe I can also be saved from the material world.

The album contained songs about his years as a Beatle and the emptiness of rock life, but its core was a clear message about life's spiritual purpose. *Rolling Stone* music critic Stephen Holden called the album "profoundly seductive" and so infused by George's devotion that it "stands alone as an article of faith, miraculous in its radiance." George Harrison the man, the myth, and the music, Holden wrote, blended into a single creation that was "vastly appealing and in places very moving." In candidly presenting his personal realizations George had invoked "the basic attraction of popular religion through the most traditional of means—by being inspirationally, opulently romantic."

According to composer Philip Glass, George's spiritual solo albums came at a critical stage in the evolution of Western music. "By the early 1960s," Glass said, "the world of new concert music had reached a virtual dead end. By that I mean there were more and more composers writing for fewer and fewer people." Glass had worked with Ravi Shankar on film sound tracks in the early sixties and, like the sitar master, was looking to open a door that would bring different sensibilities to Western music. "That door turned out to be much bigger than I thought," Glass said. "I thought it would lead to Indian music. Actually, it led to world music—and that continues to this day. You have to keep in mind that in the midsixties, if you opened up the *Village Voice* there would not be one ad for a yoga teacher. They didn't exist."

Glass had traveled to India in 1967 and discovered through his mentor Ravi Shankar that George was already immersed in India's wisdom traditions and had understood the impact Eastern music could have on the West. Glass met George shortly after his return, and they agreed that the Indian sound was a much-needed breath of fresh air.

"We were entering the same door but from different sides," Glass said. "From my side, it was the world of experimental concert music, and from George's side it was the world of popular music. It was clear to us that this had historic significance and that the foundations of contemporary music were going to shift. But I was wrong about one thing. I thought it was going to take much longer. The change happened much more quickly than I expected, and George was at the center of that change. He brought the world's attention to it through his own musicality."

Despite his success managing a solo career, George questioned how successful he was at managing a spiritual calling. Critics wondered if he had "gone crackers" from too much meditation while friends felt disconnected from him, and with good reason: he had lost interest in all-night parties with nonbelievers. He declined invitations so consistently that even old chums viewed his enthusiasm for God as wandering beyond reasonable boundaries.

"Unfortunately he was derided by certain sections," commented friend and former Beatles PR agent Tony Calder, "because they couldn't quite accept that George could be involved with . . . these kids walking up and down High Street banging a tambourine and singing 'Hare Krishna, Hare Krishna.'" Some people even wondered if his missionary zeal had contributed to the breakup of the Beatles.

George knew better, but being viewed as a weirdo troubled him. "George was under stress during *Living in the Material World*," said John Barham, who did string arrangements on the album. "I felt that he was going though some kind of crisis. . . . It may have been spiritual, but I cannot be sure."

One sign of that crisis was George's growing estrangement from his wife, Pattie. For the first few years, their life together had been a harmony of interests. They embraced vegetarianism, experimented with LSD, climbed the hills of Cornwall looking for cosmic consciousness, attended retreats with the Maharishi Mahesh Yogi, and shared an easy symbiosis of ideas and habits.

With George's accelerating enthusiasm for God and the company of God's devotees, things changed. He and Pattie continued to attend concerts together and celebrate friends' birthdays as a couple, but now she rarely took part in his spiritual activities. In 1969, inside a chapel at Friar Park that featured stained-glass windows and a vaulted ceiling, devotees installed an altar to Krishna. At night they would see George there alone, chanting quietly on his wooden beads.

The distance between them also increased as a consequence of Pattie's return to modeling. After the Beatles' final live performance, George had insisted that she abandon her career. He knew she relished her work but argued that there was danger in public exposure.

Ringo called it a "flat-cap" attitude embedded from childhood. "We were very northern," he said. "The wives stayed at home and we went to work. We dug the coal and they cooked dinner."

Pattie bridled at the restrictions. "All [Beatles] wives and girlfriends were made to feel that we shouldn't leave the 'family' at all," she said. "We mainly went out with each other. . . . We were cocooned." As early as 1968, she had already declared, "I just don't want to be the little wife sitting at home. I want to do something worthwhile." By 1971, after five years of marriage,

Pattie had grown tired of Friar Park's isolation and the incessant company of George's fellow chanters. She wanted a life of her own again.

"I never saw the breakup coming between Pattie and George," said Al Aronowitz. "Pattie was so sweet, and around them everything seemed magical. If they were having fights, no one knew it because there was never any sharpness between them. One time we were flying back to New York from California for the Bangladesh concert and George told me that he couldn't have a family, that he couldn't be a father, which turned out to be untrue if you've ever seen his son Dhani. But he blamed it all on himself. That was the kind of person he was."

Whatever the reason, Pattie did not have children. Instead, she retrieved her career and her life, and against George's wishes accepted an offer to model in an Ossie Clark fashion show. Clark, whose designs featured transparent fabrics and exposed flesh, held a midnight showing of his work in May 1971 at the Royal Court Theatre. Curvy models in glittery platform shoes gyrated down the runway. Supermodel Penelope Tree came onstage in a see-through chiffon blouse. Pattie followed, twirling a cape off her shoulders, a declaration of independence that added to the distance separating her from George.

On August 22, 1973, George maneuvered his Mercedes under the arched gateway of a Tudor-style manor in Hertforshire, where he was to meet with Bhaktivedanta Swami Prabhupada. There had been a violent thunderstorm the previous night. By daybreak, the rain clouds had dissipated and sunshine warmed the air. George trolled up a winding gravel-covered approach and parked in front of a sprawling main house. Since purchasing the property for the London Krishna Society six months before, he noted a number of improvements and repairs and new flowerbeds lining the periphery of the driveway.

It was nearly four years since his first meeting with Prabhupada at John and Yoko's estate. The elderly teacher was back in England on what disciples had confided to George might be his last tour outside India. George wanted to see the Krishna teacher while he was still there to advise him. Today's meeting might be his last opportunity to clear up a confusion that had begun to impede his search for God.

George parked and approached the front door. He wanted Prabhupada to know that, despite his doubts, he still loved Krishna, and for the meeting he had pulled his hair into a ponytail, revealing tight bands of *tulsi* beads around his neck. Twin lines of clay *tilak* marked his forehead. He wore a white linen kurta shirt over bell-bottom jeans, and a purple satin bead bag dangled from his right hand. George's friends Mukunda and Shyamsundar greeted him as he entered the vestibule. They exchanged hugs and smiles, climbed a polished wooden stairway leading to Prabhupada's quarters, and knocked gently on the door. They entered and touched their heads to the ground in traditional respect for a revered teacher. Prabhupada sat on a cushion behind a foot-high mahogany desk. He was leaning against a long wall, his eyes closed, his face illuminated by slanting rays of sunshine pouring through lead-paned windows. Prabhupada's fingers gently turned a string of wooden *japa* beads. Emerging from his prayers, he looked up. Seeing George, the elderly teacher raised his arms and laughed.

"*Jai!* All glories to George Harrison!" George and the others joined in the moment with gleeful chuckles.

"You have given us this shelter," Prabhupada said, pointing around the room and out onto the landscaped grounds, "and Krishna will give *you* shelter—at his lotus feet. We shall pray always like that." George smiled at the blessing.

"You are such a sincere boy," Prabhupada continued. "Krishna has already favored you. Utilize your favorable condition intelligently. Then everything will go on rightly." George moved closer to the low desk and sat on a cushion.

"Well, everything feels so exciting at the moment," George said, settling himself into a half-lotus position. "The future is just going to be overwhelming. There'll be more temples—in the end there'll be more temples than hotels." If George was going to reveal a crisis to his teacher, he wanted him to know that spreading the word still ranked higher than personal dilemmas. Prabhupada's first instruction to him at John Lennon's home had been that he could change the world by giving people knowledge about God, and for the past four years George had passionately followed that instruction, infusing his lyrics with descriptions of the soul, of an eternal universe beyond the covering of the material world, of a place the spirit can call home once escaping the cycle of reincarnation. The effort had not earned him much support from family or friends or from the press, and the shunning had led to sadness, the sadness to doubts.

George wasted no time in revealing his heart. "Prabhupada, I seem to be going around in circles. Maybe it's something to do with me being, you know, a Pisces—one fish going this way and one fish going that way. I have periods when I just can't stop chanting, and then other periods where, you know, I turn into a demon again and then forget to . . ."

Prabhupada smiled and shook his head. "You are not a demon. You are a devotee. Some way or other you have got attached to Krishna." He studied George's face, like a physician probing for signs that would lead to a prognosis. "Are you reading Bhagavad Gita? That will help you."

"Yes, I'm reading. You know, one verse at a time, over and over."

Prabhupada nodded his approval. "Keep reading. All answers are there."

They talked about Sanskrit and the many ways each word of scripture can be interpreted to reveal deeper and deeper meaning. They talked about the need to chant God's names attentively, without getting distracted, and how focused chanting would raise consciousness. Sunlight streamed into the room. A devotee opened a window and a breeze swept in.

"You know," George said, "when you commit yourself to something, in a way it's like putting your head on the chopping block. I find that the more commitment I make, even though, relatively speaking, it's such a little commitment, I find that now

I'm getting people angry." When word circulated that George had purchased the Letchmore Heath estate for development as a Krishna retreat, questions were raised. Was he going to renounce the world and shave his head? That was not the George people wanted.

"I'm provoking a bad reaction," George said. "The stronger the commitment on my part, the stronger the animosity becomes. You know, sometimes I get the feeling maybe there's one person who finds what I'm trying to say meaningful, and ten people—for them it doesn't mean anything. And I'm not sure if it all balances out in the end, whether reaching that one person is worth the ten or twenty who get annoyed with you. Maybe if you don't say anything, all of them will be quite friendly."

"Yes," Prabhupada said, "in preaching there is always a possibility of creating animosity. 'If you give good instruction to a fool,'" he said, quoting a popular Bengali proverb, "'he becomes angry.' But when one preaches he must tell the truth. Lord Jesus Christ—the people did not like his preaching, but he did not stop, even though they would kill him. Especially in speaking God-consciousness such things are possible, you see. We have to pay sometimes in this way."

George may have felt uneasy hearing his trials compared to those of Jesus, but the analogy carried weight. "Christ-consciousness" appeared frequently in the teachings of Paramahansa Yogananda, who urged followers to find in themselves the same "Christ-consciousness" that Jesus had exhibited through his compassion, equanimity, and love for all humanity.

"If you take risk for Krishna," Prabhupada said, "even if you stand to lose everything, Krishna comes to help and protect. Just like Arjuna. Because Krishna was there with him on the battlefield, he came out victorious. Krishna always protects his devotee."

George said he was becoming estranged, not only from the public but also from loved ones. "There's only certain times when I see Shyamsundar or a few other devotees. Most of the other people in my life, my friends—even my wife—I suddenly find myself on such a different level that it's hard to relate to them." He fell silent and no one spoke.

In their own way, everyone in the room had known doubt such as George was expressing. Not about Krishna philosophy, which was rooted in ancient scripture, but about the emotional effect of that philosophy, particularly when family expressed shock or loved ones turned away in embarrassment and the total breach with life-before-God made them question the cost of believing deeply.

"It's like I've reached a point," George continued, preparing to say what he may not have admitted before this moment, "I have to decide to either slow down and pull back in order to bring these people with me—maybe because I'm not really ready to go myself—or just cut the whole thing off. More and more the mantra builds up in me, and the effect is so subtle in a way that there's a point where I just can't relate to anybody anymore."

His friends wasted their time chasing sex and drugs and money, he said, and that distressed him. It made him sad that people he cared for didn't appreciate that death comes to us all. Still, he understood he could not just walk away from them or judge them by some lofty standard of purity. "There's a point where I'm not going to know these people anymore. So the problem is this—where to find a balance?"

"Yes," Prabhupada said with a nod, and George may have sensed the teacher's satisfaction at his willingness to admit short-comings and doubts. "You keep balance. Don't spoil your position. Keep your position. And keep the balance external and internal." He cited Ragunath Das Goswami, a wealthy sixteenth-century landholder who became attracted to the movement begun by avatar Chaitanya Mahaprabhu. The wealthy land-holder wanted to leave home and travel with Chaitanya's public chanting party, but Chaitanya advised him to be patient and not abandon his responsibilities. God could be found at home as readily as on the road, Chaitanya said.

George listened with full attention. He respected Prabhu-pada as someone who had made the journey and spoke from

realization of a place beyond material ego. George was convinced that Prabhupada knew God. He loved Krishna, spoke
with Krishna, and wanted others to reach that point. Why else
did he leave India at age seventy when most people thought only
of wallowing in retirement? His advice was precious.

Externally remain as you are, the teacher said. We can't abandon people, especially those who depend on us. Stay strong
within. That requires discipline and practice. Don't fret, he said,
or think you have to find solutions on your own. Your talent is
not ordinary karma. It has a special purpose and Krishna will
help you to fulfill it.

George appreciated the reassurance. Yet an even thornier
issue had been troubling him and had to be addressed, however
uncomfortable it made him feel—why just Krishna? Of all the
ways and paths to God, did a believer need to limit himself
to this particular expression of love? If the life of a Beatle had
taught him anything it was that masses of people could obsess
over a mental image. The Beatles may have been a great rock
band, but they came nowhere near justifying the messianic
plateau fans accorded them. What could anyone truly know of
him or his friends beyond an image portrayed by the media?
And was fixating on one deity to the exclusion of others not a
similar kind of fanaticism?

Sensitive to Prabhupada's love for Krishna, George approached the subject carefully. He had been recording Indian
songs with Ravi Shankar, he said, including "Dasha Avatar"
(The Ten Incarnations of God).

Prabhupada nodded, signaling his familiarity with the popular Hindi tune.

"I was wondering," George said, "why there is no mention
of Krishna."

Krishna was not an incarnation, Prabhupada explained as he
had at John and Yoko's home five years before. Krishna was the
origin of all incarnations. His position as Supreme Being did not
diminish the stature of other divinities, since God appeared in
many forms. Still, other incarnations were called avatar and the

Sanskrit texts called Krishna avatari, meaning "source of avatars." If that were understood, then one could see Krishna in all expressions of love for God.

"That's great," George said, relieved to have his faith confirmed and grateful as always that Prabhupada answered with reference to revealed texts.

Devotees entered the room with lunch. After the meal, when Prabhupada rose to wash his hands, George turned to Shyamsundar. "He's almost eighty. It's hard to believe he's still writing so many books, always traveling and talking to people, and almost never sleeping."

Prabhupada returned, and George turned toward the devotees. "You've really got to be prepared for the future," he said. "At the moment you have Prabhupada here to draw energy from. But sooner or later everybody's going to have to be out there on their own, you know, carrying out what he's taught." While he spoke about their future, his anxiety was about his own. Over the past four years, Prabhupada had been an important guide in his efforts to reach God. But more than once there had been indications that the teacher's remaining time was short.

"It will come by revelation," Prabhupada said, reassuring George that guidance would come even after he was gone. "That is the Vedic injunction. Nobody can understand spiritual life by academic study, but the more we become sincere and stick to the spiritual principles, the more the meaning of *shastra* [scripture] will be revealed. Become yourself purified," he said, "and Krishna will reveal himself like the sun."

George nodded, then stood up.

"Do you have to go now," Prabhupada asked, "or you will stay the night?" There was a long pause while a simple question took on deeper meaning.

"No," George said, "I must go."

"You are going alone," Prabhupada asked, "or somebody is going with you?" stretching the sense of the words.

"I go alone. Well . . ." George hesitated, and his friends laughed to see him admit his vulnerability. George trusted them with his uncertainties because he admired their dedication and devotion, but he could not tie himself to the tradition as firmly as they had. He sought the spiritual pay dirt underlying all traditions, and even advanced Krishna devotees could not do that seeking for him. Would he be going alone? George looked around the room, then back at Prabhupada sitting humbly on a cushion chanting Krishna's names on his beads.

God had to be real. How could anyone have so much love for God if he were only a myth?

"A little bit of you will be with me," George said. He joined his palms together in salutation, bowed his head to the ground, rose, and headed out the door.

11

Dark Horse

This is really a test. I'll either finish this tour ecstatically happy or end up going back to my cave for another five years.
—*George, 1974*

S hortly after his visit with Prabhupada, George learned from Pattie that she had been having an affair with his friend Eric Clapton and was leaving Friar Park to move in with him. George was no stranger to disasters; ever since becoming a Beatle, they had plagued him. They lurked around every corner, ready to ruin his success and challenge his sanity. Before yoga and meditation, his response to disaster had been to strike back. Even as recently as two years ago, when George discovered Pattie and Eric walking hand-in-hand after a concert, he had yelled at Eric that he was never to see his wife again and then shoved Pattie into their car as though she were a misbehaving teenager.

He'd changed in the past two years, and a levelheaded dispassion guided his thinking. Disasters were the product of maya, illusion, and the wise knew better than to react with fear or anger. The secret to happiness was to find sustenance in the middle ground between elation and despair, to withdraw the senses from their objects, to remember God, and see all beings as eternal souls. George didn't consider himself a very advanced devotee, but at least he could practice that kind of enlightened behavior.

Objectively, he had to acknowledge that despite the fullness of their life together he and Pattie had grown apart and were ready to move on. Her discomfort was obvious, and George acknowledged that she had as much right to determine a path for herself as he did. His own marital behavior over the years had not been without fault, after all. If she wanted to be with someone else, who was he to say no?

And who better than Eric? The two men had been friends since 1964, when Clapton's first band, the Yardbirds, opened a Christmas show for the Beatles. Over the years they had collaborated on each other's songs and become so close that looking at Eric, George said, was "like looking at myself." Eric wasn't "a leader sort of person," he said. "It's the same with me. I need someone to encourage me to do things."

At George's invitation, Eric had been the first non-Beatle to play on a Beatles song, George's "While My Guitar Gently Weeps." It was also to Eric's home in spring 1969 that George had retreated to get away from a day of bickering with Paul and John. A few bright hours walking around the Surrey estate were restorative. The day was warm, and surrounded by nature and the promise of spring, George felt inspired. He sat in Eric's garden, plucked away at one of Eric's guitars, and wrote a song that would become one of his most popular, "Here Comes the Sun." The winter has been long and cold, he sang, but the ice is finally melting and smiles are returning to people's faces.

Pattie had met Eric just after she and George were married in 1966. By 1970, Eric had grown infatuated with her and was insisting she leave George to be with him. The virtuoso guitarist struggled with drug addiction, and despite her attraction to him Pattie initially declined his advances. By 1974, with the help of electro-acupuncture treatments, he had kicked his habit, and intimations of a brighter future together prompted Pattie to change her mind.

At a reception to celebrate the completion of a new album, Clapton approached George and said, "I'm in love with your wife. What are you going to do about it?" expecting George to haul off and slug him.

"Whatever you like, man," George said. "It doesn't worry me." Then, to put his friend at ease, he joked, "You can have her and I'll have your girlfriend."

A few days later, George, Pattie, and Eric sat in the hallway of Eric's home, talking through the complexities of their relationship. Eric apologized for what he and Pattie had done.

"Fuck it, man," George said. "Don't be apologizing. I don't care."

"Well, what should we do?" Eric asked.

"Well," George said with a chuckle, "I suppose I'd better divorce her."

Eric was amazed. "He managed to laugh it all off when I thought it was getting pretty hairy," he commented later. "I thought the whole situation was tense—he thought it was funny. He helped us all through the split-up."

"George . . . could be quite quarrelsome at times," Mick Jagger recalled in later years. "But I'm talking about when he was much, much younger. I never saw that side of him later on in life."

Tony Calder, a friend who had done public relations for the Beatles in the sixties, added that George "wasn't angry [about the divorce]. He had moved on spiritually [and] there was no animosity. It was beautiful. That's all you can say about it."

Eric and Pattie eventually married, in March 1979. At a belated reception in May, George introduced himself to guests as the husband-in-law. "There comes a time when splitting is for the best," he said. "We were getting on each other's nerves, and what with the pace of my work, splitting was the easiest thing to do. In this life, there is no time to lose in an uncomfortable situation."

Seeing Pattie and Eric together actually made him happy. "I'd rather she was with him than with some dope," he said.

Over the years, popular media portrayed George and Eric as inimical; nothing could have been farther from the truth. From the rearranging of partnerships, they emerged brotherly friends who remained so throughout George's life. Friendship also marked George and Pattie's meetings with the lawyer who finalized their divorce.

"It was a clean, straightforward, sensibly arranged matter," said Paddy Grafton-Green, partner in the law firm Theodore

Goddard, which had been retained by Pattie. "They were sensitive to one another." Grafton-Green, who had worked with the Rolling Stones, noted that this kind of objectivity was particularly rare in the rock world, where "few artists know how to handle their own success. Without some sense of spirituality, they just don't survive," he said. "One has to be extraordinarily strong to come through the drugs and hedonism of that culture. There are no rules, and it is not a caring environment. Harrison was a rare exception, and he had an influence. People saw that he stood for something different. There was no overreacting, no greed or playing with each other's emotions—I wish all divorces were so well handled."

"Knowledge is supposed to lead to liberation," George said, "and I certainly liberated myself from some of the mundane things, like not talking to your friend just because you all had a divorce."

On a trip to New York, alone in his Park Lane Hotel suite, George wrote "So Sad." The song spoke of cold winds, lost love, and dreams abandoned. But he had come far in understanding how deeply entangled perfect souls became in an imperfect world. "If we were all perfected beings," he told a New York reporter that week, "we wouldn't be here in the physical world. . . . We can allow for each others' inadequacies or failings with a little compassion, you know."

To the lineup on his 1974 album *Dark Horse,* George added an old favorite by the Everly Brothers called "Bye-Bye Love," the lyrics amended to refer to Pattie. On the final mix, Clapton played guitar and Pattie sang in the chorus.

In February 1974, shortly after Pattie broke the news about leaving him for Eric, George packed his bags and flew to India to meet Ravi Shankar and revisit the spiritual world. They met in Bombay and set out on a tour of holy places, including Vrindavan, eighty miles south of Delhi, the village where Krishna had appeared five thousand years before. "In Vrindavan," Ravi said, "Krishna is everywhere, in the art, the dance, the music, the stories—you have a feeling that Krishna is a person who is still there."

For many years, prior to each trip back to America, Ravi would rejuvenate himself by spending a few days at a Vrindavan ashram on the banks of the Yamuna River. The ashram, Sri Chaitanya Prema Samasthana, dated from the seventeenth century. For many years, descendants of the Vaishnava saint Gopal Bhatta Goswami had organized the ashram's courses of devotional study.

George and Ravi arrived at the ashram and spent the next few days meditating, writing music, and discussing the art of devotion. "There is an interesting dictum," commented Shrivatsa Goswami, a descendant of Gopal Bhatta and current head of the ashram, "that says if you read the Vedas a million times, that is equal to one recitation of *japa*. And if you do a million *japas,* that is equal to once making an offering of food with love to the Lord. And a million such offerings are equal to one musical offering. Then what is superior to a musical offering? Only another musical offering. Nothing is higher. That was one of the themes of discussion when George and Ravi came to visit. We would discuss how Chaitanya took that musical offering as supreme, how it is essential to loving devotion."

In the evenings, they took walks and sat by the Yamuna River, where Krishna sported with friends as a boy. "George was writing music for his future album *Ravi Shankar and Family* and also his album *Dark Horse,*" Shrivatsa recalled. "He found musical inspiration here. It has been many years, but I remember that the mood was always calm and loving."

Every stone and bush in Vrindavan, it seemed, had a story attached to it. While touring the holy village, George's guide pointed to a grove of *ashoka* trees. That was where Krishna braided Radha's hair and decorated her with red *kunkuma* powder. Over there was the place where Brahma bathed Krishna, one of 108 bathing spots around Govardhan Hill—the hill that child Krishna lifted like an umbrella to protect his friends from torrential rains. And there, on the banks of the river, a beautiful rocket-shaped temple was built over the "mouth" of Govardhan Hill. Pilgrims poured offerings of milk and sweets into the mouth and then went for dips in the river to end their pilgrimage with a splash.

The forests and lakes of Vrindavan were havens for exotic species of water birds: long-necked egrets, red-faced *saras* cranes, and pheasant-tailed jacanas. As they walked, George heard cooing and cawing in the branches overhead. In blossoming *parijata* trees, he saw red-beaked moorhens and white-breasted kingfishers nesting, while herds of goats, buffalo, and sheep wandered freely by.

George's friend Gurudas had been stationed in Vrindavan for the past five years, working under Prabhupada's direction to build a temple in the village of Krishna's birth. The friends met and embraced. George saw Gurudas's wife, Yamuna. Grinning, George ran over and gave her a hug and a smack on the lips. Yamuna nearly fell over backward. "Hey, leave my woman alone," Gurudas joked.

They looked around at pasturing grounds where Krishna had once played as a boy, at forests that had been home to holy people since before recorded time, and marveled at the sensation of walking on sacred ground.

"How magnificent this feeling is," George said.

It was during this time with Ravi that an idea occurred to him.

"Why not get some musicians you like," he told the master sitarist, "and we'll do a tour?"

Still energized by the success of his Concert for Bangladesh and refreshed by his time in India, George returned to England in March 1974 and announced that he would soon be releasing a new album called *Dark Horse,* followed by a U.S. concert tour. He would be the first ex-Beatle to tour America. "He was definitely inspired after Bangladesh," said Billy Preston. "He wanted to [perform live] again, right away."

Within days, George pulled together a team of musicians and began recording at Friar Park. Life was short and speed counted, as *Dark Horse* bass player Willie Weeks discovered on a break from recording at Friar Park.

"We'd take a break to go for fish and chips," Weeks said, "and there were two ways you could go. One was through this very winding road through the woods from Friar Park to the little fish place. And that's the way we went. The first time, he took me in a Ferrari. Well, he really liked racing. I'm telling you, man, when we came back from fish and chips, he drove through those winding roads as if he was on a racetrack. I mean really, really going for it. It was serious, and I'm holding on, thinking, 'Wow, man, I sure hope we stay on the road because if we miss, we're history.' Well, we made it home in the Ferrari.

The next time we went for fish and chips, he took a Porsche and he took the same route. The Porsche seemed to handle the road better, so he started speeding up. I just thought, 'He's such a fan of racing, I guess there's this little racecar driver inside him.' But then he really started going, and when we got into Friar Park we were flying so fast that the car got away from him. There were these high hedges that lined the driveway to the garage, and we're running through the hedges—and I just sat there acting as normal as I could, but I was praying, O Lord, please don't let them read about us in the newspaper. Just get us back to the house. After he came out of the hedges, he shrugged and gave me a little laugh as though it never happened. I'm looking at George, and he just looks away like, Don't say nothing. Well, we went into the house and neither of us ever said a word."

Speed counted in the studio, too, with only a few weeks in which to complete an entire album of new songs. George worked nonstop, straining his voice and jeopardizing his ability to sing at all. It started as a soreness and grew worse.

George had a tough decision to make. At best he could nurse his throat and make it through okay. At worst he could injure himself and have to cancel the tour. He decided to push on.

Dark Horse was released in October. Reporters at a Los Angeles conference to launch the album received a press kit including "George Harrison Then & Now," comparing his answers to a questionnaire in a 1963 edition of *New Musical Express* to answers in 1974. Under "most thrilling experience," in 1963 he had listed "First disc a hit within 48 hours of release." In 1974 his answer read, "Seeking Krishna in Brandaban [sic], India."

One reporter queried George about his career with the Beatles. "I realize that the Beatles did fill a space in the sixties," he said. "All the people that the Beatles meant something to have grown up and want to hold on to something. People are afraid of change," he said, "but you can't live in the past."

A reporter asked if it was possible to be spiritual in the material world. "Our consciousness has been so polluted with material energy," George said, "that it is hard to see our way towards anything spiritual. But everyone has within him the same qualities as God, just as a drop of the ocean has the same qualities as the ocean. Everybody's looking for something outside—but it's all right there within ourselves." That conviction was about to be severely tested.

The *Dark Horse* album earned George the worst reviews of his career. Writers complained that the tracks seemed unrehearsed, the vocals were out of tune, the melodies unremarkable, and the lyrics weak. "Dismal," one reviewer groused, "an album which should never have happened." Another reviewer declared George a failure as a singer, songwriter, and guitarist. Two singles spun off from the album failed to reach the U.K. top thirty, the first solo Beatle records to perform so poorly. Compared with his previous grand successes, reviewers deemed George's third solo album a complete disaster.

The seven-week *Dark Horse* tour began on November 2, and things went from bad to worse. George opened each show with Ravi and a troupe of Indian musicians playing a lengthy program of Indian classical music that had fans yawning and restless. When he came on to perform the second half, George's constant exhortations to "Chant Krishna! Christ! Krishna! Christ! Allah! Buddha!" added to their unease. He came across as overzealous, alienating much of his audience. Someone in the audience yelled out a request for his hit single "Bangladesh."

"You can chant Krishna, Krishna, Krishna, and maybe you'll feel better," George said into his microphone. "But if you just shout Bangladesh, Bangladesh, Bangladesh—it's not going to help anybody."

People had come expecting at least a few Beatles memories, but George refused to be pulled back into that persona, providing concertgoers instead, with what one reporter called "a surfeit of the unfamiliar and a short-changing of the golden greats." Ravi appealed to him. "Give the people a couple of old songs," he said. "It's okay."

It was not waving a picture of Krishna over his head that fans minded. They could even go along with his insisting that God was where it was at and his yelling, "Someone's got to tell you!" After all, those were his beliefs, and so long as the music rocked, they felt they were getting their money's worth. His worst offense was when, finally relenting to sing a few Beatles tunes, he changed the lyrics to reflect his beliefs. Now his guitar "gently *smiled,*" and in his life he "loved *God* more." No one in the audience shouted what they were feeling, but the sense of betrayal was obvious beneath their indifferent applause.

Beatles songs had made them feel good. They remembered where they were the first time they heard each new Beatles song, what they were doing, and who was with them. Those memories were important to them, and playing fast and loose with Beatles lyrics came across as elitist, and worse, hurtful.

"Holy Krishna!" *Rolling Stone* reporter Ben Fong-Torres wrote. "What kind of an opening night for George Harrison is this?"

Adding to George's woes, three weeks into the tour Ravi was hospitalized with stomach problems and was unable to continue performing. Meanwhile, George's voice grew worse, prompting reviewers to dub the tour *Dark Hoarse.* George was not always graceful under the pressure. "I don't know how it feels down there," he croaked from the stage of the Forum in Los Angeles, "but from up here you seem pretty dead."

After a performance in California's Long Beach Arena, he wandered alone through the stands, looking down on bulldozers scooping up tons of broken bottles, cigarette butts, discarded shoes, T-shirts, and bras, litter of every kind. Had returning to the stage been the right thing to do?

Whether they like me or not, he thought, this is who I am. He remembered a quote from Mahatma Gandhi: we should create and preserve the image of our choice. The image of my choice is not Beatle George, he thought. My life belongs to God. That's how I feel. He was here in the world to do spiritual good, and playing the old hits would have felt hypocritical. How could he live with himself if he reinforced people's material attachment to nostalgic tunes and images? But was this better— bad reviews and mountains of trash?

From city to city, his voice continued to waver and crack. In Los Angeles, Robert Tenets of the *Herald* wrote, "Opening with 'While My Guitar Gently Weeps,' the band was cooking so fast and hard that Harrison's vocal shortcomings were easily overlooked. But as he tore into 'Something,' shouting the lyrics of this most tender ballad like a possessed Bob Dylan on an off night, you realized the voice was almost gone." Phil Elwood of the *San Francisco Examiner* wrote, "Never a strong singer, but a moving one, Harrison found that he had virtually no voice left and had to croak his way through even the delicate 'Something.'"

Still, for every fan unsure about George's religious overtures and poor reviews, there were as many who had a different take on the *Dark Horse* tour. "I saw George Harrison give thirty-five thousand fans two fine shows," wrote a fan who attended the Toronto performances on December 6, "but not according to my more lofty and so-called professional colleagues in the local press. . . . George had [the audience] standing on their seats and clapping wildly for an encore. . . . With his now usual clasped hand salute, he wished us God's blessing and pronounced, 'All glories to Sri Krishna,' then left the stage as humbly as he had arrived, but to a barrage of applause, cheers, and shouts for more."

At a December 13 concert in Washington, D.C., President Ford's son Jack invited George to meet his dad at the White House. Among those who joined George in the Oval Office was his father, Harold, sporting hair grown down to his shoulders, an ultimate tribute from a working-class dad to his rocker son. But even a presidential audience could not deter some critics from writing vicious comments about the tour. On December 15, George played Long Island's Nassau Veterans Memorial Coliseum to what one writer deemed "perceptible boredom" on the part of the audience. The review went on to claim that organist Billy Preston "salvaged" the evening with his hit songs "Nothing from Nothing" and "Outta-Space," which had the audience dancing. John Lennon attended the performance and went backstage to congratulate George on a successful show. George succumbed to his own exhaustion and foul mood and demanded to know why John had failed to side with him instead of Yoko over the Bangladesh concert. He grabbed John's glasses and threw them to the floor.

John was no stranger to anger that seethed from depression and did nothing. "I know what pain is," he said, "so I let him do it."

Despite adverse circumstances and hostile critics, George pushed on with the tour. "You either go crackers and commit suicide," he told a reporter, or "attach yourself more strongly to an inner strength."

Dark Horse drummer Andy Newmark suggested that George's solo tour would have been risky even without its religious overtones. "The Beatles survived, to some extent, because they had one another to deal with the mania," Newmark said. "They had each other to keep them grounded. I'm sure that George's whole religious thing was, in a sense, his way of keeping himself grounded while having to be on his own. He didn't have his friends with him anymore. On his solo tours, he was the boss and that can be a lonely position. By the time the Beatles broke up, he just wanted back into the human race."

"George absolutely took the press to heart," added bassist Willie Weeks. "He was not happy. He was having problems with his voice, and some people used that as an excuse to give him a hard time, maybe because of what he was trying to bring to the audiences. It was a struggle. I remember feeling hurt for him because the stress of it all was just too much. But in spite of all of that, he remained very kind to all of us, always. He'd pull little surprises. You'd check into your hotel room, and there was no telling what would be waiting for you there."

At the time of the tour, Weeks had a taste for lobster. One night, he checked into his room and found that George had had dozens delivered to his bathtub. "There was a whole lot of 'em in there. In spite of the hard time with the press, he still kept his sense of humor and generosity," Weeks said. "That stayed intact. Every night after the show, we'd board this private airplane and on one side would be all kinds of Indian food and on the other side American food, roast beef, what have you. Every night, we'd get our food, grab a seat, and cool out. Next thing we knew, we'd be in the next city, checked into our hotel, and ready for bed. And it wouldn't even be all that late. It was the classiest tour I've ever been on, the best hotels, the best everything. He wanted to make everybody happy. It was beautiful."

As for his own happiness, George felt helpless. "I don't have control over anything. I believe in God, and he is the supreme controller even down to the rehearsal," George told the press, a statement that only fueled unsympathetic writers who insisted on using print space to attack his beliefs. "In defense of his tour and new album," wrote one critic, "George Harrison has argued that if you don't expect anything, life is one big bonus. So expect nothing—is that the moral?" The reviewer went on to accuse him of using the stage to "spread his gospel" and of creating formulaic tunes "as predictable as his spiritual preoccupations."

"There will always be [criticism]," George told a reporter toward the end of the tour, "but . . . my life belongs to me." Then he corrected himself. "It actually doesn't. It belongs to *him*. My life belongs to the Lord Krishna and there's my dog collar to prove it," he said, tugging at the two strands of *tulsi* beads around his neck. "I'm lucky to be a grain of dirt in creation. That's how I feel. Never been so humble in all my life, and I feel great." Then he broke out in song: "Take me as I am or let me go."

He said to the reporter, "You know, I didn't force you or anybody at gunpoint to come to see me. And I don't care if nobody comes to see me, nobody ever buys another record of me. I don't give a shit, it doesn't matter to me, but I'm going to do what I feel within myself."

Musicians, crew, and those who understood the selfless intent behind the tour rallied to his side. Resistance was predictable, they told him, from people who were expecting rock and roll and had never heard a raga before.

George tried to see divine purpose in the debacle and reassured them that "the more they try to knock me down the more determined I am." He also accepted responsibility for his choices. "God is fair," he told them. "He's not watching over everybody and saying, 'You did that, so give him a kick in the behind.' It's ourselves who get into a mess or get ourselves out."

Publicly, he was a good sport about the all-time low in his career. Privately, he suffered.

"Every show was probably hard for him," said violinist L. Subramaniam. "He was trying sincerely to do something to benefit people. You see, in Indian tradition you cannot separate music from spirituality, and my impression was that George wasn't just looking to popularize Indian music but also a path of spirituality. He was trying to make people aware of the music because he knew gradually they would get to the root—the spirituality. But the press really wasn't always sympathetic. The press could sometimes be very harsh. Anyone else under that kind of pressure would have said, 'Okay, I'm calling it off. We'll tell the press I have a sore throat, and I'll be on the next flight home.' But he took the risk of going on, of people again writing something negative about him, of putting in all that effort. Why did he do it? I always had the feeling someone very special was occupying that body."

George may have been determined to bring spirit into music, "but like John Lennon said," he reminded a reporter during a sound check at Madison Square Garden, "Christ, you know it ain't easy. . . . For every knot I untie I might be tying ten. I don't know, sometimes it feels like that." The walls of his dressing room at the Garden were decorated with Indian bedspreads and images of his favorite deities. George lit a cigarette and took a drag. He paused and then said, "With all respect to all those silly rock 'n' rollers who have high-heeled mirrored shoes and eye makeup, there comes a time in your life when you have to decide what life is all about. There must be some other reason for being here than just jumping up and down, trying to become famous."

His career had begun on the sidelines when he had paced himself behind John and Paul like a racehorse, a "dark horse," taking his time, conserving energy, and absorbing the details of his terrain. Then when the moment was right, he broke free and gave it his all.

Why risk so much after waiting so long? Was it because the world had become such a frightening place? Crises filled newspaper headlines every day in 1974. Somewhere along the line humanity had suffered a loss of spiritual vision, and someone had to say it. John's atheism couldn't turn things around. The best that kind of existential despair had to offer was a reminder to help one another out before dying. Paul's insistence on light-hearted entertainment fell short of remedial. Strangely, Ringo's nearly Zen ability to find the eye of every hurricane seemed the most evolved of all.

Now George was confronting the greatest disappointment of his life. Not losing his wife, which in some ways had been quite liberating. Not losing his band, which had unleashed exhilarating creative energies. The price he paid for shouting out his message was losing his voice, in every sense. He grappled with the depressing realization that most people simply didn't care to hear about Krishna or maya or getting liberated from birth and death. The world wanted rock and roll. The world preferred him as a Beatle.

George had counted on at least a portion of the goodwill generated by the Bangladesh concert to follow him on the *Dark Horse* tour, but the calculation had failed. A man whose natural instinct was to share his life-transforming discoveries with others had been rejected, and he was not his jovial self anymore.

George loved live performance: it's why he had become a musician. After *Dark Horse,* he did not tour again for nearly twenty years.

It was at this vulnerable moment that Bright Tunes Music Corporation brought a legal suit claiming that George's number one hit "My Sweet Lord" plagiarized their 1963 song "He's So Fine." As an expression of his love for God, "My Sweet Lord" was considered by many to be George's signature creation. Despite his protestations, some part of him cared deeply that the world was rejecting him. He went into a deep depression. His smoking and drinking increased, and he developed a severe case of hepatitis from the "brandy and all the other naughty things that fly around," as he later described his habits. Drugs had first entered his life at age seventeen in Hamburg, when amphetamines had been an easily acquired stimulant for all-night sessions. His drug use had gone up and down in the intervening years. Now it was back.

"If you want to understand what part drugs play in the life of a rock musician, see them as a person and imagine you are entering into a relationship with that person," commented *Dark Horse* drummer Andy Newmark. "You're on the road. Your life is in planes and hotels. There's no continuity, just moving from place to place, every day a different town. You're herded like cattle. There's nothing particularly human about it. And this substance becomes your friend. It goes with you wherever you go, this constant in an inconstant life. This friend gives you a familiar feeling wherever you go, and you begin to think it makes the reality of your life easier to cope with. It's there, in a vial, in your back pocket, your buddy. Ultimately, of course, you learn it's an unhealthy friend."

After too many days and nights of free fall, George found his way back to solid ground with the help of Olivia Trinidad Arias, an administrative assistant in the Los Angeles office of his new company, Dark Horse Records. Born in Mexico in 1948, Olivia had grown up in California and studied meditation. While she was working for A&M Records, George met her in early 1974 and then hired her away to work for his own Dark Horse Records. That was when he remembered how charmed his life was.

The two became companions, and evolved a partnership in work and spiritual practice.

Everything had seemed impossible and dark, and then she was there, sensible and lovely and responsive, and everything seemed possible and bright. He never had to search far for misery; now happiness had shown up unbidden, and in her company he regained a composure and stability undermined since the *Dark Horse* tour.

Olivia insisted that George make efforts beyond prayer to recover his health. Within a few months of beginning acupuncture and following a healthier diet, his condition improved. "When you strive for something higher in the next world," she said in a rare interview, "you have a much easier time in this one." She would be George's partner for the remaining years of his life.

By 1975, George had regained strength and relaxed his missionary zeal. Compared to its predecessors, his fourth album, *Extra Texture,* was a model of religious restraint. Gone were exhortations to chant and warnings about rebirth in the material world, replaced by a modest appeal for tolerance. "Scan not a friend with a microscopic glass," he sang, quoting Sir Frankie Crisp in "The Answer's at the End." "You know his faults, now let the foibles pass." Other tracks went so far as to recommend that listeners *not* heed his advice. No one would be wise following the likes of me, he warned in "World of Stone." No longer an Arjuna, all George wanted now was to leave the battlefield behind and simply live "with no pistol at my brain."

In July 1976, George was midway through recording his fifth solo album *33 & 1/3,* when he took a break to visit Prabhupada at Bhaktivedanta Manor. The last time they had met was during George's brief visit to Vrindavan two years before. The Krishna teacher's health had deteriorated over recent months, and he was resting in bed. George entered and bowed his head to the car-peted floor. Prabhupada smiled.

"How do you feel?" George asked.

"Due to age it is becoming a little difficult," Prabhupada said. "Are you still chanting?" George assured him he was. "Thank you," the teacher said. "That is our life and soul. Wherever you live, whatever you do, chant." Prabhupada's right hand remained in a bead bag where his fingers turned wooden beads worn smooth from a lifetime of prayer. His deteriorating condition hung between them unexplored, and to lighten the mood George commented that the devotees were looking strong and well. Prabhupada nodded. Good health, he said, resulted from living a stress-free life of service to God. Pointing around the room, he again thanked George for having provided such a nice property.

"We are inviting everyone to be with us here," the teacher said, "to live here comfortably, eat nicely, and chant 'Hare Krishna.' We don't want to see people wasting away in facto-ries," he said with a chuckle. His smile dissolved into a look of concern. "Still, people prefer to go to the factory, whole day work in the hell."

"I suppose someday the whole of the world will just be chant-ing in the country," George said, wanting to reassure Prabhu-pada that a lifetime of sacrifice had not been in vain. Prabhupada shook his head. Some miracles can't be expected.

"But if some of the leading men take it seriously," Prabhu-pada reminded with a nod toward George, "others will follow. Are you reading the books?" the teacher asked.

"Mainly *KRSNA Book*," George replied. "I always take the Gita with me wherever I go. That's the one I just keep all the time. But you know, I've never been a great reader." He praised Prabhupada's prodigious writing; the teacher had written nearly a hundred books.

Prabhupada nodded, acknowledging an achievement for which he took no credit. "It is Krishna's grace—otherwise, not possi-ble." He looked across the table, and George knew the wise and devoted teacher understood more about his frame of mind than was spoken.

"I am very much pleased that you take so much trouble to come here," Prabhupada said.

"It's my pleasure," George said sincerely.

Like many of George's spiritual heroes, Prabhupada was an innovator. He taught devotional yoga to anyone interested, including people who prior had eaten meat and taken drugs—something forbidden by Hindu tradition. Caste-conscious Brahmins in India scorned his egalitarianism, arguing that anyone who did not have Brahmin parents was unfit to receive the secrets of scripture. Prabhupada paid no heed to such politics. Knowledge of God, he said, was the birthright of all souls.

George had built a relationship with Prabhupada based on the guru's purity and love for God. Nothing had changed that, but the world around them had changed. Gone were the missionary days of the sixties. Gone, too, were George's burning questions about life's mysteries. He had learned as much as he cared to know. Now he just wanted to live the truths he had already discovered. The time for intense philosophical inquiries was over.

"Are you ever going to stop traveling?" George asked. Prabhupada had already made seven trips around the world spreading the message of the Bhagavad Gita. George wondered how much more could he take.

"If that is Krishna's desire," the teacher said. He preferred to travel, teaching wherever he could. But that, he said, was not in his hands. The Swami quoted a Sanskrit verse by a long ago devotee-king. Since I will die sooner or later, the king prayed, let me die now while my health is still good and I can remember you, dear Lord. "This is the ideal," Prabhupada said. "If at the time of death one can remember Krishna, then his whole life is successful. Immediately he goes to Krishna."

"When my mother died," George said, "I had to send my sister and father out of the room because they were getting emotional. And I just chanted 'Hare Krishna.'"

"She could hear?" Prabhupada asked.

"I don't know," George said. "She was in a coma or something. It was the only thing I could think of, the only thing that may be of value, you know."

Prabhupada nodded. "If she heard 'Hare Krishna,' she will get the benefit. So let us practice in such a way that at the time of death we may remember. That is success." Prabhupada thanked George, saying that because of his example many others were now chanting.

George turned away. "I don't think it's on my account. . . . "

Prabhupada assured him it was so and looked to his disciples for confirmation. A London devotee said letters arrived regularly from people around the world who had taken to chanting after hearing George's records.

George shifted on his cushion. Subduing his ego, not inflating it, had become his avowed goal. Still, he had achieved something unprecedented, and he appreciated Prabhupada's wanting him to know how much it meant.

Hearing God's names at death was success, the teacher said. George could have added the corollary himself that since people never know when death will come, they should chant constantly. Chanting soothes the soul, Prabhupada said, quoting from scripture to authenticate his teachings. He pointed to a large volume on a shelf and asked an assistant to recite a certain verse. The young man leafed through the heavy book, then read:

> I do not know how much nectar
> The syllables "Krish-na" have produced.
> When the holy name Krishna is chanted,
> It appears to dance within the mouth,
> And we desire many, many mouths.
> When the name enters our ears,
> We desire millions of ears.
> When the name dances in the courtyard of the heart,
> It conquers the mind
> And the senses become inert.

"If you chant this verse according to the Sanskrit tune," Prabhupada said, "your admirers will take it very nicely."

George laughed and said his admirers hardly understood much even when he sang in English. Time stretched on. Prabhupada looked tired. George bowed and rose to leave. They looked at one another for a moment in silence.

"Long life," Prabhupada called out as George left.

In November 1977, on a thin mattress in a room of the Krishna Balaram temple in Vrindavan, Prabhupada lay dying. Around him disciples tried as best they could to chant, but tears and sobs got in the way. Prabhupada removed a ring and handed it to an assistant with instructions that it be conveyed to George with his blessings.

12

Laws of Nature

Every blade of grass has its angel
That bends over it and whispers, "Grow, grow."

—Saying from the Talmud

T he sounds of a stream ran through Friar Park, and a hush of
wind rustled the hemlocks and oaks. God came to George
now through trees and gardens, through the simple miracles that
had drawn him as a child and continued to lure him as an adult.
He luxuriated in tilling the earth, planting jasmine bushes, free-
ing a magnolia tree from wild brambles, and nursing abused
ground back to beauty. He had seen people worshiping nature
in India where they called the earth God's "Universal Form."
Trees were the hairs on that divine form, mountains and hills the
bones, clouds the hair, rivers the blood flowing through the
veins. Gardening from that vantage point took on holy dimensions, a caressing of God's body.

As in all things that held his interest, George went about
gardening as though there had never been any other calling in
life but this, to know nature and commune with her. Soil was
not mere earth; it was a universe of microorganisms that served
trees and flowers and deserved the tools to do so: food and water,
sunshine and air. He was a servant, too—a servant of the servant—and went about his work with courtesy and a composer's
sense of composition and grace. George's creative impulse mi-

grated from music to nature, and over time there emerged at Friar Park one of England's most unusual and inspired gardens. George had little interest in creating anything overly formal. Instead, he sought ways to facilitate nature's own purposeful spontaneity, to assist something to flourish that might seem at first glance random or unruly. Some sections he set aside for themes, Japanese or Hawaiian, but his intention overall was environment in the raw, contrasting colors and sizes that would flow freely as though no human hand had dictated their grouping. George did in his garden what he did onstage: he stepped back away from the limelight to allow others to show what they could do.

By the mid-seventies, the young people who helped make George Harrison a superstar had become adults. Sixties-era protesters went home to find jobs and have families. Idealism moved aside to make room for mortgages and retirement portfolios. Many musicians left music and found more dependable careers elsewhere.

George knew no other life and could not imagine one. His way of communicating had been shaped by his years as a Beatle, and he would forever make sense of the world through music and song and the natural poetry of his soul. But the desire to do so publicly wasn't as urgent now as it had been.

George and Olivia enjoyed simple pleasures that had eluded them in previous years. Olivia later recalled that in those days George might wake his family with a morning raga or chant or a Mozart concerto or ukulele rendition of a Hoagy Carmichael tune. There was time to attend flower shows and time to cheer favorite drivers at stock car races.

Ringo and Maureen divorced in July 1975. Now he and his new girlfriend, Nancy, joined the Harrisons at the races. There never was any friction between George and Ringo, who seemed as capable as George of shrugging off shadows and seeing the humor in things. "Ringo would bounce in here and there, make a simple statement, and smile," Gurudas remembered of their time together during devotee recordings. Concerning reincarnation, "Ringo wanted to know if he could come back as a cat. 'I like cats,' he told me and laughed."

There was time now for George and Olivia to travel the world, to walk on beaches and visit with friends. He continued working, although at a leisurely pace. New albums emerged periodically from his home studio, and he collaborated now and then with fellow musicians on their tunes, including Monty Python's single "The Lumberjack Song" and an album of original songs by the band Jiva. Mixes were done in the privacy of Friar Park. London held nothing for him anymore.

"He was more relaxed than when I knew him in 1974," commented drummer Andy Newmark, who recorded the album *George Harrison* at Friar Park. "Nothing was quite as traumatic. He only got mellower from 1974 onward."

"The best thing anyone can give to humanity is God-consciousness," George told a friend that year, "but first you have to concentrate on your own spiritual advancement. So in a sense, we have to become selfish to become selfless." To a reporter from *Crawdaddy* magazine he explained, "There are a lot of people in the business that I love, friends, you know, who are really great but who don't have any desire for knowledge or realization. It's good to boogie once and a while, but when you boogie all your life away it's just a waste of life and of what we've been given. I can get high like the rest of them, but it's actually low. The more dope you take, the lower you get, really. Having done that, I can say that from experience."

On visits to Los Angeles, George spent time at the Self-Realization Fellowship estate in Encinitas, overlooking the Pacific Ocean and only three miles from Ravi Shankar's home. Ravi had met SRF founder Yogananda in the 1930s and had given his first U.S. concert at the Encinitas retreat in 1957. The organization strictly honored its members' privacy, a privilege George appreciated after the notoriety of his affiliation with Krishna devotees. The quiet ambience of the Encinitas estate and the organization's focus on achieving heightened awareness through kriya-yoga had a calming effect.

Not much has been printed about George's private life in later years. The press, so garish in covering every twitch of the young Beatle George, lost interest in pursuing the real person into adulthood. Why bother if it wouldn't sell papers? Some details emerge from celebrity sightings columns. In January 1977, he and Olivia traveled to India for the wedding of Ravi's niece, then to Mexico for a holiday with Olivia's family. He wrote no songs that year, calling 1977 "the year I took off from music" and "went to the races."

In May 1978, at the Harrison home in Appleton, George's father died in his sleep. As he had done for his mother, George now did for his father and sat by his side chanting, appreciating the love this man had given him and wishing him safe passage back to God. George had been a handful growing up, rebellious, defiant, dropping out of school, and joining a band—all against his father's wishes at the time. As much as his success, George's ability to remain a gentleman and lead a spiritual life had made his father proud. On the eve of his father's death, George dreamed that Harold came to him and bade him farewell.

In August 1978, a son was born to George and Olivia. They named him Dhani, after notes in the Indian musical scale— Sa-Ri-Ga-Ma-Pa-DHA-NI-Sa—and through his newly minted father's eyes George caught a glimpse of what his own father must have seen when George was a boy. "With a child around, I can realize what it was like to be my father," he told *Rolling Stone* magazine. George enjoyed the fatherly pleasures of watching Dhani exploring nature, Dhani growing a few years older and going crazy over the Beach Boys' "Surfin' USA." George told him, "That's really good, but do you want to hear where that came from?" and played him Chuck Berry's "Sweet Little Sixteen." Dhani fell in love with rock and roll, coming to understand who his father was and what he meant to others.

"You can relive certain aspects of being a child," George said. "You can watch him and have all these flashbacks of when you were a kid. It somehow completes this generation thing."

George didn't think much about his Beatles days, and if he did, it was with a grin. He felt rather like Charlie Chaplin or

Laurel and Hardy, a relic from the past. His former bandmates had long since tired of suing one another and were just friends again. He hadn't heard from John in a couple of years, other than an occasional postcard, but he saw Paul and Ringo from time to time.

George's preference was to spend time with his own family. George, Olivia, and Dhani attended concerts by Ravi Shankar at Royal Albert Hall and screened classic films such as *Singin' in the Rain* for friends at Friar Park. They appeared at a Boys' Club Christmas show and ventured out to participate in an anti-nuclear march through the streets of London. How could people hope to progress spiritually if they allowed God's planet to be neglected or destroyed? And how were seekers interested in only their own salvation any less selfish than outright materialists?

"As an ordinary member of humanity and of the British public," he told a reporter sometime later, "the only vote I have ever cast is Green. The whole planet is operating on the ways of overindulgence. It's just ridiculous."

By 1982, his attentions had shifted from music to movies, and his company HandMade Films was doing well, spurred by the success of its main asset, the Monty Python comedy team.

"He was a huge Python fan," said founding member Terry Gilliam. "We started the year the Beatles quit. He was absolutely convinced whatever that spirit was that animated the Beatles just drifted across to Python." George relished the Python group's scathing send-ups of Britain's upper class and their ribald slashes at people who took themselves too seriously, especially religious types. He invested huge sums to fund the group's projects, to the point of mortgaging Friar Park to finance their 1979 hit film *Life of Brian*.

"I remember watching the very first Monty Python show that ever came on, on BBC 2," George told *Melody Maker* magazine. "Derek Taylor and I were so thrilled by seeing this wacky show that we sent them a telegram saying 'Love the show, keep doing it.' . . . I couldn't understand how normal television could continue after that."

George bought a house in Maui, Hawaii, with grounds that led to a rocky bluff overlooking the ocean, and gave himself over to loving his wife, raising their son, tending his garden, enjoying the view, and remembering what it was like to be a regular human being. Aside from occasional appearances for a noble cause, he luxuriated in the peace, privacy, and predictability that had evaded him all his life. For a while it felt as though he had achieved everything he wanted.

By the midseventies, many people who had come of age in the postwar years were waxing nostalgic for the sixties. Beatlemania resurfaced with a vengeance. In 1976, reissues of ten-year-anniversary Beatles singles climbed the charts to become seven of the United Kingdom's top forty. *Beatlemania: The Musical* opened on Broadway in June 1977. *Sergeant Pepper: The Musical* opened on the West Coast a few months later. Liverpool inaugurated "Magical History Tours" of places where the Beatles had lived and played: the Cavern and the tiny house in Wavertree where George was born, the club where the Beatles had played for Janice the stripper. Beatles conventions were held in cities across the United States and England. *Reveille* magazine declared "Beatles Boom," and the BBC ran weekend-long Beatles television specials. Looking to cash in on the craze, a Los Angeles promoter offered the grotesque sum of $100 million for one Beatles reunion concert. George, John, Paul, and Ringo flatly refused.

"It's a joke," George told an Amsterdam television interviewer. "It's trying to put responsibility for making the world a wonderful world again onto the Beatles. I think that's unfair."

As Beatlemania again spread, peace and privacy—the possessions George most coveted—crumbled under a barrage of media.

In September 1976, a federal circuit court judge in New York announced that George had "subconsciously" plagiarized the tune of "My Sweet Lord" from the sixties hit "He's So Fine" and ordered him to pay a fine of $500,000. The verdict was a terrible blow to someone whose intentions had been selfless. "It killed him," said a friend close to the case.

The Beatles were once again everywhere in the press, and the adulation led to tragedy. Everyone knew where John Lennon lived. A group of fans always gathered outside the Dakota building in New York, where he and Yoko had their apartment. John had mellowed. Where previously he may have waved them off without a word or at most a snide remark, these days he usually had a moment to shake hands and say hello. On the afternoon of December 8, 1980, as he and Yoko left the Dakota, a man approached and asked John to sign a copy of his album *Double Fantasy*. John obliged. Later that night, when they returned home, the man stepped out from the shadows of their building. He fired five shots with a revolver, and John fell to the ground.

Not long after, George's sister heard of John's death on a radio broadcast and called George at Friar Park.

It was the end of a brief time of sanity. Things seemed to have righted themselves in his life, and if there were still a few problems, they got solved. Now this. John murdered. Nothing was smiling down from anywhere on anyone anymore. What possible mechanism could digest this horror? What faith could ever indemnify him or anyone else against such evil? George kept peering in from outside himself, looking at his own life through the distorted mirror of what had just occurred and trying to rationalize it. But he couldn't.

Where could he go, what could he do? His song called "Dream Away" said the sky was "black as day." It said a man dreamed of fabulous treasure and traveled through thousands of years of history to find it. It said the man found his treasure, and then it was stolen and his dream came undone. What a heavy task it is, the song said, to share a dream.

Weeks later, after the initial shock had worn down sufficiently for conventional speech to return, George allowed himself to be interviewed.

"We saw beyond each other's physical bodies," he said, seeking to reassure fans that John's soul lived on. "If you can't feel the spirit of some friend who's been that close, then what chance have you got to feel the spirit of Christ or Buddha or whatever else you may be interested in?" On the popular British talk show *Aspel & Company* he added, "I believe what it says in the scriptures and the Bhagavad Gita: 'Never was there a time when you did not exist, and there will never be a time when you cease to exist.' The only thing that changes is our bodily condition. . . . I feel him around here."

No one could blame George for wanting to transform the grim substance of John's execution into a declaration of rebirth. Eulogies were a sign of normality. Hope was what allowed you to get up the next day. But if martyrdom was the price for rising so high in this world, neither could anyone fault him for wondering if he would be next.

"He was by no means a recluse [before then]," remembered Monty Python founder Michael Palin. "We used to have a drink in a pub near his house. He didn't mind going there and mixing with people. After John was shot, that's when things changed. George became quite paranoid. He put barbed wire up around his home and retreated."

"It really shook him," recalled Mina Robb, whose husband, George, was a stonemason at Friar Park. "He used to say that if he landed after a flight, he'd come out onto the steps of the plane and wonder which person might have a gun."

The Beatles wanted only good for the world, and the world stalked them down. The post-Beatles George wanted only spiritual good for the world, and now he lived in fear of the same retribution visiting him. He needed some place to go where no one would find him.

A song George recorded around this time, "Sat Singing," describes his experience of leaving his body during meditation. It is midday. The sun shines in a clear blue sky. He sings of drifting away, with no memory of what has come before. An unseen lover appears in his heart. I am here for you, the lover says. Going deeper, the meditation awakens him from his dream of embodied life. Moving deeper still into his ecstasy, he senses himself drifting in a golden flow. In the undulating glow, he feels himself becoming part of the unseen lover. The song extends the moment of oneness through gently textured slide guitar and a lulling patter. Then, slowly, George emerges from his reverie and realizes he has been in a state of bliss for a long time. The sun is setting. There is no disappointment over losing the reverie, only joy. He calls his lover's name. If only he could return to that place, he would never regret leaving the world behind. He would gladly kiss it goodbye if he could just stay in his lover's company.

The title played on the Sanskrit term *sat-sang,* an abbreviation of *sadhu-sanga,* a term used in Hindu, Buddhist, Jain, and Sikh traditions to mean the company of holy people. In the company of holy people George had discovered meditation, prayer, knowledge of a reality beyond what his senses registered. Everything, even his friend John's death, could filter through that lens and assume at least a semblance of likable color. But it required effort and undisturbed quiet. Unrelenting persecution had finally driven him to the only places where he could still salvage an ounce of sanity: at home, with family, and inside himself. It would be several years before he emerged for more than short stretches from the cloistered security of Friar Park.

George's films did well, but his only album between 1982 and 1987, *Gone Troppo,* performed poorly and failed to make the *Billboard* chart. The songs gave the impression of a man in retreat, content to sway in a hammock and eat papaya, someone recording for his own pleasure rather than for a record-buying public.

People say I'm not what I used to be, he sang on "Mystical One." No matter, since I'm happier now than a willow tree. There wasn't much tooth to these vacationlike songs. Even the album's cover design lacked imagination, and any foray the songs did make into weightier topics came across as weak. With each birth our soul takes on a body, he sang in "Circles." Along life's road the soul reincarnates, round and round in circles. The lyrics bordered on indifference, their only discernible emotion a lament for the fate of a world gone mad.

"There's a point in me where it's beyond sad," he told his devotee friend Mukunda shortly after the album's release in 1982, "seeing the state of the world today. It's so screwed up. It's terrible. And it will be getting worse and worse." From the back patio of his home, they looked out on a lavish vista of nature restored by years of George's gardening. "More concrete everywhere, more pollution, more radioactivity—there's no wilderness left, no pure air. They're chopping the forests down. They're polluting all the oceans. I'm pessimistic about the future of the planet. These big guys don't realize that for everything they do there's a reaction. You have to pay. That's karma."

"Do you think there's any hope?" Mukunda asked.

"Manifest your own divinity first," George said. "The truth is there. It's right within us all. Understand what you are. If people would just wake up to what's real, there would be no misery in the world. I guess chanting is a pretty good place to start."

George had not lost sight of the spiritual journey revealed by Prabhupada, Vivekananda, Yogananda, and other teachers. His life's mission was still to know God, but in 1982, with a wife and four-year-old son to care for, he had other priorities. "When I was younger," he said, "with the aftereffects of the LSD that opened up something inside me in 1966, a flood of other thoughts came into my head, which led me to the yogis. At that time it was very much my desire to find out. It still is, though I have found out a lot. I've gone through the period of questioning and being answered, and I feel I've got to the point where there isn't anything really that I need to know. Maybe in my youth I was more exuberant about it. Now I've had more experience of it, and it's inside me. I don't talk about it that much."

In 1982, Paul McCartney commanded forty-six lines in the annual *Who's Who,* while George nestled in obscurity between 1950s rocker Bill Haley and entertainer Noel Harrison in the "Whatever Happened To" section of a pop nostalgia book.

The loss of status didn't bother him. "Some of the best songs that I know," he said, "are the ones I haven't written yet. And it doesn't even matter if I don't ever write them, because it's only small potatoes compared with the big picture."

But the farther sixties idealism faded into memory, the more adamantly fans insisted on keeping it alive by deifying their idols.

That year, Liverpool launched its first annual "Mersey Beatles Extravaganza" and renamed public thoroughfares George Harrison Close and John Lennon Drive. A Beatles museum, "Cavern Mecca," opened a short time later. A few months after that, Abbey Road Studios began Beatles tours of their premises. Beatlefest conventions spread across the United States. In 1984, New York City dedicated a Central Park memorial garden to John Lennon and named it Strawberry Fields. On March 9, scientists at the Anderson Mesa Station of the Lowell Observatory discovered a minor planet, which they named George Harrison 4149.

Each new "honor" stoked the flame of celebrity and threatened to consume George's most prized possession, privacy. That year, the *Los Angeles Daily News* reported his purchase of a California home, allegedly so hidden away it could only be accessed by helicopter. The farther away he could get, the better he felt.

"They're not interested in me as a human being," he told the *Australia Sun Times*. "They're only interested in the Beatles— what guitar I played on *Sergeant Pepper* and all that crap."

Shunned by music companies for his indifference to popular trends, abandoned by the record-buying public yet still hounded by graying baby boomers, all he wanted now at age forty-two was the one thing a celebrity-obsessed culture refused to grant: to be left alone. If people insisted on feeding their habit with his life's minutiae, he couldn't do much about it.

"I just have to accept that," he said. "Ex-Beatle George—it's just part of keeping the mundane world turning. . . . There's so much they've written about the Beatles that is wrong. It just shows me that most of the stuff I learned in school, in history, is just—I mean, if they're wrong about us now, and we haven't even died yet, just think what really happened to Christopher Columbus and all them people, you know. History must be totally twisted."

"I don't want to be a film star," he told the press in 1985. "I don't want to be a pop star. I just want to live in peace."

Later that year, George ventured out to browse in a Los Angeles record shop. CDs stood at attention in Plexiglas bins, each one bar-coded and protected by a hologram-encrypted safety strip. What a difference from the days when Brian Epstein stocked his store's wooden bins with vinyl records in cardboard jackets and taped little bits of sewing thread to the last copy of each record—his invention for knowing when inventory was running low.

A young woman glanced at George from across the aisle. "Look," she whispered to her friend, loud enough to be heard. "There's that singer."

However far from public view he may have receded, George would always be "that singer," and however much he enjoyed his privacy, he still loved playing with a band. When a band was in sync and fellow musicmakers intertwined their craft with his, it was the biggest high in the world, pure magic, and despite his hesitations about appearing in public, by the mid-eighties he was like the fisherman who had had his fill of rough tides but missed the smell of the sea.

The return to performance began in October 1985, when he was invited to appear with Ringo, Eric Clapton, and other musicians in a television salute to singer-songwriter Carl Perkins, one of George's early music heroes.

"If I ever want to get over my fear, my inhibitions about going on and playing," he said, "if I can't play Carl Perkins songs there's not much chance of me ever playing anything." The concert had George energized, exuberant, happy to be back in the fire, singing "Everybody's Trying to Be My Baby" and "Glad All Over."

He harnessed the energy from the Perkins celebration and produced his first album in years, *Cloud Nine,* released in 1987. The difference between this revitalized composer and the indifferent creator of *Gone Troppo* was, in the words of one music critic, "intergalactic." Gone were exhortations to chant and call upon the Lord, but gone, too, were the existential despair of *Dark Horse* and the indifference of *Extra Texture. Cloud Nine* featured driving rhythms, layers of crystal-clear guitarwork, and a wide range of well-polished musical motifs. More than one reviewer declared it his best album since *Living in the Material World.*

The album's title track invited listeners to accept his love, his smile, his heart, his hope, his jokes, and to leave aside any part of him that hurt or didn't fit. His lyrics sounded almost apologetic, as though excusing himself for his youthful proselytizing. In "That's What It Takes" he slightly altered the message of those early years. Instead of urging people to get free from the material world, he sang of needing to be "in this life together." Changing the world mattered less than seeing it clearly for what it is. In "Just for Today" he wished not only to escape life's problems but also not to *be* life's problem. Of the album's eleven songs, only one exuded sadness: "Someplace Else," the lament of a man who has finally found love and knows it can only last one lifetime. Even this wistful note was balanced by a promise to leave all sadness behind.

Cloud Nine rose to number nine in the U.S. top ten. One of its singles, a just-for-fun rocker called "Got My Mind Set on You," reached number one. *Billboard* magazine called the album "one of the greatest comebacks in rock history." At a promotional gathering, a reporter from *Melody Maker* magazine noted how George's lighthearted demeanor contrasted with the media's portrait of him as a sober, reclusive mystic. Mellowing into the celebratory mood with a few pints of Guinness, George offered loud and surprisingly frank observations about the Beatles.

"People think I did fuck-all in the band," he said with a chuckle, "but it wasn't true." Guests approached him for his autograph, and George obliged by signing not only his own name but also exact replicas of the other Beatles' signatures as well. He even signed "Bob Dylan" for one fan, leaving his admirer speechless.

"I was tagged as somber because I did some spiritual things," he told a reporter, "and sang a lot of songs about God or the Lord or whatever you want to call him. . . . I've got a very serious side of me, but even with that I always see the joke, too." To a reporter from *People* magazine he confided, "I still believe the purpose of our life is to get God-realization. There's a science that goes with that, the science of self-realization. It's still very much a part of my life, but it's sort of very personal, very private."

Three years after the Carl Perkins show, in spring 1988, George once again joined a band, teaming up with a few best friends to make great music and just have a good time. Like many of the most enjoyable moments in his life, this one happened without planning. He was in Los Angeles putting together tracks from his *Cloud Nine* album. Bob Dylan lived nearby, and George called to ask if he could use Dylan's garage recording studio. Jeff Lynne, who was coproducing the tracks, drove over and brought their mutual friend Roy Orbison. George had left his guitar at the home of Tom Petty a few nights before. George called, and Petty drove over with the guitar.

Dylan prepared a barbecue while the others jammed. Behind the garage door, George spied a cardboard box stenciled with the words HANDLE WITH CARE.

"Give us some lyrics, you famous lyricist," George said to Dylan, pointing to the box. Dylan improvised a few lines. George strummed a few chords and out came the group's first song, "Handle with Care."

Playing with his friends was fun and easy. They had no deadlines. They were under no pressure to perform. Songs rolled out one after another; the verses and harmonies were shared more or less equally among them. The group was spontaneous and silly, like quirky gremlins who made weird stuff happen during recording sessions—what they called "Wilburys." The Traveling Wilburys were born.

George and Roy Orbison had become friends in 1963 when the Texas-born singer headlined a European tour with the Beatles. Orbison, who was seven years older than George, had built a worldwide following in rock and roll with original love songs and a voice that seemed almost operatic by popular music standards. What struck George was the purity of Orbison's sound. While other bands, including the Beatles, used physicality to establish their presence onstage, Orbison stood stock-still in front of his microphone and commanded audience attention solely with the timbre of his voice and an astonishing three-octave range.

The Wilburys released their first album in October 1988 and it went double platinum, selling more than two million copies. In December, Orbison died of a heart attack. He was fifty-two.

"He was a sweet, sweet man," George told the press. "We loved Roy and still do." Not one to miss an opening, he added, "He's out there, really, his spirit. You know, life flows on within you and without you. He's around." The remaining Wilburys produced a second album, but only as a quartet. "You can't really replace somebody like Roy," George said. "For now, it's just us four." A short time later, the group disbanded; it just wasn't the same without Roy.

In the past, life's disappointments had made George miserable, something he'd expressed in songs such as "Isn't It a Pity" and "Art of Dying." But those were the expressions of a younger man writing before death became as familiar as it was now. Stuart Sutcliffe died when George was twenty-one, Brian Epstein two years later. George's mother passed away in 1969. The Beatles died in 1970, along with his marriage. His father passed away in 1977, Prabhupada later that same year. Now Orbison was gone, and George viewed death with greater dispassion: part of the fabric of things, something even to be welcomed. "Just think," Paramahansa Yogananda had written in the 1950s, "no more repaired tires on the body vehicle, no more patchwork living." Those with no knowledge of death may contemplate dying "with dread and sadness," Yogananda wrote, but those who have learned death's true meaning knew it as "a wondrous experience of peace and freedom."

When asked if he still missed John ten years after his death, at first George said no. "There's no point. It can happen to anybody. You can fall under a truck." Then he backtracked and said, "Yeah, we miss him. We miss him around because he was so funny." He had finished discussing death and he preferred revisiting a few fond memories.

"One of the disc jockeys," he said, "gave me a little bootleg. It was just the talking between songs, mainly John and Paul trying to get their harmonies right, but it's really funny. John says, 'Did you see that movie the other night?' And Paul says, 'What—Humph?' And John says, 'Yeah, Humph Boge.' And Paul says, 'Humph Boge's fab'—just real silly stuff like that. God knows how we got through all them years. It was just bedlam, really. It was madness."

By assimilating death with such ease, he wasn't surrendering to fate, he was merely being pragmatic. The body falls, the soul moves on. Why belabor the sadness? Remember the good parts. "We would walk around the grounds together," noted Derek Mann, who became head gardener at Friar Park in 1991. "Sometimes he would have a ukulele with him and play a few chords while we wandered around. There were a couple of spots in the garden where George would sit, watch the sun go down, and meditate. There I planted night-scented stock plants, which gave off a very strong perfume." George thanked him and said the fragrance reminded him of his mother, who used to plant the same flowers around their home in Speke. The heady fragrance evoked remembrances of loving parents, of a garden growing amid the rubble of war—of the good parts worth remembering.

Ever since John's murder, George had hesitated to perform in public. Memories of the *Dark Horse* tour and the misery it put him through had also conspired to keep him off the stage. But in 1991 Eric Clapton convinced him to come on tour once more, this time to Japan.

Clapton tendered the offer to perform together five years after he and Pattie had divorced. George never allowed their shared history with the same wife to mar their friendship. But touring? The thought of again going in front of an audience and again becoming an entertainer left him cold. If only he could be as simple as the legend of George Harrison concocted by fans. Climbing back onstage meant putting aside the frightening memories of Beatlemania, the bitterness of his last tour, the despair over John's murder. Why run those risks again?

Clapton assured him that playing together live in Japan would not be nearly as difficult or dangerous as Europe or America.

At a press conference in Tokyo prior to the tour, Clapton explained, "George can go onstage here and get over his stage fright without being right in the international spotlight."

How have you remained friends so long? asked a reporter. Clapton smiled.

"George has always been like the elder brother I never had— you're how old now? Seventy-nine?" he joked. "I've always respected his judgment and his values. He's a unique man."

"I knew that eventually I'd have to try it again," George said, "and I thought I'd better do it soon before I got too old to take the trouble. Besides, I wanted to stop smoking, and having to sing every night was the best motivation I could think of."

The series of Harrison-Clapton concerts started on December 14, 1991, in the Tokyo Dome. The fifty-six-thousand-seat auditorium sold out as soon as tickets went on sale, earning more than $10 million in a few hours. The tour comprised a dozen concerts over three weeks, and by his fourth performance the joy of live performance had returned. George even dressed for the occasion: a flashy black sequined jacket with black pants and a red shirt, reminiscent of the clothes Elvis wore when they had met twenty-six years before.

George walked out and began singing an old Beatles song, "I Want to Tell You," and the fans roared their approval. His voice was strong and self-assured. Next, he played a toe-tapper, "Old Brown Shoe," followed by yet another Beatles tune, "Taxman." Clapton appeared for a series of duets. For "My Sweet Lord" George doubled with the chorus, singing the mantras over and over and ending with a rousing cry of *"Jai Gurudev!"*—a Sanskrit salutation acknowledging all the teachers who had helped him progress on his spiritual path.

On the second night, George surprised everyone with a rock-out encore of "Roll Over, Beethoven." Thirteen-year-old Dhani walked onstage, grabbed a tambourine, and joined in the chorus. As the song ended, George put an arm around his son, and they strolled off as the cheers mounted behind them.

* * *

By the early 1990s, meditation had become a daily necessity for George. After the *Dark Horse* tour, his daily practices had dwindled in a fog of drugs, parties, all-night recording sessions, and business woes. The ensuing despiar forced him to recognize, "Jesus, I've got to do something here." And that was when he remembered. "What about meditation? I had forgotten totally that that's what it was all about—to release the stress out of your system."

He compared his need for daily meditation to a drinker's need to attend an Alcoholics Anonymous program. Meditation was something that had become necessary "to keep myself focused and keep the buoyancy, the energy, and also to realize that all this stuff that's going on is just bullshit. It's hard to be able to not let that get next to you."

"All this stuff" had recently included the Persian Gulf War, Rajiv Gandhi's assassination by terrorists, the collapse of the Soviet Union, and genocide in the former Yugoslavia. America's highest-grossing films that year were *Terminator 2* and *Silence of the Lambs.* The world had bought into a culture of death, and none of England's major politicians had the courage to call it a spiritual crisis.

On April 6, 1992, in London's Royal Albert Hall, a benefit concert was held for the Natural Law Party, a political group formed by the Maharishi's followers, and George agreed to play. He also contributed a statement that was passed out before the concert. "I will vote for the Natural Law Party," the statement read, "because I want a total change and not just a choice between left and right. The system we have now is obsolete and is not fulfilling the needs of the people."

He harbored no illusions about a student of the Maharishi actually winning a national election, just as he had not expected the Concert for Bangladesh to bring peace to a war-torn nation. It was sufficient to "do his bit," knowing that over time little drops of water could wear away a mountain.

That evening he sang to a warm, receptive audience. Any doubts about meditation's impact on his talent were laid to rest as one hit after another rolled off his guitar. The applause was deafening. His self-doubts, though, once again came out.

"Thank you very much," he told the audience. "It really overwhelms me, you know. I'm always really paranoid about whether people like me, I don't know." Even in 1992, after a quarter century of meditation and yoga, he was haunted by insecurity.

"You always seem very self-deprecating about your songwriting," said one reporter.

"Self-deprecating," George repeated. "The story of my life."

The insecurity surfaced again later that year. In Los Angeles to receive *Billboard* magazine's first ever Century Award for musical achievement, George stared out at a packed audience in the University Amphitheatre, with television cameras rolling, and said, "I don't know why I got it, somebody like me. Bob Dylan should get one, too."

Dark Horse concert drummer Andy Newmark commented that George's insecurity also emerged during shows. "He was a worrier. He would turn to musicians he invited to play with him and want to know, 'Do you like this? Are you having fun?' If something was wrong, he would wonder, 'What have I done wrong?' In day-to-day stuff, he could be quite jittery."

A short time later, according to a report by journalist David Quantick, George visited the Maharishi and asked that he forgive him and his friends for how they had behaved in Rishikesh. "We were very young," George said.

The Maharishi replied that the Beatles were "angels in disguise" and that there was nothing to forgive. "I could never be upset with angels," he said.

The Natural Law Concert on behalf of the Maharishi's candidate for president was the last full-length program George performed in his life.

13

Sacred Ground

Where's the big man?
—*George, 1996*

It was June 1993, twenty years since George had purchased Bhaktivedanta Manor for Prabhupada and his disciples. Gurudas, Mukunda, and Shyamsundar arrived in England to join in the anniversary celebration mounted by British devotees and their growing congregation. They also came to have their first reunion with George in more than a decade. On a sunny morning they drove out to Friar Park. George embraced each one, staring at deep trenches in familiar faces. He nodded with pride at Mukunda's saffron swami robes and shaved head. He circled Gurudas, now huge with a scruffy beard and a head of hair resembling Einstein's.

"Ten years," Gurudas managed through tears.

Appraising George's sweatshirt and togs and plucking at a lock of his graying hair Shyamsundar asked, "How are you, Dad?" The two old friends hugged and laughed over the signs of aging.

They stumbled into the vestibule, fumbled with laces, tumbled through the vaulted entry, and stopped. Immaculate forty-foot-high beamed ceilings, gleaming stained-glass windows, panels of ancient oak polished to a mirror sheen—the restoration George had achieved since their last visit was magnificent.

Above a massive stone fireplace hung life-size photographs of Yogananda and Vivekananda. Bric-a-brac peppered the spacious living room: ukeleles, songbooks, vases of fresh-cut flowers, tapestries and Turkish rugs, statuettes and photographs. Across the vast room stood an old Wurlitzer jukebox. George played guide, pointing to this and that, clowning with the instruments. Then he opened the glass doors and they took a tour of the grounds. The guests marveled at all that had been done and at the many varieties of trees and flowers George had planted.

George showed them his racing cars. Looking at one up close, the devotees noticed tiny Hare Krishna mantras painted across the entire body. Racing was dopey to a lot of people, George admitted, but good racing involved heightened awareness, he said. As far as he could tell, the best drivers had had some sort of expansion of consciousness.

As they walked, they yearned to ask George about Krishna in his life now that Prabhupada had passed on. He sensed their curiosity and steered the conversation back toward them. "What's it like now at the temple? Many devotees?"

"Hundreds," Shyamsundar said. "They've come from all over for the anniversary celebration. The new ones are so bright and shining. We're old-timers now. It's definitely the graying of the Hare Krishna movement." He nodded at the others, saying how good it was to see them again. When it hit, that sense of having lapsed, it hit hard. "I'm not a very good example anymore," Shyamsundar said. The gravel crunched under their shoes as they walked toward a lake shimmering in the distance. "I mean, I feel like an impostor compared to those pure souls. All the new kids ask us questions about Prabhupada and what it was like in the old days, but my memory's shot. I can't even remember how to tie my friggin' dhoti." He tugged at the cloth robe around his waist.

"Yeah," George responded, acknowledging the reality of growing older. They walked some more.

"What about you, George?" Gurudas asked. "You still chanting and all that?"

It wasn't a small question somehow, despite casualness in the asking. From the beginning of their friendship, George had known Gurudas to make simple statements that carried critical weight. "Washing your hands is like chanting," Gurudas had told him at their first meeting, "a cleansing process." And now an offhand inquiry about chanting, on which so much rested.

George looked off at nothing in particular. "I have my little ..." He turned to them, faking a serious expression with knitted brow, and in a deep comic voice said, "moments of doubt." Then he laughed. "Yeah, I try to chant and meditate a little every day. It's easier for me here. Or in Maui, with the gardens and the peace."

They walked on, everyone chanting softly on beads, and passed by the miniature Matterhorn that Sir Frankie Crisp had installed on the Friar Park property. When the devotees had first seen it back in 1970, the hill hardly had any grass growing on it. Now it overflowed with shrubs and plants.

"When you go back to Vrindavan," Gurudas told George, "you must visit Govardhan Hill." He reminded George of a story from *KRSNA Book* that recounted how Krishna once displayed his mystic powers by lifting Govardhan Hill as a giant umbrella to protect the people of Vrindavan from torrential rains sent by demigod Indra.

Turning a corner of the Friar Park property, the group came upon a fountain featuring a life-size carving of Shiva that George had purchased from devotee sculptors in Los Angeles. Gurudas took photos of the gang with George's castle looming in the background. It was a feel-good day. The Om flag flew from the castle tower. They played hide-and-seek like kids in the topiaries. Gurudas got lost in a tangle of bamboo. George reached in and pulled him out. "Beware the hand of Maya!" he cried. As they continued on around the grounds, he impressed everyone by rattling off the names of each plant in Latin: *romneya* and *echinacea* and *cercis canadensis*.

They walked on, crossing a little wooden bridge that spanned a stream. "Which is the reality and which is the illusion?" George asked Gurudas, pointing to a reflection of Friar Park in the pond.

Gurudas snapped a photo while reciting a verse from the Bhagavad Gita that described the material world as a reflection of the spiritual world. "It looks the same," Gurudas said, "but the material world is only a shadow of true reality. It can get entangling if you confuse the two."

The four men leaned on the bridge's wooden railing and stared across at the sun gradually setting behind George's manor in the distance. George noticed that Shyamsundar seemed worried and asked what was the matter.

The American sighed. His wife, he said, had waited until they were driving to the airport to tell him that she was filing for divorce and leaving home. There was a long pause, then the group looked at one another from the corner of their eyes and burst out laughing. The material world. What a dump. As if on cue, they applied the secret formula for rising above it all: Monty Python.

"You think *you've* got problems?" Gurudas chided, stabbing a finger toward Shyamsundar. "At least you *have* a home. When I was growing up we were so poor we lived in a cardboard *box*."

"A box? You had a *box*?" said another. "At least you had a *box*. When *we* were growing up, we were so poor all we had was a *hole* in the ground."

"A *hole*? You had a *hole*?" George retorted.

In the last light of day, they headed back. The party moved to the dining room, where Olivia had prepared vegetarian treats and tea. Gurudas and Olivia talked about yoga and spirituality. George's son, Dhani, and a few teenage school chums showed up lugging amplifiers. They had formed a rock band. Shyamsundar helped move the equipment to an upstairs practice room. The devotees expressed amazement at how much the son resembled the father. George smiled. The similarities extended beyond the physical. Dhani shared his passion for motor racing, and they enjoyed many of the same friends, including his Monty Python mates.

George's spiritual beliefs had made their impact as well, through gentle reminders to his son that "you're not that body" and time shared chanting.

The guests reminisced. George mentioned the trouble he had had getting people to hear his spiritual message but acknowledged that the preaching part of his life was behind him now. "I'd rather just sit in my garden and chant."

Olivia talked about her work on behalf of children orphaned by civil strife in Romania. A visit to shelters in the battle-weary country had left her overwhelmed and shocked. With help from friends, she had raised more than $1 million in relief funds. Mukunda reciprocated with a description of Food for Life, a program fellow devotees had organized in Bosnia. Deep inside the war zone, devotee chefs prepared nutritious meals and delivered them to thousands of locals stranded during periods of fierce fighting. They agreed that spirituality needed to make a tangible difference in the world.

Mukunda remembered a gift he had brought. He dashed out to the car and returned with copies of a huge book called *Krishna Art.*

"This is for you, George, and a couple more copies for friends."

George's eyes lit up as he examined large oil paintings of Krishna in his many pastimes. One painting depicted infant Krishna hiding from his mother, Yasoda. Another showed child Krishna playing with his cowherd boy friends. In another, Krishna danced with Radha. The *KRSNA Book,* which he had financed twenty years before, had given rise to an entire school of transcendental artists who contributed to the oversized volume of paintings.

George's friend and the former press agent for the Beatles, Derek Taylor, arrived carrying a box of videos. Taylor was overseeing production of *The Beatles Anthology,* an ambitious ten-hour retrospective, and had rough cuts to show.

At first George had been a reluctant participant in the documentary. Bob Smeaton, who conducted interviews for the series and took part in determining its content, favored revealing all there was to reveal about the Beatles, including scenes of arguments that led to their dissolution. "I'll play whatever you want me to play," George was saying in one of the clips.

"Oh, we don't want to say that," George said in an edit session. "I hate that. I hate that period."

"Yeah, but the fans want to see it," Smeaton said. "They've never seen it before, George."

When it came to showing footage of their time in Rishikesh and explaining rumors about the Maharishi that prompted their departure, George said, "Look, Bob, it's bullshit, that whole thing. You shouldn't even pay lip service to it, because if you do, you're saying that it's true. That thing didn't happen, despite what people have said. I was there. And if you put that sort of stuff in there, all you're doing is sensationalizing something. If you talk about something, people will think it really happened."

Eventually George warmed to the project, seeing that it offered a chance for him and John and Paul and Ringo to talk about their music and tell their story in their own words.

The devotees followed George and Derek into a study. Derek pushed the start button on a VCR, and a photo of a boyish Ringo appeared on-screen. "My dad made cakes," Ringo said in voice-over, "but he left us when I was three. After that, I'd sing 'Nobody's Child' and that would make my mum cry." George appeared on-camera talking about his childhood. Photos dissolved on and off: there he was as a boy in Liverpool, playing his first guitar, emerging from a swim at age eleven, posing for a school photo at age twelve in tie and jacket, his hair piled high over a baby-faced grin. Paul's voice came on, saying how he always used to talk down to George because he was younger and how it probably was a failing of his to have done that. George appeared on-camera, interviewed just a few weeks before, confirming that Paul was indeed nine months older than he.

"Even now," he said, "he's *still* nine months older."

On the floor above, Dhani and his friends let loose with a decent rendition of Jimi Hendrix's "Purple Haze." George smiled proudly. "Like father, like son," Gurudas mused.

To top off their visit, the group retired to a quieter room for a bit of kirtan. George grabbed a ukulele and strummed verses of "Govinda," then played a few new tunes. They gathered around the jukebox to hear old favorites: Radha Krishna Temple singles, some Slim Whitman numbers about lonesome trains and cattle, a Bob Dylan eulogy to Woody Guthrie. George looked up, dreamy-eyed. "Bobby Dylan. He's greater than Shakespeare."

No one wanted to break up the party, so they listened to record after record, sprawled on the stairs, stretched out on the floor, and kept each other's company late into the night.

For years, George had spoken with his devotee friends about taking a trip together to Vrindavan, the village southeast of Delhi where Krishna had appeared five thousand years before. In April 1996 George flew to Madras, South India to record an album of traditional Indian songs and mantras with Ravi Shankar. Taking advantage of his proximity to Krishna's birthplace, George met up with Mukunda and Shyamsundar at the Taj Hotel in New Delhi, and the following morning they set out for India's holiest of holy places.

George looked back from the front seat of their taxi, chatting excitedly about the Vedic chants he was recording with Ravi and telling stories about the last time he had visited Vrindavan, all the while mimicking the driver's wild attempts to speed through crowded intersections and marketplaces. Time passed quickly as they jerked and jolted their way through the three-hour ride. The taxi arrived at the outskirts of Vrindavan, where cars and trucks trickled out in an imitation of rush hour. There was nothing of interest in Vrindavan for businesspeople, no matters of consequence or reasons for noisy traffic, and the group fell silent. Sound here traveled through filters of heat and light and ethereal space and entered the ear so spare and clean that birdcalls seemed muted, footsteps padded.

To the uninitiated, Vrindavan looked like a neglected village. Skinny dogs and mischievous monkeys scampered down its dusty roads. Loudspeakers blared kirtans from dilapidated temples. Ramshackle buses belched diesel fumes and honked weakly at creaking bullock carts that blocked crossings. Nonbelievers considered Vrindavan too hot during the day, too cold at night, and its residents too ignorant of how the real world operated. Believers, though, saw the village's hidden dimension: Vrindavan was the spiritual world. Sixteenth-century scholar Viswanath Chakravarty had written that a devotee whose eyes were smeared with "the ointment of love" saw Vrindavan as "resplendent with exotic trees blossoming with fruits and flowers, splendid ponds and lakes replete with multicolored lotus flowers, swans, and waterbirds, earth overflowing with precious gems, and trees and bushes made of gold and crystal."

In the sixteenth century, Chaitanya's followers had developed the holy town and restored its many places of pilgrimage to rustic dignity. By the time of George's visit, the population had grown to thirty-five thousand full-time residents. Once, thirty years before, Prabhupada lived alone in a tiny room on the grounds of Vrindavan's Radha Damodar Temple. He had left India on a tramp steamer in 1965, and after four years of vigorous preaching in America and Europe returned to Vrindavan with his first Western disciples. He predicted that many pilgrims would visit in years to come and wanted them to be comfortable. With Gurudas and his wife, Yamuna, leading the effort, he constructed a white marble temple and guesthouse. Five thousand temples, some no bigger than a hole in the wall, decorated the roads and lanes of this small village, but residents considered Prabhupada's Krishna Balaram Temple to be the most beautiful.

Two blocks from the temple stood a white three-story villa owned by Prithu Das, one of Prabhupada's most senior German disciples. Prithu had invited George and his devotee friends to stay with him during their visit.

The taxi caromed down narrow alleys and screeched to a halt at the head of a footpath leading to Prithu's villa. The husky, shaven-headed fifty-year-old came quickly up the path, holding the edge of his robes in one hand and reaching out with the other to take George's suitcase. George waved him off.

"Why should a big man carry his own bag?" Prithu joked.

"That's true," George agreed. "But where's the big man?"

The group entered the villa and parked their bags in a hallway lined with potted plants. It was too late to begin their pilgrimage that day, and someone suggested they plan tomorrow's itinerary from the roof. The group made their way up a scrubbed stone staircase. From the flat roof, they gazed out on orchards of flame trees grouped in giant orange clusters. Ornate temple domes rose in the distance. The sun began its descent behind hills and trees. Prithu pointed a camera and waved the threesome into a clutch.

George put his arm around Mukunda and Shyamsundar. George laughed, shook the hair back from his eyes, and raised his cotton bead bag above his head. "Still Krishna after all these years," he called out.

The day had been long. They bowed to one another, recited prayers of thanks, and George trudged off to his room. All-night kirtan singers kept vigil in temples lit with candles, while in the forest, tradition held, Krishna and the Gopis danced in the moonlight.

By 11:00 A.M. the next day, George still could not rouse himself from bed. Then he heard someone tinkering in the hallway and investigated: a thermos of Earl Grey tea sat steaming outside his door. The elixir worked wonders, and soon he emerged from his room in crisp white cotton pants and kurta shirt, his *tulsi*-bead necklace tight around his neck, his bead bag strapped to his right hand, eager to start the day. He joined his friends, and they went off in a bicycle rickshaw. First stop was Prabhupada's *samadhi,* the domed marble memorial beneath which the teacher's body lay buried.

The *samadhi* had been built alongside the Krishna Balaram temple, and as they approached, pilgrims came and went, pointing to details in the carved marble facade. The friends entered, bowed to the *samadhi,* and sat in a row, chanting quietly on their beads. George closed his eyes. He opened them after a moment and said softly, "To think that Prabhupada is right here." He stared into space and whisked away a tear with his bead bag. "Starting to get a little misty. Shall we go down to Starbucks for a double cappuccino?" he joked.

The group piled into a bicycle rickshaw and jumbled their way down Vrindavan's narrow streets. Arriving at Radha Damodar

Temple, they bent down to enter Prabhupada's tiny room. Outside the room's one small window they spied fragrant eucalyptus and tamal trees. Residents considered Vrindavan's trees to be evolved souls that were undergoing a last incarnation before returning to the spiritual world. The trees outside Prabhupada's room had been rubbed smooth by caresses from pilgrims over the years. The visitors imagined what it must have been like for Prabhupada, approaching seventy, to have looked out this window and contemplated leaving Vrindavan for an unfamiliar and inhospitable Western world. Why had he done it? And if he had not come, what would their fate have been?

George chanted furiously on his beads. Instruments provided for visitors lined one wall. Prithu pumped a portable harmonium and began singing. Mukunda picked up a mridanga drum and kept time. George tapped a brass gong with a stick. They sang the old standard Hare Krishna melody. As the tempo built, the mystery overcame them, where they were, how the most secret of all secrets had come to England and America, how little they had done to deserve being invited into the heart of that secret, how their lives had been saved, the impossibility of it, feeling deeply the inadequacies that kept them from seeing God, from realizing the bliss of his love.

The kirtan ended. There was a long silence. Tears flowed down their cheeks.

"It was only a moment," Shyamsundar recalled, "but Prabhupada was really there. And we felt his love for us and his pleasure at seeing us all together."

They strolled around the town of five thousand temples. George and his friends walked by a group of singers seated roadside. The lead singer stretched his hand toward heaven. The Gopis—cowherd women—hear Krishna's flute, he sang in Braj, the local language, and run to him in the dead of night. Krishna multiplies himself into an equal number of Gopis so that each Gopi may be happy believing she alone dances with her beloved. In that moment of pleasure, the Gopis become proud and Krishna disappears from their sight and the cowherd women go mad from separation.

George did not speak Braj, but he understood the gist of what the man was singing—sorrow and yearning were universal. Yet there was nothing irreconcilable about the man's sadness, for in the next moment the group broke into rapid drums and a joyous chorus. People stood and danced, hands above their heads, then swooped down, executing slow turns, then rose again with a jump. No one led; the waxing and waning rhythms and spontaneous dance came from intuition. There seemed to be no logical sequence to their actions. This was a display without notation or orchestration and, in that sense, not a performance at all—simply hearts drifting on waves of devotion, a song that would never be repeated exactly the same way.

George and his friends moved down the road. It was a long time before anyone spoke. They passed one kirtan, then another. Temple bells mingled with drums and bells, clappers and clapping. The world seemed afloat in music. Spirit for the people of Vrindavan was not a weekly class or a weekend retreat—they breathed it in at every moment and breathed it out in song.

George's party descended an embankment and arrived at the Yamuna River. After haggling with a dispatcher over price for a rowboat and guide, they drifted along Vrindavan's sacred waterfront, identifying temples and the ruins of ancient palaces. George sang out, "Rollin', rollin', rollin' on the riv-v-ver." Packs of red-rumped monkeys shadowed their cruise, leaping and swinging from stone parapets and balconies along the shore. Mukunda pointed out some huge turtles lounging in the sun, and the three Westerners debated what the turtles ate. Dead bodies, they guessed.

They disembarked and made their way down narrow streets and alleyways. A wrinkled old man sat on his haunches while tinkering with an ancient bicycle. A huddle of little boys coaxed water from a creaky iron pump. With his video camera, George traced their faces and captured images of architectural oddities. "Look at this," he called out, focusing on a doorway painted a rainbow of colors.

In a hovel promoting itself as a "God Shop," the group examined deities and items of worship: brass trays, copper water pots, carved wooden incense holders. A gaunt shopkeeper, his mouth stained red with betel juice, squatted beside his wares and haggled the price with George and Prithu for three-foot-high marble deities of Radha and Krishna.

They arrived back at Krishna Balaram Temple by three o'clock. An American man about thirty walked up to George and put his arms around him.

"Your song 'My Sweet Lord' turned my life around," he said, choking back tears.

"Well," George said glancing down, thankful for moments like this that made up for court cases and charges of plagiarism, "it's nice to have been of use sometimes."

The temple hall was filled with devotees waiting for the altar doors to open. "Let's do some service," George suggested, "and sing for them." They sat with half dozen other devotees in a shaded portico before the altar and sang "Hare Krishna." At first a pensive expression creased George's face. "Headache," he claimed. Then, as the kirtan built and resonated in the vast marble temple, he closed his eyes and his voice swelled with an intensity and beauty that his friends had not heard before.

In the temple that day was a young American woman named Karnamrita, who had come to India to study classical singing. From childhood she had played George's recording "Hare Krishna Mantra" and knew its every nuance by heart. Hearing a voice that sounded like a young Yamuna's, George opened his eyes. He turned to Karnamrita and smiled, gesturing for her to sit next to him. Together they sang as the London crew had sung thirty years before. The torch was passing to a new generation, one that might do better than their parents at setting the world aright.

"He made me feel like we were all simple devotees chanting for Krishna," Karnamrita recalled. "I've been around gurus all my life. They're supposed to be, you know, different. Nothing like that came to mind being with George. We were just absorbed in chanting. I was just in the temple room, in Vrindavan, George was there, and we were chanting."

It was dusk, and a smudge of light rimmed temple roofs. The friends gathered in the living room of Prithu's home, talking and listening to tapes of Prabhupada lecturing and of devotional music from around the world. George picked up a guitar and strummed for a while, singing snippets of his own songs and a smattering of others, such as Dylan's "In Every Grain of Sand." The group had rediscovered a lost paradise in Vrindavan, and even if only for a few days the demands of a world growing more and more material were left behind.

On the day of their departure, George and his friends packed, thanked Prithu for his hospitality, mounted a taxi, and set out for Delhi. The taxi rocked from side to side and hit every pot-hole. Temples and forests gave way to roads and fields. Farmers worked with their dhotis tucked up between their legs and turbans wrapped around their heads against a hazy afternoon sun. Trees and bowers yielded to low-lying scrub brush and then to crumbling concrete roads. Delhi was in the throes of a thick, steamy rush hour. Perhaps it had been a dream. Maybe they had never been away at all. Or perhaps it had been real, and it was only now that they were falling into a dream.

The driver lost his way in a circle of traffic and drove into a motor scooter. Drivers jumped out in the middle of a crowded street, yelling and shaking their fists. The Harrison party sat silently, waiting for the brouhaha to end. It was an abrupt reentry into the material world.

From the backseat, George sighed. "Say, one of you blokes wouldn't have a smoke, would you?"

Everyone laughed.

Inspired by his visit to Vrindavan, George assembled musicians at Friar Park to finish the work that he and Ravi Shankar had begun in Madras on *Chants of India*. The album was unlike anything either had done before. It was to be a collection of mantras sung according to traditions extending back before recorded history. For Ravi, *Chants of India* posed what he called "one of the most difficult challenges in my life."

For *Chants of India,* George and Ravi intended to step back away from their own extraordinary musical abilities and allow *Nada Brahma,* God in sound, to flow unimpeded. Their job was not to produce an album but rather to create an environment in which sacred sound could emerge. The music had come down through the ages in oral tradition, improvised and with no written notation; as far as collective cultural memory would allow, George and Ravi would record original melodies. The repetition of such chants "would invoke a special power within oneself," Ravi explained. With help from a Sanskrit scholar, Ravi chose fourteen chants for peace and harmony among nature and all creatures. He selected one verse from the Bhagavad Gita, composed three original musical interludes, and wrote one original prayer.

The sessions took place in the warmth and hospitality of Friar Park. From their positions on the carpet of George's drawing room, the musicians and singers looked out tall French windows onto manicured gardens. Cables from microphones and video cameras snaked across the floor and up the wooden staircase to a studio where the engineers kept track of the session on television monitors.

The album opened with a single tambura drone. The chorus entered and offered an invocation to elephant-headed Ganesh, the deity who removes all obstacles. Next came a prayer to Saraswati, "blessed presiding deity of learning," and another prayer honoring the guru as an incarnation of God's compassion. These opening prayers shared a common message: do not neglect those who help you, even if they are unseen.

The next track offered musical instructions from a teacher to disciples preparing to enter the world. You may achieve everything this world has to give, the guru sang, but if you multiply the happiness of those worldly achievements one hundred times, and then multiply this number again one hundred times, and again and again, still you cannot calculate even the smallest fraction of happiness known by those who have realized their oneness with the Supreme.

As the album unfolded, a cello provided a handful of notes, a chorus sang, and a violin echoed the music of their prayer. There were few solos, none lasting more than a moment; the artists maintained a modest place in service to the prayers, and the chorus sang as one voice, without harmonies. The tracks that followed called for unity among people of the world, praised life in its many forms, and reminded listeners that all creation is interconnected.

George played on each track and occasionally sang with the chorus. He overdubbed instruments, mixed the voices, and submitted the results to Ravi for his review. It was an ultimate offering to his seventy-seven-year-old teacher, a man George credited with lifting his life to a realm of sacred sound and setting him on a course to God. The result was more than Ravi had dared hope.

"Fantastic," Ravi said, shaking his head. The recording gave him "goose bumps and a deep spiritual awareness."

A few days later, finished master in hand, George approached Ravi and embraced him with tears in his eyes. After half a century of mortal life, George had moved at last from the sounds of war to the sounds of peace. "Thank you," he said, "for this music."

When asked later about the album by an interviewer from VH-1, George said, "I believe in the thing I read years ago in the Bible. It said, 'Knock and the door will be opened.' And it's true. If you want to know anything in this life, you just have to knock on the door. . . . That's really why for me this record is important, because it's another little key to open within each individual. Just sit and turn off your old mind, relax and float downstream and listen to something that has its roots in transcendence. The words of these songs carry a very subtle spiritual vibration that goes beyond the intellect, really. If you let yourself be free . . . it can have a very positive effect."

Chants of India was warmly received, although in terms of sales it made hardly a dent compared to those of reissued Beatles albums. "In 1996," the London *Observer* wrote, "The Beatles have achieved what every group since them has failed to do—become bigger than the Beatles." By November 1996, more of the group's records had been sold that year than in any year of their entire working career. In addition, sales of the newly compiled *Anthology* albums had surpassed more than twenty million copies. In the eyes of the world, despite thirty years since the group's last concert, George was still a Beatle.

In July 1997, George was outside, gardening. The sun shone brightly, and as he reached up to wipe sweat from his neck he felt a lump. In early August, he underwent surgery. Doctors removed several enlarged lymph nodes through a small incision. A biopsy revealed that the nodes were malignant. Most people hearing that cancer has invaded their body progress through a series of documented stages, denial and anger among them. George went back to his garden, chanting and planting.

A few days later, light rain fell on the rolling hills of Hertfordshire. George was planting trees when he heard a car coming up the approach. He mounted a tiny golf cart and tooled silently across the lawn and around the corner of his towering Gothic manor in time to see his old friend Shyamsundar parking a battered Vauxhall by the front staircase. George knew he had changed—he saw it in the American's eyes as he assessed George's grayer hair and heavier jowls. In the thirty years they'd known each other, George had gone from a skinny beam of kinetic energy to a middle-aged meditator. The American smiled and waved but seemed nervous, uncertain perhaps over how George would be toward someone who no longer lived the full-time devotee life. George gave him a reassuring smile, and they embraced.

"What's it been?" George said warmly. "How long since we were together in Vrindavan?" He watched Shyamsundar's trepidation melt away. A quick moment of small talk and they were back to their jovial selves. George tossed out wry remarks, and his old buddy encouraged him with a laugh.

Shyamsundar looked at George's frayed Levi's and mud-spattered rain boots. "Quite the country squire these days," he said, then, pointing to the tiny golf cart, asked, "Where's the MacLaren?" George's purchase of the exclusive sports car had been big news a few years back. Only two were manufactured each year, at a sticker price of $750,000 and a top speed of 235 miles per hour.

"Oh, it's out back, but this is all I need these days," George said, pointing to the cart. "I don't go to London anymore."

They walked the grounds. Shyamsundar glanced up into a massive oak and stopped. Staring down at them were life-size carvings of Krishna, Prabhupada, Yogananda, Yukteshwar, and other spiritual guides laminated into the tree trunk. George said he came here some mornings to sit and chant. "Shall we have a look round the garden?" he said. "There's something I want to show you."

George motioned him into the electric golf cart. "Please buckle up," he ordered. "Put away your tray tables and bring your seat to the upright position." Off they went at a breakneck five miles per hour. The tiny cart chugged past lakes where swans visiting from the nearby Thames River silently glided by, over fairy-tale bridges, around statues and gazebos. Rhododendrons in full bloom bobbed gently in the summer drizzle. Shyamsundar noted spots where they had played together thirty years before and marveled at how much work George had done since then. They puttered past a Japanese garden decorated with sundials, dwarf pines, and willows. They gazed at a Polynesian glen choked with bamboo thickets and flowers of brilliant hue. Their cart topped a slight rise, and through a rainy mist they looked down on a small rustic cabin.

"I come here to chant and meditate and listen to music," George said. Rain fell in sheets now as they dashed inside. Sliding glass doors along one wall opened onto a stand of pine trees.

George opened the door and lit incense that mingled with wet forest smells. Half the room was taken up by a platform bed covered with an ornate embroidered quilt. A potbellied woodstove radiated heat from a corner. Along one wall stood a large wooden box. He opened the box, which held a CD player and boxes of CDs, grabbed a CD, and put it in the player.

"Remember this?"

The opening bars to George's recording of "Hare Krishna Mantra" spilled out of speakers mounted on walls. The two friends sprawled out on the quilt and laughed over old memories. George reached over and changed the music. Out came melodic voices from his latest recording of traditional Sanskrit chants. Then he switched to some bluesy numbers by Slim Whitman, a few Dylan classics, and a taste of stand-up from Lenny Bruce. George put on a tape of Ravi playing a rainy-afternoon raga, and the two friends chatted about how the world had been treating them over the years.

"What's all this about some cancer thing?" the American asked, trying to sound as casual as possible. "I saw something in a newspaper."

George pulled down the collar of his shirt to reveal a tiny pucker in his neck. "You know, they told me at the clinic I had a small malignant, this tiny spot, and they could cut it out, and I thought, Why bother? I don't really care about sticking around this material world any longer than I have to. I mean—I didn't even want to tell anyone, just let it go. I had it removed, but really there's nothing, I mean, I've done it all, I've had it all."

"No more material fantasies?"

George chuckled. "No. No more gigs on Dave Letterman's show. I'll just go now, anytime, doesn't matter. I'm ready, Krishna, whenever you want to pull the plug. I just want to be with—I mean, can you just imagine the spiritual sky."

George fell silent and saw in his friend's face the same anticipation over moving on that inspired him. Was this what the scriptures had been talking about? When yogis of the Himalayas spent years in caves preparing to see God, was this what they felt?

George lowered his eyes. Raindrops played gently on the roof of the hut.

"You're there, George," Shyamsundar managed softly. "You made it."

"Yeah, well," George said.

*   *   *

A few weeks later, George underwent surgery for a suspected recurrence of throat cancer, followed by several weeks of radiation therapy. "I didn't really relate to it, to be honest," he said. It was other events he found hard to reconcile. Shortly after the surgery, his old friend Derek Taylor died of throat cancer. Three months after that, his guitar hero Carl Perkins also died of throat cancer. Less than three months after that, Paul McCartney's wife, Linda, died of breast cancer at age fifty-six. "The Beatles had an expression," Paul told the press shortly after her death, "something will happen. That's about as far as I get philosophically. There's no point mapping out next year. Fate is much more magical."

Whether the litany of deaths was magical, karmic, or just sad, George saw in them a reminder of mortality and a need to make every moment count. When Ringo asked him that month to compose guitar music for a new song, "King of Broken Hearts," George put his own heart into it. One reviewer would later describe his beautiful slide guitar work as "sharing a little of his soul . . . [a] moving musical statement [that] spoke of the musician's inner peace."

George sent the tape off by mail. Ringo took the package to his recording studio and sat with his hands behind his head, listening to an unexpected poetry of notes.

"You're killing me, George," he mumbled. "You've got me crying, you bugger."

In September 1997, Gurudas sent George a letter expressing love for his old friend and admitting to distress over reports of his cancer. George wrote back to thank him and offered words of reassurance. I don't feel as bad as the newspapers make out, he wrote. Besides, there was always the gardening to make him feel better. "See you soon," he signed off, "somewhere."

George returned to the hospital for observation in January 1998 and again in May. Doctors reassured him that the cancer had not recurred.

* * *

By the end of the year, the three remaining Beatles were the third-highest-paid entertainers in the world, behind Oprah Winfrey and Steven Spielberg. Sales figures released that month confirmed the Beatles to be the most successful recording act in history. An online religion began, called Beatlism, exhorting followers to get in touch with their "inner Georgeness" and "inner Ringo." Press coverage of the resurgent Beatlemania grew exponentially, and incursions into George's private life increased.

Thieves climbed a ten-foot wall at Friar Park, evaded security cameras, and stole two bronze busts valued at a total of £50,000. In December, a deranged woman broke into the Harrison retreat in Hawaii and made herself at home eating pizza and doing laundry until police arrived to take her away. "I thought I had a psychic connection with George," she told them.

George learned that Michael Jackson, who had quietly purchased the Beatles music library, was licensing "Drive My Car" for use in a car commercial. George lamented that unless something was done to stop the exploitation, every Beatle song would end up advertising bras and pork pies. "The history of the Beatles was that we tried to be tasteful with our records and with ourselves," he said. "We could have made millions of extra dollars doing all that [commercial licensing] . . . but we thought it would belittle our image or our songs. As the man [Bob Dylan] said, 'Money doesn't talk, it swears.' Some people seem to do anything for money. They don't have any moral feelings at all."

His past refused to leave him alone. On October 9 he arrived with Olivia and Dhani at London's Barbican Center for a concert by Ravi Shankar. A fan stepped forward, holding out a copy of *Abbey Road* for him to sign. George brushed it aside and continued inside the theater.

"I've come all the way from Germany," the young man shouted.

George turned. "I don't give a fuck about the Beatles!" he shouted back.

To emphasize his point, George delivered a dramatic statement that year in a lawsuit to block release of an unauthorized

Hamburg recording. "Unlike the Beatles experts who wallow in Beatles trivia," he told a London high court, "I spend a lot of time getting the junk out of my mind through meditation. So I don't know or don't remember—I don't *want* to know or remember—every detail, because it's trivial pursuit."

At 3:30 A.M. on December 31, 1999, a crash from the ground floor of their home woke George and Olivia in their upstairs bedroom. George ran out and from the top of the stairs he saw a figure silhouetted in the moonlight. A statue from the Friar Park grounds lay on the floor surrounded by broken glass from one of the tall French windows.

"You get down here!" the intruder yelled. "You know what it is!"

George could see a lance in the man's hand from another statue in the hallway. "Hare Krishna! Hare Krishna!" George chanted, hoping to distract him. A lawyer would later argue that the intruder, a heroin addict who had scaled the walls of Friar Park, suffered from "an abnormality of mind" that had him believing George's chanting was "the language of Satan spoken backwards" and that "such sorcerers should not be allowed to live."

If he gets by me, George thought, he might go after Olivia or Dhani or Olivia's mother, who was also in the house. Finding courage, he tackled the intruder to the ground. The man jabbed at George with a six-inch blade. Olivia came out from the bedroom and ran at him from behind with a poker. The man turned and grabbed her by the throat. Despite his injuries, George jumped on him and forced him to release his grip. Olivia fell to the floor and crawled away. The intruder pushed George down and stabbed, over and over. Olivia grabbed a table lamp and brought it down on the intruder's head. The man slumped to the ground. Dhani, awakened by the noise, rushed to his father's side to console him. "Dad, you are with me. It's going to be okay."

Police burst in and arrested the intruder. An ambulance arrived. At the hospital, doctors examined George's wounds. He had been stabbed eight times. The knife had come within an inch of essential arteries.

George recovered and, being George, managed to keep a sense of humor. Asked by reporters who his attacker was, he quipped, "He wasn't a burglar—and he definitely wasn't auditioning for the Traveling Wilburys. Adi Shankara, an Indian historical spiritual and groovy-type person, once said, 'Life is fragile like a raindrop on a lotus leaf.' And you'd better believe it."

Monty Python member Michael Palin recalled with admiration the difference between George's reaction to the attack on his own life and his reaction after John's death. "Amazingly, after that awful event with the break-in, he had become so serene that he was able to talk about it with complete ease, without any of the anger I'd seen before, without any of the distress or concern that had been there before. There was precious little anger or blame. He'd changed."

Paul and Ringo learned of the attack and sent messages of love. News of the break-in was featured on front pages around the world, focusing on George yet again a spotlight he did not want. Ironically, this one came on the final day of the millennium. At midnight on New Year's Eve, inside London's Millennium Dome a band played "All You Need Is Love." Outside George's hospital room, two professional security agents stood watch against further madness and hate.

George turned fifty-seven on February 25, 2000. "Now I understand about ninety-year-old people who feel like teenagers," he said. "It's just the body that changes. The soul in the body is there at birth and there at death. The only change is the bodily condition." Spectators that March were treated to the sight of a recovered George in attendance at the Australian Grand Prix, as were London concertgoers later that month at two performances by Ravi Shankar. By August, George was back at work completing unfinished songs.

In September 2000 he made his next-to-last trip to India.

"Sometimes he comes here and spends a few days," Ravi told a reporter. "He's not really studying or practicing sitar now. But he's got much deeper into music itself, listening, understanding, and getting a lot of spiritual pleasure out of it. He's very happy and he's done a lot of recordings. We are all telling him to bring out a record soon."

The Beatle-madness of the world continued unabated. In May, thieves made off with two eight-foot-tall gates from the Strawberry Fields children's home in Liverpool; the gates were valued at £5,000. In November, a CD collection of Beatles number-one hits went straight to the top of the charts in nineteen countries, earning an unprecedented thirty-five platinum discs.

If any of this hysteria made an impact on George, he did not let it show. Cresting a Friar Park hill, he paused more often than before to catch his breath, and pruning a tree went slower than when he planted it nearly thirty years before. But his voice remained clean and bouncy, even if air kept escaping piecemeal from a lung damaged in the attack. Friends listening to him sing against such resistance thought it about the bravest thing they had ever heard.

George planted four hundred maple trees that year, and when he strolled around the garden he would pick up a flower or a leaf whose unique shape he admired. "I think he saw in that garden an affirmation that life goes on," said Michael Palin. "That seemed to give him great pleasure in the last years of his life. It was almost as though the body might be weakening, but everything around him was an affirmation of life and the continuity of life."

When friends came to visit, George would remind them to take time to live fully. He would ramble on about plants and flowers and hug them for minutes on end, not wanting them to leave before knowing how much he loved them. In their eyes he glowed with the truth that the worth of a person dwells inside, in something eternal and pure regardless of karma or politics or religious beliefs.

In December 2000, George began work on a rerelease of "My Sweet Lord." He wanted to "freshen it up a bit," he said, "to remind myself that there is more to life than the material world. . . . It is my attempt to put a bit of a spin on the spiritual side, a reminder for myself and for anybody who's interested."

*   *   *

In March 2001, doctors at the Mayo Clinic discovered cancer in George's lungs. A growth was removed, but within a month the cancer spread. Soon a malignancy was found on his brain. This, too, he took in stride, knowing that death would mean he had finished his work here and was at last entitled to leave.

"He never sat around moping, 'Oh, I'm ill,'" his son, Dhani, later said. "Even when he first found out that he was ill years ago and the doctor gave him—what, six months to live? He was just like, 'Bollocks!' He was never afraid. He was willing to try and get better, but he didn't care. He wasn't attached to this world in the way most people would be. He was on to bigger and better things. And he had a real total and utter disinterest in worrying and being stressed. My dad had no fear of dying whatsoever. I can't stress that enough, really."

Soon after the diagnosis, George took his family by private jet to Varanasi, India, where he bathed in the Ganges—a traditional practice for one who is preparing to die.

After their return, Olivia tried everything possible to find a cure. While staying near a hospital in Staten Island, New York, George received a few select visitors. Ringo visited and stayed for hours.

George's sister, Louise, arrived. They had not seen one another in several years. Louise had become a grandmother in 1990. Her son had taken up Transcendental Meditation, while she had joined the Self-Realization Fellowship and become a dedicated advocate of environmental awareness. "I believe this is your dharma," George told her. "This is what you have to do." Looking back, she remembered him at that final meeting as kind, loving, and completely fearless in the face of death.

Later, Paul visited the hospital and they told jokes, hugged, and cried. George and Paul had known each other nearly half a century. That last visit was the first time they ever held hands.

14

Going Back

When you separate from your body and mind you will perceive that which is subtle yet dazzling and glorious—the radiance of your own real nature.

—*Tibetan Book of the Dead*

The *KRSNA Book* that George had helped publish was part of a longer Sanskrit history, *Srimad-Bhagavatam*, which told the story of a great king who learned he would soon die. . . .

The king chose a select circle of friends and holy people to be present with him at the end. He left his kingdom behind, went to a secluded place, and sat down to meditate and prepare for leaving his body.

Throughout his life, the king had only one wish: to know God. He never allowed wealth or privilege to distract him from that goal. Every day he meditated and prayed. Throughout his reign, he organized festivals of sacred music for the benefit of his citizens. When he learned he had only a short time to live, the king did not despair over fate's cruelty but prepared himself with a cheerful heart.

"Let death come at any time," he told those gathered around him. "I am ready. My only request is that you sing the glories of God and never stop singing."

"We will be with you," they said. "We will sing, and we will not stop singing." They consoled one another, saying that there is no cause to lament when a person of great devotion passes away: the soul goes to God. Still, sorrow pulled at their hearts, for the company of such a beautiful soul is rare. The assembly gathered around the king in his final hours. They sang and prayed, creating a musical passage for his soul out of the material world. He could no longer eat or drink yet he felt no distress. He was the witness to his pain, and there was no pain in witnessing.

"Your music and prayers are my nourishment," he told the assembly. "Kindly go on chanting."

"He has already attained eternal life," those around him whispered. "In his heart dwells only devotion." One of those in attendance knelt by the king's side. "You will never die," he said through tears. "Death can never claim such a master of the self as you. You have conquered all dangers on the path."

The king was indeed already liberated from the material world. No plans crowded his thoughts, no pleasures tempted his senses, no doubts troubled his heart. He felt no fear or anger. As he listened to the chanting of God's names, he consecrated the elements of his body to their source: earth to earth, fire to fire, water to water, air to air. At the appointed moment, all movement ceased. There was silence, and as those present looked on, his soul left his body.

A friend in attendance turned to the king's son. "It was God Himself," he said, "who took your father back."

The king's journey was achieved, and the silence of that moment was not empty. It was filled with spiritual sound, with symphonies of purpose and the rightness of things, and with the harmony of hearts rejoined. It was the silence only of all material sound, and into that space flooded ragas and kirtans and a chorus of welcoming voices. It was a glorious orchestral silence that calmed the pain of those who suffered from knowing they would never again in this life have the sweet pleasure of his company.

News of the king's demise spread. From all corners of the kingdom came cries of sorrow and outpourings of affection, for the king was loved by one and all. Gradually from the

ashes of lament rose a bright, joyful flame of celebration.
A great soul had returned home.

From the beginning of his spiritual journey, George knew that his frame of mind at death would determine where his soul would be reborn. "Whatever state of being one remembers when quitting the body," he read in the Bhagavad Gita, "that state one will attain without fail," and from that time on, he was rarely without the holy names of God on his lips. "Om Hari Om," he prayed, walking down the street. "Govinda jaya jaya, Gopala jaya jaya," he sang, driving in his car. "Hare Krishna, Hare Krishna," he chanted on beads when traveling by plane or sitting in his garden.

Because thinking about God was his life, George never needed to make separate arrangements for death. Liberation was not some place he would go to later, but a way of being now. To stop judging, to stop racing, to stop wishing for something grander than this moment—to manifest divinity at every second; that was the real yogi life. Living this life and living the next had become one and the same for him. There was no fear of leaving his body, no concern for what would happen next, only selfless love and the anticipation of going on with selfless love in some other place. Having recognized the immortal, indestructible nature of his soul, he had transcended death's tragic dimension. It was a gift he wished to share with everyone he knew.

In August 1966, a reporter had asked George to describe his personal goal. "To do as well as I can do," he replied, "whatever I attempt, and someday to die with a peaceful mind." He was twenty-three years old when he set that goal for himself. He never gave up.

"You know, I read a letter from him to his mother that he wrote when he was twenty-four," his son, Dhani, said. "He was on tour or someplace when he wrote it. And it basically says, 'I want to be self-realized. I want to find God. I'm not interested in material things, this world, fame—I'm going for the real goal. And I hope you don't worry about me, Mum.' And he wrote that when he was twenty-four! And that was basically the philosophy that he had up until the day he died. He was just going for it right from an early age—the big goal."

"He gave his life to God a long time ago," Olivia explained. "He wasn't trying to hang on to anything. He was fine with it. ... Sure, nobody likes to be ill and nobody likes to be uncomfortable. But he went with what was happening." George dedicated his life to obtaining a good end, she said, and she had no doubts that he was successful.

George died on November 29, 2001, less than three months after the devastation of September 11. A memorial service was held in Los Angeles. The sun shone brightly that day, and after the service George's family and friends gathered outside. "It was an extraordinary sky," remembered his friend Jim Keltner. "I mean extraordinary, without exaggerating. The clouds were swirling in slow motion, and the color was a deep orange—it was so *George,* man, and I can say from my heart that George was out there on the astral plane. I just felt him. Everybody agreed. We just knew.

"To this day, I feel George like that. I'm a Christian, and a friend of mine has a beautiful way of explaining the difference between our faith and his. She says he had a kind of advanced scientific version of who God is. Not that I understand that, and I don't need to, really. But I like it. I like how it makes me feel, because if that's true then it means we're all connected and we'll all be together again someday. If God is a gracious God, a God of love, as I understand Him to be, then I believe that there is some reward for this man in God's kingdom, and he'll be there when we think of him. Anytime we think of him, he'll be with us. I just love the idea of that."

A year after George's death, Dhani completed production of a final album of his father's songs. The album "is not about death and dying," he told a reporter. "We talked about putting a chant at the end—a really nice vibration to leave you in a good place. He never liked sad stuff, and this is a lighthearted record—much more than *Art of Dying* or *All Things Must Pass,* written back when he was more serious. This is a joyous thing."

As a result of his son's efforts, *Brainwashed,* George's final album, is glorious, irreverent, happy, touching, loving, and beautiful. Even the heavy parts are light. The opening track, "Any Road," evokes an image of an old geezer rocking on his porch, his thumb hitched beneath a frayed red suspender, welcoming folks to the material world. Need directions? I can help, he offers. Been most everywhere myself, by boat and plane and car and bike—been through it all, sometimes by the skin of my teeth. Don't know where you're going? Well then, any road will get you there. But if you are looking for a way out, then best to bow to God because "the way *out* is *in.*"

The album journeys through funky Dylanesque goofs on organized religion, rustic ballads about finding an ocean of bliss that flows through all beings, a calm Hawaiian raga played out on an elegant slide guitar, odes of love to Olivia, and a closing title track that might be a summation of his entire life. We're in a mess here, he sings in "Brainwashed." Drums and electric guitars pound it out. We're under attack by teachers, leaders, the stock market, governments—God, God, God, he sings, you are the wisdom, the lover we seek, and your nature is existence, knowledge, and bliss.

The rock and roll disappears, and in flow slide guitar, harp, and tablas. Gently he lifts his listeners above the chaos into a cloud of celestial harmonies. An angelic voice recites second-century master Patanjali's yoga aphorism. Those who achieve enlightenment, Patanjali wrote, are one with love, knowledge, and eternal existence.

Then he takes us back—dropped like a rock, drums and bass and more attacks from businesses, computers, mobile phones. O God, lead us out of this concrete mess. If we have to be brainwashed, then let it be you, Lord, who does the washing.

Again the music dissolves away. This time the journey is complete, and all sounds fade except for a harmonium's drone, a single note as the album draws to a close. Its final moments pay homage to wisdom's transmission through the ages and into the future as George and Dhani chant together:

namah parvati pataye hare hare mahadev
namah parvati pataye hare hare
shiva shiva shankara mahadeva

"Homage to the Lord of Parvati, O great God, O sublime Supreme Cause of all creation." Over and over, two voices singing as one, in soulful prayer.

The sound of perfect union.

Afterword

Soon after completing the manuscript for this book, I took a few days to visit my son outside Savannah, Georgia, where he flies for a regional airline. On the way down from New York, I reread passages from a book commemorating George's life. His fellow Wilbury and friend Tom Petty was quoted as remembering that in his last years George always said there was nothing to be gained by bitterness or anger or hatred. He was pure love, Petty said. Still, he always had a desire to leave the maya world behind. Petty's daughter used to visit George at Friar Park and remembered walking with him in the garden one evening when he turned to her and said, "Sometimes I just wish I could turn into a light beam and go away."

The plane landed in Savannah, and my son picked me up. We drove into town and strolled along River Street, watching tourists boarding riverboats. We stopped to browse in souvenir shops. A notice tacked to the door of one shop announced that a local author would be signing books that day. Feeling sympathy for a fellow writer, I went in. A man about my age (mid-fifties) sat with his hands folded behind a small metal card table. On the table, a short stack of books waited for customers. While my son perused T-shirts, I made friends with Murray Silver, whose previous book *Great Balls of Fire*, about 1950s rocker Jerry Lee

Lewis, had been made into a film starring Dennis Quaid. He asked me what I did, and when I mentioned this book, Murray's eyes grew big.

It turns out he had been a photographer for the *Dark Horse* tour in 1974 and had spent days asking George all about his spiritual interests.

"George was doing his preaching onstage back then," Murray said, "but it didn't go down in the South. Ask a bunch of Georgia crackers to start chanting? The crowd just tuned him out. They went to go get beer, milled around grumbling—it just wasn't going down." Murray signed a copy of his book of Savannah stories for a lone customer and then resumed. "You have to remember," he said, "at that time religion was considered a very personal thing, a divisive force on the planet, so you didn't bring it up. And George saw he couldn't engage people in a serious discussion. They just wanted to talk about the Beatles, sex, drugs, and rock 'n' roll. So he figured the best thing he could do was lead by example."

While my son went next door for an ice cream, Murray explained that he became a Buddhist shortly after his time with George and encountered the same kind of resistance when serving as road manager for the Dalai Lama's monks. "Americans are spiritual teenagers compared to the people of India," he said. "You have to wade through so much crap before you can get to the heart of an issue. It's just exhausting."

It was a lazy day, and the conversation moved easily between stories about George and watching seagulls outside the gift shop as they circled over the Savannah River.

Maybe it was because of writing the book, but I had noticed George showing up a lot lately. A friend had called a few days earlier to tell me he had just had lunch in a Seattle restaurant named My Sweet Lord. "My Sweet Lord" was playing in the plane as it landed in Savannah. And now I was bumping into the *Dark Horse* photographer.

"It's a shame George wasn't able to share more of his message with people," Murray said. "The atmosphere of the time, the indifference from Christian America—it was impossible for him to hold forth on spiritual matters."

I asked Murray if he thought George had been trying too hard to get a message through. "Maybe at first," he said, "but from what I saw of him, he was just trying to put information out there and hoping it would take root. He was planting seeds. That's all the man was doing. Planting seeds." Images of Friar Park came to mind.

"By the time he reached the South," Murray said, "it was clear that whenever he made overt personal statements, they exploded in his face. Remember John's comment about the Beatles being more popular than Christ? People never forgave that. George told me he wasn't about to wade back into that now by saying, 'Maybe you should take a peek at Krishna.' He was concerned the same thing would happen to him."

We discussed my book. Murray said, "You could spend a whole chapter just talking about the cover of *Sergeant Pepper.* George told me that was where he deposited his first clue. A lot of people aren't even aware that there's a photo of Yogananda in there. That was the first of his clues. He asked me if I remembered the rumor about Paul being dead. People were running around for years playing albums backward and finding evidence that Paul was dead. He said it even reached a point where *he* began believing that Paul was dead. He was absolutely amazed how people would study this stuff. Well, he wanted the spiritual side of his life to be revealed the same way. If people wanted it, they'd have to look for it. He felt his role was to bring this light that otherwise people wouldn't know about, and he was hoping that one day the clues would blossom into something."

Murray and I went over some clues from George's album covers. There were obvious ones, like a Krishna and Arjuna poster that came inside each copy of the *Living in the Material World* album, and the little "Jai Sri Krishna" logos printed here and there, and Om signs that decorated nearly every album he ever made. There were less obvious clues, such as making the album title *33 & 1/3* look like three Om signs combined. We were enjoying our treasure hunt and glad for a friendly chat on a sunshiny day with jazz pouring from a jukebox next door and everything more or less anesthetized by the warm, hazy air. We agreed it was a shame that George never knew how deeply his spiritual message had influenced people.

"If he were doing his spiritual thing today," Murray said, shaking his head in wonder, "the Earth would tilt on its axis. The time is right now. But he didn't live long enough to see that day. He started something in the sixties, something that—"

My son came back at that moment, anxious to show me a model airplane he'd found in an antiques store nearby. As I prepared to leave, I asked Murray what he meant by his reference to something George had started.

"Well," he said, "maybe it was a continuation of something from history. Or maybe it was meant to be a new beginning." We said good-bye. Connecting with another human being who appreciated the mystery of things was a gift, and we agreed to stay in touch. "Or maybe," he said as my son and I stood in the doorway, "that thing George started—maybe it was simply causeless grace."

That sounded about right.

Acknowledgments

In 1969, while studying at the Sorbonne in Paris, I met Umapati Swami (known back then as Wally Sheffey), who urged me to visit the London Radha Krishna Temple. He was the first person to speak with me about George and Krishna consciousness, and my acknowledgments begin with him. I thank the late Tamal Krishna Maharaja, who took me under his wing in London and invited me to play harmonium at Abbey Road Studios on the *Radha Krishna Temple* album. In those days, Gurudas, Shyamsundar, Mukunda, and their partners Yamuna, Malati, and Janaki showed by example that spirit means friendship as much as philosophy. I thank them for their affection and their dedication to Krishna's service.

There are more than 1,000 books about the Beatles currently in print and more than 5.5 million Web sites tracking every detail of their lives. The framework for this book emerged from examining hundreds of books, thousands of Web sites, dozens of filmed and transcribed interviews, documents in the British Museum's Sound Archive and other libraries, as well as magazines, chronicles, newsletters, videos, and digests. Christopher Wood at Oxford University helped verify much of this voluminous data, and I thank him for his help. By applying their astonishing command of Beatles history, biographer Alan Clayson and Liverpool Beatles Fan Club president Jean Catharell saved me from the special purgatory reserved for those who misrepresent details of Beatles history. For their kindness in reviewing the manuscript, I am both indebted and relieved. Albert Sussman took that skill to yet another dimension by offering insights known only to the truly Beatles obsessed. He has my thanks and my sympathies.

Written sources failed to say much about George Harrison's motives, fears, or reasons for wanting to explore life's deeper mysteries. The most telling details came from remembrances by people who knew him. For allowing me to interview them, or for offering valuable recommendations and perspectives, I thank Karen Addison, the late Al Aronowitz, John Coates, Prithu Das, Sripati Das, Karamrita Desi, Joel Dorn, Barry Feinstein, Larry Geller, Giriraj Swami, Philip Glass, Shrivatsa Goswami, Paddy Grafton-Green, Louise Harrison, Bill Harry, Judith Jamison, Norman Kauffman, Jim Keltner, Pamela Keogh, Donovan Leitch, Dave Mason, Joey and Kathie Molland, Cousin Bruce Morrow, Andy Newmark, Michael Palin, Alan Parsons, Paul Saltzman, Ramesh Sawhney, Murray Silver, M. K. Srinivasan, L. Subramaniam, Godfrey Townsend, Jan de Villeneuve, Willie Weeks, Michael Zagaris, and the many other people whose input helped enrich this story.

For their help in vetting the manuscript for philosophical accuracy I thank Professor Graham Schweig, Steven Rosen, Hridayananda Goswami, Professor Klaus Klostermaier, and Hari Sauri Das. Even before this work began, Erik Jendresen, one of the finest screenwriters around, assured me that if motivated by the heart, a writer could do justice to the life of another human being. I'm grateful to him for that encouragement. I owe a special thanks to Iain McCaig for his uncanny ability to sniff out story-line gems in piles of broken verbiage. I thank my brother Brian Greene for his comments and for using his command of physics to reveal the elegance of creation. Adele Greene, who happens to be my mother, deserves acknowledgment for her suggestions on how to improve both the manuscript and my wardrobe. From the outset, Robert Campagnola and his partner Kamala saw the value of this undertaking and supported my research for more than a year. I gratefully acknowledge their role in helping bring this book to completion. For their recommendations and guidance I wish to thank Beatlefest founder Mark Lapidos and historian Leonard Primiano.

I also thank my literary agent Linda Chester and her partner Laurie Fox for their enthusiastic support of this book from its inception. My editor Kyra Ryan is hereby awarded a brass filigree with gold-leaf clusters for her expertise in raising the manuscript through an awkward childhood and seeing it through to publication. She has my gratitude for fully capturing the spirit of this effort. My editor Tom Miller of John Wiley & Sons deserves special thanks for having seen the potential in the work at hand and for having offered insightful recommendations at its various stages of evolution.

The many teachers who have helped bring *sanatan-dharma*, the eternal religion of all souls, into the world also deserve acknowledgment, along with my apologies for not adequately representing all of them here.

Finally, I offer more thanks than words can express to my wife, Esther Fortunoff-Greene, for her unwavering love and support, without which this book could not have been written.

Notes

Preface

xi   In her preface to a tribute: *Harrison,* by the editors of *Rolling Stone* (New York: Simon & Schuster, 2002), p. 8.

Chapter 1: Beginnings

1   He wondered how he came to be in that family: see George Harrison, *I, Me, Mine* (San Francisco, Chronicle Books, 1980), p. 20.

3   "It was rough then":   Interview with Bill Harry, December 13, 2004.

4   George's sister-in-law Irene: Harrison, *I, Me, Mine,* p. 26.

4   As a boy, George had dreams: *Crawdaddy,* February 1977, interview by Mitchell Glazer.

6   "Not many people understand how brilliant":   Interview with Louise Harrison, September 8, 2004.

6   "I was raised Catholic":   Interview with Murray Silver, August 25, 2004.

7   For George, starting at Liverpool Institute: Harrison, *I, Me, Mine,* p. 21.

7   "Harrison was the greatest surprise to me of all":   Quoted in Bill Harry, *The George Harrison Encyclopedia* (London: Virgin Books, 2003), p. 266.

8   "He had a wicked sense of humor":   Interview with Rod Othen in the documentary *George Harrison: The Quiet One* (London: Waterfall Entertainment, 2002).

9   Psychologist Francis J. Braceland, then president: Cited in David Pichaske, *A Generation in Motion: Popular Music and Culture in the Sixties* (New York: Schirmer Books, 1979), p. 38. Also cited in Barry Werth, "How the Church Used Psychiatry to Care for—and Protect—Abusive Priests" (*New Yorker,* June 9, 2003).

10   "There was a sense of staying together":   Interview with Joey Molland, September 2, 2004.

11   "Shut up, Mimi," John said: *The Beatles Anthology* (San Francisco: Chronicle Books, 2000), p. 11.

11   "You watched your p's and q's around her":   Len Garry interview in "The Beatles: A Long and Winding Road" documentary (North Hollywood, CA: Passport Video), episode 1.

11   "How can I do my ballet without tight jeans?":   Hunter Davies, *The Beatles* (New York: Dell, 1968), p. 51.

12   After that, "John always had a thing about authority":   Julia Baird interview in "The Beatles: A Long and Winding Road" documentary, episode 1.

12   "George was terrified that I was going to die next":   Hunter Davies, *The Beatles* (New York: Dell, 1968), p. 54.

12   "That was one thing to be said about us":   *The Beatles Anthology,* p. 83.

13   G. J. Peat, one of the managers, wagged a finger: Cited by David Peat, "George Harrison Tributes," newswww.bbc.net.uk/2/hi/talking_point/1685036.stm, posted December 17, 2001.

14   "The night they first played here":   Allan Williams interview in "The Beatles: A Long and Winding Road" documentary, episode 2.

15   Satisfied by their trial run: Allan Williams and William Marshall, *The Man Who Gave the Beatles Away* (New York: Macmillan, 1975), p. 76.

Chapter 2: George among the Savages

19   "The Kaiser Keller was a black hole in hell":   Tony Sheridan interview in "The Beatles: A Long and Winding Road" documentary (North Hollywood, CA: Passport Video), episode 3.

20   In later years, George remembered Hamburg: *The Beatles Anthology,* p. 78.

20   At other times, he would describe Hamburg: *Time Out,* September 4, 1988. Cited in Alan Clayson, *The Quiet One* (London: Sanctuary Publishing, 1996), p. 69.

20   "Oh, you just wait till we're as big as the Shadows":   Quoted by Astrid Kirchherr in *The Beatles Digest* (Iola, Wis.: Krause, 2000), p. 29.

21   "My darling Little Georgie":   Astrid Kirchherr, "The Last Word," *MOJO Beatles* (London: EMAP Metro, 2002), p. 146.

22   "As soon as I announce you":   Pritchard and Lysaght, *The Beatles: An Oral History* (New York: Hyperion, 1998), p. 54.

23   In his column for . . . *Mersey Beat:*   Cited in Davies, *The Beatles,* p. 105.

25   Louise recognized her and called out: Cited in Peter Brown and Steven Gaines, *The Love You Make* (New York: New American Library, 2002), p. 45.

25   On October 28, 1961:   In his book *With the Beatles* (London: John Blake Publishing, 2003, p. 16) Epstein's assistant Alistair Taylor calls this well-known story "rubbish" and states that he fabricated a teenager named Raymond Jones—a name he picked at random—to justify the NEMS record shop's ordering copies of "My Bonnie" from its German distributor Polydor.

28   "Not to mince words," Rowe said: Cited in Shawn Levy, *Ready, Steady, Go! The Smashing Rise and Giddy Fall of Swinging London* (New York: Doubleday, 2002), p. 65.

32   "We just fell about laughing":   Cited in Badman, *The Beatles off the Record* (London: Omnibus Press, 2001), p. 41.

32   For nineteen-year-old George: *Western Morning News,* March 29, 1963. Cited in Clayson, *The Quiet One,* p. 125.

33   "It sounded like pigs were being slaughtered": Quoted by Dave Thompson, "The Beatles Meet the Loog," in *The Beatles Digest,* p. 51.

Chapter 3: A Price to Pay

34   "I don't want to sound ungrateful":   Cited in Badman, *The Beatles off the Record,* p. 70.

35   "After every concert, the best-looking female":   Alistair Taylor, *With the Beatles* (London: John Blake, 2003), p. 90.

35   At an annual meeting of the Church of England: Davies, *The Beatles,* p. 207.

37   "It's funny," George told a Manchester television reporter: From an interview filmed on August 28, 1963, and broadcast that October as part of a BBC documentary, "The Mersey Sound."

41   "Well, what could I do?":   Davies, *The Beatles,* p. 226.

41   On George's twenty-first birthday: Interview with Louise Harrison, October 21, 2004.

41   "Have you got to put up with this all the time?":   Davies, *The Beatles,* p. 279.

42   "Ten pounds, two shillings," his father said: Davies, *The Beatles,* p. 280.

46   "We made fun of ourselves":   Interview with Louise Harrison, September 8, 2004.

47   "A good romp? That was fair in the films":   Harrison, *I, Me, Mine,* p. 39.

47   "I'm not meeting Shirley Temple":   Recounted by Derek Taylor in *The Beatles Anthology,* p. 155.

48   "It was like the eyes of a deer":   Pritchard and Lysaght, *The Beatles: An Oral History,* p. 227.

49   "Sorry, lads," Epstein said: Cited by George Martin in *Beatles Anthology,* p. 221.

51   "Even in those early days":   Interview with Bruce Morrow, September 28, 2004.

52   By the time of their Shea Stadium concert: Sales statistics of Beatles merchandise are quoted from Levy, *Ready, Steady, Go!: The Smashing Rise and Giddy Fall of Swinging London,* p. 260.

53   "George is a very nitty-gritty person":   Cited in Pritchard and Lysaght, *The Beatles, An Oral History,* p. 190.

54   It happened in the spring of 1965:   See *The Beatles Anthology,* p. 177. John and George both said that they thought the dentist was trying to keep them there by force for an orgy.

54   By this time, they were smoking marijuana for breakfast: John, quoted in Badman, *The Beatles off the Record,* p. 162.

55 "To be shaken out of the ruts of ordinary perception": Cited in Stephen A. Kent, *From Slogans to Mantras: Social Protest and Religious Conversion in the Late Vietnam War Era* (Syracuse, N.Y.: Syracuse University Press, 2001), p. 12. Also see Aldous Huxley, *The Doors of Perception* (London: Chatto & Windus, 1954).

55 "You can take it and take it": Interview by David Swanson of the *San Francisco Chronicle*, August 7, 1967.

56 "They just looked up at him": Interview with Larry Geller, September 13, 2004.

Chapter 4: A Father to His Spirit

60 "We were open to anything": *The Beatles Anthology*, p. 197.

63 "I felt I wanted to walk out of my home": *MOJO*, 2001. Cited in Badman, *The Beatles off the Record*, p. 191.

64 "He's trying to figure out life:" Cited in Badman, *The Beatles off the Record*, p. 244.

66 "What is your personal goal?": Ibid., p. 13.

Chapter 5: Rebirth

67 "Oh, no," he said with a sigh. "Foxes have holes": *Beatles Anthology*, p. 223.

68 "I believe much more in the religions of India": Interview by Donald Milner for the BBC program *Lively Arts*, September 29, 1966.

70 "I'd heard stories about men in caves": Cited by Pritchard and Lysaght in *The Beatles: An Oral History*, p. 229.

71 Did people who attain cosmic consciousness: *The Beatles Anthology*, p. 179.

73 "Taking a guru," Ravi said: As quoted in his biographical film *Raga* (1971, directed by Howard Worth).

73 "Throughout the Beatle experience," George said years later: Interview by John Fuglesang with George Harrison and Ravi Shankar on the VH-1 program "George Harrison & Ravi Shankar: Yin & Yang," July 24, 1997.

73 Thousands of pilgrims had assembled: Followers of Hindu devotional tradition date Rama's appearance much earlier than scholarly calculations, to the Treta-Yuga or Silver Age of Earth's history, nearly two million years ago.

74 "Too many people have the wrong idea about India": *New Musical Express*, May 27, 1967.

Chapter 6: In the Land of Gods

76 "Everybody talks about Lennon and McCartney": Quoted in David Simons, "The Unsung Beatle," *Acoustic Guitar*, February 2003, p. 60.

76 Despite a growing sense of his artistic ability: Clayson, *The Quiet One,* p. 181.

76 "I'd give up everything if I could be a monk": Cited in Belmo, *George Harrison: His Words, Wit & Wisdom,* p. 75.

77 "George was having to put up with an awful lot": Quoted in Bill Harry, *The George Harrison Encyclopedia,* pp. 268–269.

78 "When I first met George in 1963, he was Mister Fun": Cited in Steve Turner, *A Hard Day's Write* (London: Carlton Books, 1994), p. 129.

78 Juan Mascaro, a professor of Sanskrit: Cited in Harrison, *I, Me, Mine,* pp. 118–119.

79 "The realization of human love reciprocated": *Disc,* July 16, 1966.

80 "They've tried everything else": *The Beatles Anthology,* p. 258.

81 "Six hours we sang": *Chant and Be Happy* (Los Angeles: Bhaktivedanta Book Trust, 1997), p. 8.

81 "It seemed as if we were sailing": Taylor, *With the Beatles,* p. 177.

82 "We were great at going on holiday with big ideas": *The Beatles Anthology,* p. 258.

83 The hippies were "hypocrites": *Creem,* January 1987.

83 As their car pulled away: Harry Pules, "George Harrison in Haight-Ashbury," *Melody Maker,* August 19, 1967, p. 11.

84 "George's visit to the Haight-Ashbury neighborhood": As startling as Haight-Ashbury and the spiritual explosion of the sixties may have seemed, the "mystic revolution," as George called it, had been percolating for a long time. Many nineteenth-century intellectuals had foreshadowed George's own dissatisfaction with Western religion by adopting Eastern philosophy in their writings and lectures. Author Herman Melville referred to Vishnu's fish incarnation in his 1851 work *Moby-Dick.* Henry David Thoreau so adored the Bhagavad Gita that Mahatma Gandhi called Thoreau his guru. Hindu philosophy influenced Walt Whitman's lyrical work "Passage to India," and his fellow transcendentalist Ralph Waldo Emerson was reading Sanskrit poetry by age seventeen and protesting America's infatuation with maya or illusion. "The Goddess of Illusion is stronger than the Titans," he wrote, "stronger than Apollo."

The heyday of the transcendentalists ended with the Civil War in 1865. Industrialization was spreading across America, and as the public's interest in foreign ideas dwindled, the more intolerant Christian churches began subjecting Hindus to vicious attacks.

Hindu leaders protested. "I came here not to thrust my religion upon you," pleaded Swami Premananda Bharati, who had arrived in 1907, "but to help you to understand your own God and your own religion. If I have talked of Krishna and the Vedas and Hindu philosophy, it was only to illuminate the teachings of your own Christ, to present him before you in the light of the Vedas." Nothing could slow the tsunami of hostile public opinion, and in 1914 anti-Hindu prejudice led to passage of legislation denying entry to immigrants from most Asian countries. Hinduism would remain nearly extinct in America for the next three decades.

World War II rekindled interest in peaceful, spiritual cultures, and by the early 1950s, Hindu, Buddhist, Taoist, and other Eastern beliefs were influencing a new generation of thinkers who included philosophers Thomas Merton, Herman Hesse, and beat writers Gary Snyder, Alan Watts, Jack Kerouac, and Allen Ginsberg. In 1965 the U.S. government at last rescinded its nearly fifty-year-old anti-immigration laws, and by the time of George's visit to Haight-Ashbury, Indian gurus and yogis were flocking to Western shores.

85   It was, in the words of historian: Cited in David G. Browley and Larry D. Shinn, *Krishna Consciousness in the West* (Bridgewater, N.J.: Associated University Presses, 1989), p. 106.

86   He didn't know much about him: *The Beatles Anthology,* p. 260.

87   "It's like going somewhere without your trousers on":   Davies, *The Beatles,* p. 261.

88   "The Maharishi provided us with a device":   From a presentation at Beatlefest, New Jersey, July 2003.

89   "What is it you fear most in life?":   Interview with Brian Epstein by Mike Hennessey, *Melody Maker,* August 5, 1967.

90   "George himself is no mystery":   Cited in *Harrison* by the editors of *Rolling Stone,* p. 18.

91   "Is it a new song, George?" he asked: Paul Saltzman, *The Beatles in Rishikesh* (New York: Penguin Putnam, 2000), p. 77.

95   "The way George is going":   *The Beatles Anthology,* p. 281.

95   "It's hard to actually explain it":   Quoted in Badman, *The Beatles off the Record,* p. 341.

96   "Within three months," the Maharishi told press: Ibid., p. 342.

98   "We are now setting ourselves":   Karlheinz Stockhausen, "Manifesto for the Young," originally printed in Paris, *Journal Musical,* June 16, 1968. Cited in Arthur Marwick, *The Sixties* (Oxford, Eng.: Oxford University Press, 1998), pp. 330–331. Composer Karlheinz Stockhausen was supposed to meet the Beatles in New York in January 1969, to discuss a joint concert, but bad weather delayed their arrival, and the meeting was never rescheduled.

98   "He's found something stronger than the Beatles":   Davies, *The Beatles,* p. 356.

99   Donning an advertiser's persona: "Sour Milk Sea" was never recorded by George, who gave it to singer Jackie Lomax for his album *Is This What You Want.*

99   "If you're in the shit":   Harrison, *I, Me, Mine,* p. 142.

99   "Even though [the song] was [about] me getting pissed off":   *Musician,* November 1987. ("Not Guilty" was never released by the Beatles. George issued a solo version in 1979.)

Chapter 7: Devotees

104   Devotees worshiped Krishna as God's original personal form: See Louis Renou, *Hinduism* (New York: George Braziller, 1962), pp. 167–168.

106   Shyamsundar introduced Yamuna: Readers interested in vegetarian cooking might enjoy Yamuna Devi's award-winning book *Lord Krishna's Cuisine: The Art of Indian Vegetarian Cooking* (New York: E. P. Dutton, 1986).

107   On the altar stood eight-inch brass figures: Worship of deities in the bhakti tradition differs from idolatry. Unlike idols or other objects invented by artistic inspiration, Vedic deities are prepared according to elaborate scriptural guidelines. When properly fashioned, the Vedas describe these deities not as symbols but as God himself in visible form, appearing to facilitate worship by his devotees. Seeing the deity is called *darshan,* literally "a vision of Truth."

111   He marched Taylor into his dining room: Taylor, *With the Beatles,* pp. 213–214.

111   "This group by itself," wrote critic Carl Pelz: Cited in Marwick, *The Sixties,* p. 464.

112   "What's happened to the Beatles?":   Editorial in the *Daily Mail,* cited in Badman, *The Beatles off the Record,* p. 289.

113   George thought he was quite capable: *Beatles Anthology,* p. 316.

113   "Everybody else thought they were for the teenyboppers":   Anthony DeCurtis and James Henke, with Holly George-Warren: *The Rolling Stone History of Rock & Roll* (New York: Rolling Stone Press, 1976). Cited in *In My Life: Encounters with the Beatles,* edited by Robert Cording, Selli Jankowski-Smith, and E. J. Miller Laino (New York: Fromm International, 1998), p. 12.

113   "I'd hate to think that putting Bob together":   Al Aronowitz, *Bob Dylan and the Beatles* (Elizabeth, N.J.: 1st Books, 2003), p. 13.

114   George called those who walked out of the concert: Bill Harry, *The Ultimate Beatles Encyclopedia* (New York: MJF Books, 1992), p. 211.

114   "Even his stuff which people loathe":   *Melody Maker,* November 6, 1975. Cited in Clayson, *The Quiet One,* p. 172.

114   "What was interesting about that day":   Interview with Judith Jamison, August 18, 2004.

115   "Dylan's influence was incredible":   Interview with Barry Feinstein, August 18, 2004.

115   "There are two 'i's":   *Beatles Anthology*, p. 319.

116   "George had to leave":   Cited in Badman, *The Beatles off the Record*, p. 411.

117   Once he might have considered striking back: See Harrison, *I, Me, Mine*, p. 21.

119   John's soon-to-be-recorded "Give Peace a Chance":   On October 1, 1969, John watched on television as demonstrators chanted the song for the first time during New York's Vietnam Moratorium Day gathering.

Chapter 8: Looking for Krishna

140   "George was very meticulous":   Interview with Alan Parsons, December 31, 2004.

142   "Actually," George said, "it's about Krishna":   George seems to have offered different explanations of whom he had in mind when writing certain songs. "Creative artists have always had their muses," Pattie told *Hello!* magazine in August 2004 (p. 75). "I was young and very shy, so when George told me 'Something' was for me, it didn't seem a big deal. I had no sense of being part of history." On a different occasion, George explained that the song "wasn't about Pattie. Everybody says it was, but it wasn't. It was just a song." (Cited in Badman, *The Beatles off the Record*, p. 469.)

142   Apart from recollections by those who were there: The ambivalence in "Something" over love's outcome echoed themes that had pervaded India's devotional poetry for centuries as in odes by fourteenth-century poet Vidyapati and sixteenth-century poet Chandidas, that glorify the Gopis, cowherd women of Krishna's village, for whom Krishna was "like no other lover." (See Deben Bhattacharya's translation of *Love Songs of Vidyapat* [Delhi: Motilal Banarsidass, 1987]). The bhakti tradition describes love for God as taking place in evolving stages, called *rasas* or tastes. Rupa Goswami's *Bhakti-rasamrita-sindhu* (available from the Bhaktivedanta Book Trust under the title *Nectar of Devotion*) compares the early stage of love for God to sugarcane juice: liquid and pure, but easily shaken. This early stage is called *shanta-rasa*, a peaceful, passive knowledge of God's presence. *Shanti* or peace receives much attention in Western yogic circles, but for Krishna bhaktas it is only the beginning. When stimulated by a desire to actively demonstrate that love, this peaceful stage erupts into *dasya-rasa* or servitude. Rupa Goswami compares this sentiment to cane juice boiled and thickened into syrup. Servitude, however, implies higher and lower stations. When that distinction disappears, love between equals emerges: *sakya-rasa*, the "taste" of friendship, which is compared to syrup thickened further into molasses. When friends interact, they treat each other casually. Further evolved love for God sheds that informality and attains

vatsalya-rasa or parental affection. When love for God achieves its most intense stage, the parental sense of duty disappears. What remains is reckless, total ecstatic love that cares nothing for social conventions: *madhura-rasa*, conjugal affection. The cowherd women of Vrindavan express this highest level of love, which is compared to rock candy.

142   "That's good," George replied: *Crawdaddy*, February 1977, interview by Mitchell Glazer.

145   "Go away? I've thought about it for years":   Quoted in Badman, *The Beatles off the Record*, p. 438.

146   "I never stop chanting the Krishna mantra":   From transcript of press conference, Sydenham, South London, August 28, 1969.

147   The "key cultural artifact" of the sixties: Marwick, *The Sixties*, pp. 734–735.

150   "There is a verse in Bhagavad Gita":   from transcript of conversation recorded at the Lennon estate on September 11, 1969.

152   Maybe he was underestimating Prabhupada: *Chant and Be Happy*, p. 25.

155   "A lot of people say, 'I'm *it*'":   Ibid., pp. 25–26.

156   George called their brand of revolution superficial: *International Times*, September 11, 1969.

162   Everybody is looking for Krishna: Preface to A. C. Bhaktivedanta Swami Prabhupada, *KRSNA Book* (Los Angeles: Bhaktivedanta Book Trust, 1970), pp. ix–x.

Chapter 9: All Things Must Pass

172   The owner, Konrad Engbers: "Tributes to George Harrison: A Very Special Person," posted on www.henley-on-thames.com, December 7, 2001.

173   "Did you hurt your hand?" people would ask.   Ibid., p. 11.

177   The four of them had grown up together: "We all felt so close," Ringo once described. "We knew each other so well that we'd know when any of us would make a move up or down within the music, and we'd all make it. No one would say anything or look at each other. We'd just know. The easiest word is telepathy." Cited by Robyn Flans in "The Fab 4/4," *The Beatles Digest*, p. 233.

178   "For all I know," he said: *Chant and Be Happy*, p. 35.

181   "I wanted to show that 'Hallelujah'":   Ibid., p. 32.

183   "I still get letters from people":   Ibid., p. 17.

Chapter 10: The Sky beneath His Feet

187   "George was very nervous":   Cited in Simon Leng, *The Music of George Harrison: While My Guitar Gently Weeps* (London: Firefly, 2003), pp. 84–85.

192 Backstage, Dylan picked George up: As described by George in an interview with Anthony DeCurtis, *Rolling Stone,* November 5, 1987.

193 "It was a thrilling moment": Farida Majid writing for *News from Bangladesh.* Cited in Leng, *The Music of George Harrison: While My Guitar Gently Weeps,* p. 88.

193 The concert was "rock reaching for its manhood": Jon Landau, "The Concert for Bangladesh," *Rolling Stone,* February 3, 1972.

193 "The money we raised was secondary": Cited in Bill Harry, *The George Harrison Encyclopedia,* pp. 135–136.

194 Songwriting, he wrote, helped him: Harrison, *I, Me, Mine,* p. 36.

194 "I drove for about twenty-three hours": *Chant and Be Happy,* pp. 6–7.

195 "By the early 1960s," Glass said: Interview with Philip Glass, September 24, 2004.

196 "Unfortunately he was derided": Interview with Tony Calder on the documentary *George Harrison: The Quiet One,* Waterfall Entertainment, 2002.

197 As early as 1968: Davies, *The Beatles,* p. 359.

198 "I never saw the breakup coming": Interview with Al Aronowitz, July 27, 2004.

200 "Prabhupada, I seem to be going around": From transcript of conversation recorded at Bhaktivedanta Manor on August 22, 1973.

203 Still, other incarnations were called avatar: See David Kinsley, *The Sword and the Flute* (Berkeley: University of California Press, 1975), pp. 66–73.

Chapter 11: Dark Horse

207 "I'm in love with your wife": Cited in Bill Harry, *The George Harrison Encyclopedia,* p. 38.

208 "George . . . could be quite quarrelsome": *Harrison,* by the editors of *Rolling Stone,* p. 227.

209 "It was a clean, straightforward": Interview with Paddy Grafton-Green, August 26, 2004.

209 "Knowledge is supposed to lead to liberation": Mark Ellen, "A Big Hand for the Quiet One," *Q Magazine,* January 1988, pp. 54–56.

211 "He was definitely inspired": Cited in *Harrison* by the editors of *Rolling Stone,* p. 126.

212 "We'd take a break to go for fish and chips": Interview with Willie Weeks, December 14, 2004.

213 "I realize that the Beatles did fill a space": Los Angeles press conference, October 23, 1974.

214 People had come expecting: Larry Sloman, "George's Tour Winds Down in New York, and Mr. Harrison Goes to Washington," *Rolling Stone,* January 30, 1975, p. 10.

215 "The image of my choice is not Beatle George": Ben Fong-Torres, "Harrison's Return," *Rolling Stone*, December 9, 1974, p. 59.

215 "I saw George Harrison give thirty-five thousand fans": Jeremy Weeks, "Hari's on Tour 1974," *The Harrison Alliance*, no. 54/55, October 1984–January 1985.

216 *Dark Horse* drummer Andy Newmark suggested: Interview, October 3, 2004.

217 "In defense of his tour": Jim Miller, "*Dark Horse*: Transcendental Mediocrity," *Rolling Stone*, February 13, 1975.

218 George tried to see divine purpose: Interview with *Rolling Stone*, January 30, 1975.

218 He also accepted responsibility for his choices: Interview with *Tanned Equine*, December 20, 1975.

218 "Every show was probably hard for him": Interview with L. Subramaniam, September 30, 2004.

218 "But like John Lennon said": Sloman, "George's Tour Winds Down in New York," p. 20.

220 His smoking and drinking increased: Interview with Mick Brown, *Rolling Stone*, April 19, 1979.

Chapter 12: Laws of Nature

228 "The best thing anyone can give": *Chant and Be Happy*, p. 31.

229 "With a child around": Interview with Anthony DeCurtis, *Rolling Stone*, October 22, 1987.

229 He felt rather like Charlie Chaplin: Interview with Mick Brown, *Rolling Stone*, April 19, 1979.

230 "As an ordinary member of humanity": *Daily Express*, July 29, 1989.

230 "I remember watching the very first Monty Python": "George Harrison," *Melody Maker*, December 23, 1987, p. 65.

232 "We saw beyond each other's physical bodies": Interview with Anthony DeCurtis, *Rolling Stone*, November 5, 1987.

233 "He was by no means a recluse": Interview with Michael Palin, January 2, 2005.

233 "It really shook him," recalled Mina Robb: "Tributes to George Harrison: A Very Special Person," posted on www.henley-on-thames.com, December 7, 2001.

234 "There's a point in me where it's beyond sad": *Chant and Be Happy*, pp. 36–37.

235 "When I was younger": Anthony DeCurtis, "George Harrison Gets Back," *Rolling Stone*, October 22, 1987, p. 44.

235 In 1982, Paul McCartney commanded: Clayson, *The Quiet One: A Life of George Harrison*, p. 386.

236 "They're only interested in the Beatles": *Good Morning Australia*, 1981.

236   "I just have to accept that":   "George Harrison," *Melody Maker*, December 23, 1987, p. 62.

237   "Look," she whispered to her friend: Cited in Clayson, *The Quiet One*, p. 413.

237   "If I ever want to get over my fear":   "George Harrison," *Melody Maker*, December 23, 1987, p. 58.

238   To a reporter from *People* magazine: *People*, October 19, 1987, p. 64.

239   "Give us some lyrics":   the *London Guardian*, May 3, 1988.

239   What struck George was the purity of Orbison's sound: See *The Beatles Anthology*, p. 94.

240   "He was a sweet, sweet man":   cited in Harry, *The George Harrison Encyclopedia*, p. 293.

240   "There's no point":   "George Harrison," *Melody Maker*, December 23, 1987, p. 63.

241   "We would walk around the grounds together":   "Tributes to George Harrison: A Very Special Person," posted on www.henley-on-thames .com, December 7, 2001.

242   At a press conference in Tokyo: Quoted in *Daytrippin'* Vol. 18, spring 2002, p. 7.

244   "You always seem very self-deprecating":   "George Harrison," *Melody Maker*, December 23, 1987, p. 59.

Chapter 13: Sacred Ground

249   "Oh, we don't want to say that":   Cited in Gillian G. Gaar, "The Long and Winding Road: The Making of the Beatles' Video Anthology," in *The Beatles Digest*, p. 256.

256   "He made me feel like we were all simple devotees":   Interview with Karnamrita, April 28, 2004.

259   "Thank you," he said, "for this music":   Raga Mala, *The Autobiography of Ravi Shankar* (New York: Welcome Rain, 1999), p. 308.

263   "The Beatles had an expression":   "Paul McCartney," *USA Today*, October 15, 1999, p. 8E.

263   One reviewer would later describe his beautiful slide guitar work: Simon Leng, *The Music of George Harrison* (London: Firefly Publishing, 2003), p. 218.

264   "The history of the Beatles":   Anthony DeCurtis, "George Harrison Gets Back," *Rolling Stone*, October 22, 1987, p. 44.

264   "I've come all the way from Germany":   Cited in Keith Badman, *The Beatles Diary*, vol. 2: *After the Breakup 1970–2001*, p. 637.

267   He wanted to "freshen it up a bit," he said: "George Harrison Renews His Faith in 'My Sweet Lord'," the *Daily Telegraph* (London), December 23, 2000.

268   "He never sat around moping":   Christopher Scapelliti, *Guitar World*, interview with Dhani Harrison, January 2003, p. 112.

Chapter 14: Going Back

269 The story of Maharaja Pariksit's demise is summarized from A. C. Bhaktivedanta Swami Prabhupada's translation and commentary of the *Srimad-Bhagavatam,* cantos 1–12 (Los Angeles: Bhaktivedanta Book Trust, 1973).

271 "You know, I read a letter from him": Christopher Scapelliti, *Guitar World,* interview with Dhani Harrison, January 2003, p. 120.

272 "He gave his life to God": "Tribute to Brave Beatle," *Sunday Times* (London), November 29, 2002.

272 The album "is not about death and dying": Dhani Harrison interview on National Public Radio, November 29, 2002.

Afterword

275 Petty's daughter used to visit George: *Harrison* by the editors of *Rolling Stone,* p. 225.

275 "George was doing his preaching": Interview with Murray Silver, August 25, 2004.

Credits

The author is grateful for permission to quote from the following copyrighted material:

Harrison by the editors of *Rolling Stone* © 2002 Rolling Stone Press. All rights reserved. Reprinted by permission.

"The Concert for Bangladesh" by Jon Landau from *Rolling Stone,* February 3, 1972, © 1972 Rolling Stone. All rights reserved. Reprinted by permission.

"Lumbering in the Material World" by Ben Fong-Torres from *Rolling Stone,* December 19, 1974, © 1974 Rolling Stone. All rights reserved. Reprinted by permission.

"George's Tour Winds Down in New York" by Larry Sloman from *Rolling Stone,* January 30, 1975, © 1975 Rolling Stone. All rights reserved. Reprinted by permission.

"George Harrison Gets Back" by Anthony DeCurtis from *Rolling Stone,* October 22, 1987, © 1987 Rolling Stone. All rights reserved. Reprinted by permission.

"All Things Must Pass" by Ben Gerson from *Rolling Stone,* January 21, 1971, © 1971 Rolling Stone. All rights reserved. Reprinted by permission.

"Living in the Material World" by Stephen Holden from *Rolling Stone,* July 19, 1973, © 1973 Rolling Stone. All rights reserved. Reprinted by permission.

"Dark Horse: Transcendental Mediocrity" by Jim Miller from *Rolling Stone,* February 13, 1975, © 1975 Rolling Stone. All rights reserved. Reprinted by permission.

Chant and Be Happy © 1992 The Bhaktivedanta Book Trust International. Used with permission.

Foreword to *KRSNA, The Supreme Personality of Godhead* © 1997 The Bhaktivedanta Book Trust International. Used with permission.

Bob Dylan and the Beatles © Al Aronowitz. Courtesy of Al Aronowitz.

Photo Credits

Page 121 top, © Michael Ochs Archives.com; page 121 bottom, © Jurgen Vollmer/ Redferns; pages 122 top, 133 bottom, 134, © Getty Images; pages 122 bottom, 123 top, © Mirrorpix; page 123 middle, bottom, © Daily Mail/Associated Newspapers; page 124 top, © Hulton Archive/Getty Images; page 124 bottom, © David Hurn/ Magnum Photos; page 125, © John Loengard/Time Life Pictures/Getty Images; page 126 top, Thomas Picton/Camera Press, © Retna Ltd. USA; page 127 top, © Stories To Remember; pages 126 bottom, 127 bottom, 128 top, © Bettmann/Corbis; pages 128 middle, 128 bottom, 130, 131, 132 top, 133 top, 136 bottom, © Bhaktivedanta Book Trust Int'l; page 129, painting by Ramadasa-Abhiramadasa, photo © Bhaktivedanta Book Trust Int'l; page 132 bottom, © Ron Howard/ Redferns; page 135, © Rex Features; page 136 top, © WireImage.com; page 137, © Judy Totton/Rex Features; page 138, © Steve Wood/Rex Features.

Index

Page numbers in *italics* refer to illustrations.